Postville

STEPHEN G. BLOOM

Postville

A Clash of Cultures in Heartland America

Harcourt, Inc.

New York   San Diego   London

www.harcourt.com

Library of Congress Cataloging-in-Publication Data
Bloom, Stephen G.
Postville: a clash of cultures in heartland America/Stephen G. Bloom.
p.   cm.
ISBN 0-15-100652-0
1. Jews—Iowa—Postville—History. 2. Hasidim—Iowa—Postville—History. 3. Postville (Iowa)—Ethnic relations. 4. Postville (Iowa)—Politics and government. 5. Bloom, Stephen G.   I. Title.
F630.J5 B56 2000
977.7'33—dc21   00-038928

Text set in New Caledonia
Designed by G. B. D. Smith

Printed in the United States of America
First edition
K J I H G F E D C B A

To Iris and Mikey,
The adventure continues

Author's Note

Some of the people interviewed for this book requested that their real names not be used. I have complied with these requests, and have indicated, either within the text or on the list below, where substituted names have been used in place of real ones. Except as so indicated, no other names have been changed, and I have made no changes to the facts and statements reported.

The following names have been substituted for real ones:

Alicia Gustafson
Nahum Leibowitz
Beverly Schaeffer
Harold Schaufenbuel
Dawn Schmadeke

Contents

The Threat

The signboard went up early that day, at the intersection of Tilden and Lawler Streets, on the first Tuesday of August 1997, around the corner from Dr. John R. Mott High School, where the polls would be open until eight in the evening. It was a plastic sign with a flimsy frame and moveable white letters, the kind you see in coffee shops to announce the special of the day.

IT'S FAIR
IT'S EQUAL
IT'S TIME
VOTE YES

This pleasant, balmy summer day, when the Iowa sky was a shade or two lighter than robin's-egg blue, when an ever-so-slight breeze billowed white sheets pinned on clotheslines in backyards, this was the day Postville would get to vote for or against annexation.

I'm not sure anyone in Postville knew exactly what annexation meant—that is, in a technical sense. Maybe a state attorney in Des Moines could have explained it, but that probably would have left even more people confused. Annexation had something to do with land and government and taxes; it was something about platting, maps, and surveying, but to explain anything more—I don't even think I could spell it out very clearly.

If voters approved annexation, 703 acres of unincorporated land would become part of the city of Postville (population: 1,465). It would mean that $8 million in taxable property would be added to the city's tax base. If the referendum passed, property owners in the annexed area would have to pay slightly more in local taxes. In exchange, they would get city services such as police and fire protection. Included in the annexation plan were the local motel, a feed store, the Postville Farmers Cooperative Society, the gun-and-rifle firing range, a small plastics factory, a turkey-processing plant, and a kosher slaughterhouse.

But the technical points of annexation were never at issue. What annexation *really* meant was an opportunity to tell the Hasidic Jews to leave the God-fearing city of Postville, a quiet town nestled among the cornfields in the northeast corner of Iowa.

It was a vote to tell the ultra-orthodox Jews who had taken over Postville to get out. Leave us alone. Don't ever come back.

Today, eleven years after the first Hasidic Jews set foot in Postville, was the showdown. Annexation had been a ticking clock ever since the Jews had arrived in Postville, and today the alarm was going to ring.

By seven in the morning, an hour before the polls were to open, ten people had already lined up outside the high school, and when poll workers Joyce Kuhse and Lavon Kregel pushed open the school's heavy metal doors, the people in line streamed forward, waiting to take their places inside the seven metal voting booths, each with red, white, and blue curtains. One thousand, two hundred and twenty people were eligible to vote in the referendum, and Bill Roe, Jr., the Allamakee County Registrar of Voters, expected a good turnout.

For months, Sholom Rubashkin had bragged to his cronies at the packinghouse that the locals would fall in line, and if they didn't, then the people of Postville would be sorry. "They vote for annexation, and we'll pack up and leave," he liked to boast. "We'll take the goose that gave them all their golden eggs. And then where will they be?"

"Don't go threatening us," replied Leigh Rekow, a blue-eyed corn farmer and member of the city council. "If Sholom and the rest of the Jews want to pack up, that'll be fine with us. Just don't let the screen door hit you in the butt when you leave."

With little fanfare, a hardy band of Hasidic Jews had transformed Postville, a stagnant community that had held little future for its next generation, into what at first seemed like a Promised Land. In 1987, a Brooklyn butcher by the name of Aaron Rubashkin, Sholom's father, bought the town's abandoned slaughterhouse and turned it into a kosher meat-packing plant. By 1996, the packinghouse had become the world's largest owned and operated by the Hasidic Jews known as Lubavitchers. Each week, 1,300 cattle, 225,000 chickens, 700 lambs, and 4,000 turkeys were trucked into the renovated plant, and each week 1.85 million pounds of beef, chicken, lamb, and turkey came out in refrigerated trailer trucks bound for Chicago, New York, Los Angeles, Miami. The meat was so prized that some was even flown to Jerusalem and Tel Aviv.

At first, the kind of money the Rubashkin family was channeling through Postville was like a dream come true for the locals. The Jews had created 350 jobs at the slaughterhouse. No one could have dreamed that the Jews would have been able to make the run-down slaughterhouse hum to the strains of such a magnificent aria.

That dream, though, turned into a nightmare for some of the people of Postville. The Jews and many of the Postville locals were like two masses of oppositely charged air colliding in this remote land where twisters come and go without warning. That the Jews had made so much money in Postville only made matters worse. Because of the Jews, Postville hadn't turned into a heartland town of boarded-up shops on Main Street—that was Wal-Mart's contribution to the rural Midwest. By giving back life to the abandoned slaughterhouse, the Jews had resuscitated Postville. With the slaughterhouse operating around the clock, save for Friday nights and Saturdays, Postville had become a mecca of jobs. Not that educated Iowa kids would want to work in a bloody slaughterhouse, or even that their parents would let them. No matter. The Jews had breathed life back into Postville.

But their success was a kick in the shins to the locals. It said the Jews could achieve what the locals had failed miserably at. In becoming the town's modern-day saviors, the Jews had also become Postville's ruling class. They were in charge, and the locals didn't like that at all.

Of course, many of the locals thought that Postville had already sold its soul to the devil the day the Jews moved in, and whichever side won today wouldn't make any difference. It was already too late. Even if Postville people voted to annex the land where the slaughterhouse stood, there was no way the Jews would leave. Packing up would hit them too hard in their pocketbook, and that's all the Jews cared about, wasn't it? Sholom Rubashkin and the olive-skinned men with their little skullcaps and their curled sidelocks, they all were bluffing. They had too sweet a deal to close down the plant and move somewhere else.

But that wasn't reason not to vote, preached Leigh Rekow, the popular farmer who owned 240 acres on the outskirts of town. Today's vote would be Postville's last gasp, the last chance to save the city and its Lutheran heritage from being swallowed up by these Jews. Postville Lutherans knew the story of Jonah.

The vote that day proved to be a watershed for the Jews, the local Postville people, and for me. The vote was the culmination of four years of my life searching for meaning in Iowa. At first, I had sought out the Hasidim as guides and mentors. I went to Postville to learn about these strangers in a strange land. The reason for my own fascination with these devout men was one part of a mystery I was to solve as the months and years passed. I was attracted to the Postville Jews by my own deepening curiosity, a desire to belong. The Jews beckoned me to join them. They beseeched me to move away from what I had known to be true, so that I could come closer to their sense of *tzedaka*, "righteousness and justice." They sought to insinuate themselves into my life.

At first, I welcomed their attentions. I was entranced by how foreign these Jews were, by the cadence of their walk— their shoulders hunched, heads bobbing, as though they were carrying on imaginary conversations with themselves. When they *davened*, "prayed," they faced east, rhythmically swaying back and forth, tipping their chests, shoulders, and heads in a single movement from their waists so far forward that I thought they would topple over. They told fanciful allegories.

They relied on kabalistic strictures based on numerology and superstition. These biblical men were somehow a part of me, part of the viscera that my own ancestors had passed down to me.

Gradually, though, I came to realize my own truth. To understand Postville and the Jews whose business came to dominate the town was to learn about influence and power. The Hasidic Jews brought unimaginable turmoil to Postville, so much that few of the Postville elders or their children would ever forget what these newcomers had done.

CHAPTER 1

Can of Worms

The only time I had ever been in Iowa was when I was a fourteen-year-old Boy Scout on the way to Philmont Scout Ranch in New Mexico, and our horny troop spent the night in a dormitory at Iowa State University on the lookout all evening for sex-crazed college coeds we never found. Now, three decades later, I was leaving San Francisco for Iowa on a chilly, foggy morning in the middle of March. At the time, I knew next to nothing about Iowa except that there were more corn, pigs, and cows there than I could ever imagine.

The Midwestern winter in 1993 was still in full force. From the airplane, I saw the ground covered in a deep, thick blanket of snow. The fields were a continuous sweeping layer of white. Gusts of wind picked up mounds of snow, sprinkling powder into the air like soft talc. Through the swirling white particles, the earth looked hard and barren. A sense of slumber lay over these plains. I imagined that under the banks of snow lay thousands and thousands of acres of dormant land that, come spring, would produce fields of lush, vibrant green.

1

The airport north of Iowa City is in the middle of a giant cornfield. My welcoming committee that day consisted of a bespectacled professor who had warned me to dress warmly— a cold front was coming in from Canada that evening. The temperature was fourteen degrees, and as soon as I stepped outside, the wind swooped under my down jacket and blew me up like the Michelin Man. Driving south on the freeway, we bisected icy land so flat that the only elevation seemed to be meringue-like snowdrifts. The arc of early-evening bluish sky reminded me of a planetarium as the lights begin to dim. I noticed darkening silhouettes of grain silos, wooden fences, barns. The pigs and cows had to be in the barns, but what did I know about pigs and cows?

When we got to Iowa City at twilight, stray students plodded to and from classes, but what struck me was how empty the town was. Everything seemed in slow motion. I took a late-night walk and went into a restaurant called The Brown Bottle. Never in my life, except at Disney World, had I seen such large and such white people. As I slid into a booth, I noticed that the space between the table and vinyl bench must have been three feet wide. It wasn't just the abdominal girth of the hulking people around me, it was their necks, hands, fingers, arms. I felt like a shrimp.

I turned on the local TV news. I had read somewhere that television news directors across the nation seek broadcasters who speak "Iowan," that is, with nary an accent, and sure enough, the newscasters in front of me spoke with a nonregional speech that was clear as a bell, what rhetoric teachers call Standard American Articulation. The lead items that night were about an eighteen-wheeler that had skidded into a ditch (no one was injured), a farmers' meeting at which the stench from hog lots was discussed, and a car dealership that planned to give away a pig with every vehicle sold. The commercials were for pickups, crop fertilizers, seeds, herbicides, and a giant hardware store called Menards.

The next morning, I turned on the radio and heard the lunch menu of the public schools, along with obituaries (and funeral visitation schedules). I listened to an auction (called Radio-Tradio), during which these items were put up for sale: an albino ferret, a Weber grill, forty-three Hardy Boys books, a rollaway bed, and a wedding dress ("hardly ever used, still in the box"). Over breakfast, I saw on page one in the Cedar Rapids *Gazette* a color photo of last night's big-rig accident. I picked up a copy of the local "alternative" newspaper, which rated the best restaurants in town. In the seafood category, Red Lobster came in first, followed by Long John Silver's.

I dialed my wife, Iris, from the hotel. She anxiously asked about Iowa.

"Bleak," I muttered. "Very bleak."

We wanted out of San Francisco, but were we ready for Iowa?

I was in Iowa for a job interview to become a professor of journalism at the University of Iowa, and during the rounds of interviews that day, everyone wanted to know why I would ever want to leave San Francisco. My answer was less stress, more rewarding work, a better place to raise our three-year-old son, Mikey. Over the next three days, I gave a lecture to a class of fifteen students, spoke at a brown-bag lunch with a dozen professors, and attended a faculty cocktail party at which precut vegetables were arranged around a tub of onion dip. Two male faculty members took me to Iowa City's fanciest restaurant and asked me whether I liked to fish or hunt. Pheasant hunting in Iowa is known throughout the world, they said. I gulped.

For my last night in Iowa, two professors and a graduate student took me to dinner at a Chinese restaurant, called Yen Ching, which had red vinyl booths, Chinese lanterns, and a tropical fish tank that needed its water changed. One professor looked and talked like Burl Ives; the other chain-smoked hand-rolled cigarettes. In Chinese restaurants in San Francisco, place settings come with chopsticks only. If you want a fork, you have to ask. In this restaurant, it was the opposite. When I asked the waiter for chopsticks, it sparked a lively ten-minute discussion that culminated in my hosts asking me for a lesson, as they awkwardly clicked the plastic sticks.

Before I left Iowa the next day, I followed the suggestion of a California friend who had urged me to pay a visit to the sole synagogue in town. "You better find out where the Jews are," Ernie had advised me. "You might need them." It was an oblique reference, based more on "fly-over" stereotype of the rural Midwest than anything else. But what did I know about life in small-town Iowa? So before returning to San Francisco, I begged off a couple of hours from my hosts and met with the rabbi in town, Jeff Portman, a slight man in his mid-forties with a salt-and-pepper beard. "My experience is that Jews who move to Iowa City from big cities go one of two routes," the kindly rabbi told me. "The lack of *Yiddishkeit* here makes them much more active than they ever would have been—or they turn into nonpracticing Jews. It's one or the other."

"Can you find a good pastrami sandwich in town?" I asked out of genuine curiosity.

The rabbi shook his head, then smiled benignly. A chain restaurant called Bruegger's, which bakes fresh bagels, had opened in Iowa City a year earlier. "They're not New York bagels," the rabbi warned, shrugging his shoulders, sounding like the bagel maven he ought to be. "Too small, something about the water. But you get used to them."

Sitting in a window seat on the airplane later that day, as we left the mass of snow for evanescent blue air, I tried to see myself in front of a classroom. Living in a community where the only industry was a university of young people and academics seemed like an unbelievable luxury. Iris and I wouldn't be dependent any longer on the whims of the newspaper business. That it was in Iowa, a place we didn't know at all, added to the adventure. Moving to Iowa would be an opportunity to accomplish what we wanted: to trade city flash for small-town pleasures. We probably would be able to buy a comfortable farmhouse for a fraction of what we had paid for our Victorian two-flat in San Francisco. The worst traffic in Iowa City was what everyone called "rush minute," at 5:01 P.M. when drivers scurried to get home. During my three days in Iowa, everyone raved about the public schools. What I heard over and over again was "This is a great place to raise a family." Iris's dream, ever since I had met her, had been to go to law school. This would be her chance. Mikey's fantasy was to get a dog, and in Iowa, Iris could walk it at midnight without packing an Uzi.

Two weeks later, while sitting before a plate of Shanghai chicken at our favorite restaurant in San Francisco, we said yes to the job offer, a little unsure of ourselves, clinking our wineglasses. What did we have to lose? If our new Iowa lives didn't work out, we could always move back, tails between our legs, all the wiser for the experience.

When we shared our plans to pack up and head for the Iowa plains, we figured the rejoinder would be "You're moving *where?*" But the response was loud and clear, even from hard-core San Franciscans who could tell you what Bobby Bonds went for last night, as they juggled a *Chronicle,* double *latte,* and briefcase, all while standing in the aisle of a packed Muni bus. "Wow, how'd you ever arrange *that?*" they asked. "I wish *I* could pick up and move!" Maybe they were just making us feel that we hadn't lost our marbles.

Saturday, the week before we left, we held a garage sale to get rid of everything we didn't want. We were jettisoning our old lives to start new ones. Two friends hosted a going-away party at a bar in the Richmond District called the Russian Renaissance. They rented wooden cutouts of a pair of black-and-white cows, and with the cows as a backdrop, Iris and I posed, *American Gothic*–style, each holding a broom. Everyone raised shots of iced vodka and toasted our success in the heartland.

Four days later, we strapped Mikey into his car seat and waved good-bye to the city we once swore we would never leave. We pointed our 1979 Volvo east and drove across the Bay Bridge, confounding everything Horace Greeley, America's great newspaperman, had advised one and all about seeking fame and fortune a century earlier. We had a giddy sense of discovery, even after the Volvo's air-conditioning conked out on the Nebraska plains when the mercury peaked at one hundred. As we approached Iowa City on Interstate 80, Iris and I both felt a palpable sense of excitement. This was to be our new life. While Mikey slept contentedly in the backseat, our hearts raced.

Within a week, we rented from the university's track coach a gray-and-white two-story house on Court Street, fifteen blocks from Iowa's gold-domed original capitol building. The first weekend in our new home, a neighbor brought over her Dirt Devil and vacuumed as we unpacked. The Welcome Wagon lady, who looked and dressed like June Cleaver, came by and gave us a wicker basket full of refrigerator magnets, key chains, and coupons. In early November, when Iowa City got its first snowfall of the season, another neighbor called us at seven-thirty on a Saturday morning and excitedly told us to open the blinds to see the "winter wonderland" (her words). No one baked us a cake, but our across-the-street neighbor built a Jacob's ladder in his basement woodworking shop and presented it to Mikey for Christmas.

The other professors at the journalism school welcomed me, eager to have a colleague with real-world experience. The often-repeated tract on academic politics—that university politics are vicious because the stakes are so small—never came into play. Any rancor was minor-league stuff compared to the rough-and-tumble world of newspapers. My students did their homework, showed up for class on time, and lined up outside my door during office hours, a boon to any new professor's ego. They were big healthy kids, and in many ways, I felt as though I was in a time warp around them. The boys wore loose-fitting jeans and T-shirts, and many of the girls wore hippie skirts and blouses—the same clothes that college kids had worn twenty-five years earlier when I was a student at Berkeley.

San Francisco had been fast, exacting, and impersonal. In Iowa, we had entered a wholly different cosmos. In many ways, life in Iowa was a throwback to years past, and it took us city slickers some getting accustomed to, but we were prepared to like it. The concept of road rage didn't exist. Most Iowans drove large American-made automobiles, and they drove them ever-so-slowly, almost never over the speed limit.

They rarely passed other cars. On Iowa freeways, motorists gladly allowed merging cars into the stream of traffic with a smile and a pleasant horizontal wave, as though they were patting the butt of a newborn. Parking tickets were three dollars.

An ice-cream parlor in Iowa City was called Whitey's, yet there was no NAACP to protest the name. At many restaurants, credit cards weren't accepted, but local checks were. The True Value hardware store had one of the most popular bridal registries in town. Iris and I were floored by how honest Iowans were. In the local newspaper, I saw this classified ad with a telephone number: "Found money on sidewalk near Journalism School, around 11 A.M. on Wednesday." In San Francisco, we used to hear foghorns in the distance. Here we listened for a train whistle every night at eight, which we told Mikey was the train's way of letting him know it was bedtime.

After our first year in Iowa, we decided our experiment had worked. We wanted to sink roots and buy a house. We settled on a two-story brick farmhouse built in 1861, the oldest house on a tree-lined street with dappled sunlight, around the corner from where *American Gothic* artist Grant Wood used to live. We had front and back yards and a patch of dirt on the south side of the house that Iris promptly turned into a vegetable garden. The wild rabbits soon did their best to nibble away at our fresh pea pods and tomatoes, but they entranced Mikey, who had just learned to sing "Here Comes Peter Cottontail." The school Mikey would eventually attend, Henry Wadsworth Longfellow Elementary, was a three-story, eighty-year-old brick building three blocks away. A shortcut went through two backyards and a split fence that barely allowed a grown-up to squeeze through. The path was well worn by kids who had used it for years; the homeowners waved as troops of boys and girls scurried to get to school before the eight-thirty bell rang.

The best thing about the house, though, was a wooden porch that wrapped around the front. Iowans love their porches, which almost always have swings that hang from ceilings painted sky blue. One sweltering summer day, I drove over to Payless Cashways and bought our own swing. It came boxed—a do-it-yourself number, with screws, bolts, fifteen slats of wood, and a green metal frame, all of which I laid out on our front lawn. I looped the ends of the twin chains onto the hooks, and tentatively we tested the swing, Iris, Mikey, and I, rocking gently at first. During the twilight that evening, the front yard was full of fireflies—blinking, flickering bugs that Mikey found amazing. I punched holes in a lid to a peanut-butter jar, and Mikey scampered in his bare feet on the grass, swooping and swerving to catch as many lightning bugs as he could.

"Dad! Mom! They're all over!" he whooped.

We looked out, witnessing our sole progeny in the midst of a child's bliss that knew no limits. We uncorked a bottle of wine and toasted our new life.

On Sundays in the fall, we drove through the countryside, past working farms in the rural counties surrounding Iowa City. Even in our second year, we still were consummate city folks, and Iris and I were continually amazed by what we saw. We were wowed by pigs rolling in goopy mud, a sight we thought we would never tire of seeing.

"Smell that stuff!" I exhorted Mikey, as he dozed in the backseat.

We all had a long way to go before we would know what

it meant to be Iowan. As soon as he was eligible, Mikey announced that he desperately wanted to join the Cub Scouts. There is something about uniforms, badges, and knots that goes to the heart of young boys, and our son was no exception. Cub Scouts meant oaths, salutes, dens and packs, special handshakes, hiking, camping, and fishing.

At a den picnic at nearby Kent Park, after Mikey and I stuffed ourselves with grilled hot dogs, mayonnaisey potato salad, and Sterzing's potato chips, it was suddenly time to go fishing. One of the fathers went to the back of his pickup and magically produced fishing poles. Soon, sixteen fathers and sons lined up at the lake's edge. Another father went to his pickup and came back with a can of worms. And then it dawned on me. I had used the expression "can of worms" hundreds of times, but never did it have anything remotely to do with a can of live worms. To these Iowa guys, a can of worms meant one thing—a coffee can filled with worms dug up from your backyard, usually after a rainstorm. "Hey, Randy, pass that can of worms over here, will ya?" I yelled out with no small amount of pleasure. The slimy, pinkish worms we plucked from the can that day were tasty enough to catch five fish, which Mikey enticed by dropping his line into a "honey hole" (one of the fathers' terms) as dozens of fish slithered by.

Later that year, Mikey became friends with a blond kid whom I'll call Jimmy Reynolds. Jimmy invited Mikey to his house in the country for a sleepover. Jimmy's father, Kurt, had offered to take the boys on a camping trip. They were going to pitch a tent in a cow pasture, roll out sleeping bags, light a campfire, and roast marshmallows. This was what growing up in Iowa was all about, and Iris and I were excited about the prospect—until Mikey told us that Jimmy's dad had a large gun collection and that father and son often went target shooting. This headline instantly appeared in my head:

GUN ACCIDENT KILLS
6-YEAR-OLD; PARENTS
HAD PREMONITION

Like most city people who were neither vigilantes nor drug dealers, we knew nothing about guns and wanted to keep it that way. In our first year in Iowa, we had probably met more than half a dozen men missing fingers or portions of their hands from hunting or farming accidents. After much family debate ("But, Dad, Jimmy's father has lots of ribbons and medals," Mikey pleaded. "He teaches safety courses on how to shoot"), Iris called Kurt Reynolds.

"We're not from here, and we're unfamiliar with guns," Iris said haltingly. "We were concerned when Jimmy said you had a gun collection."

Silence.

Iris went on to ask where Kurt stored his guns and whether he kept them in a locked case.

Silence.

I was wondering whether Kurt Reynolds had covered up the mouthpiece and was either laughing or cursing.

Kurt assured Iris that his guns were stored in a locked case in a locked room to which only he had the key. He said he would be working Saturday night, so he wouldn't even be around for the sleepover, which wasn't going to take place in a cow pasture, but in Jimmy's room, with Jimmy's mother presiding.

"So, you're sure that the boys won't have access to the guns?" Iris asked.

"Ma'am," Kurt replied stiffly, "I teach safety courses for

the local NRA chapter. My son knows how to shoot and clean three kinds of rifles. But no one gets into that gun case when I'm not around. And if anyone does, that's when my belt comes off."

I believed the part about the belt, but that only scared us more. Against our instincts, Mikey went to the sleepover. Iris and I probably got less sleep that night than either Mikey or Jimmy, but when I picked Mikey up the next day, he said he had had a great time. "We got to play Nintendo before breakfast!" Mikey announced.

We did have some disquieting thoughts about Mikey's growing up in this kind of rural environment, but no matter how hard we tried to impart the vibrancy of big-city life to Mikey's little head, he was becoming less and less an urban kid. On our first trip out of Iowa, when we drove on the freeway past downtown Davenport on the way to Illinois, Mikey pointed to an old eight-story hotel, and shouted, "Daddy, look! Tall buildings!"

The Iowa landscape did, in fact, take some getting used to, even for two people who came searching for a change. Iowa, we discovered, was a rural canvas of extremes. From 110-degree summer days to −16-degree winter nights, there was no moderation in seasons. The in-between times were short and transitory. By mid-October, fall was over, and we had to brace for bone-chilling cold that lasted until the end of April. For weeks, the winter skies would be pewter-colored without even a tentative ray of sun. Formerly light and fluffy banks of vestal snow turned into cold, hard, blackish gray ice mounds. The days were short. By mid-February, unless you liked ice-fishing, hockey, or snowshoeing there was little to do except stay indoors. To prove how cold −50 degrees below zero is (with the wind-chill factor) a friend suggested that I pee outside to see urine freeze in midair, but I never attempted the experiment. I was afraid once I whipped out my pecker, it, too, would freeze. The summers were just as extreme. July and August were baking, mosquito-swatting months with the only relief being air-conditioning, jumping off the high dive into the City Park swimming pool, or if you were under ten, running through sprinklers in your backyard. During the brief spring, the sun could be shining, the temperatures rising nicely to the seventies, and then all of a sudden, the sky would turn coal black. Golf-ball-sized hail would come pounding down, bouncing off streets like ice cubes, or burrowing deep in the brown dirt of cornfields.

Starting in our third year in Iowa, that first radiant blush began to fade. Iris and I started appraising our lives more and more. We were enjoying Iowa; everything we had hoped for had come true. But we were lonely. We didn't fit into the local social order—neither the arcane world of university professors nor the humdrum world of the blue-collar locals. We had occasional pangs of homesickness for the big city and missed people who were like us.

Iowa City wasn't exactly rural Iowa, but I began to understand what Edna Ferber, who grew up as a Jew in the southeastern Iowa town of Ottumwa, wrote about in her 1938 autobiography, *A Peculiar Treasure*. "Business was bad, the town was poor, its people were frightened, resentful, and stupid. There was, for a place of its size and locality, an unusually large rough element. As naturally as could be, they searched for a minority on whom to vent their dissatisfaction with the world. And there we were, and there I was, the scapegoat of the ages."

We never found such blatant anti-Semitism in Iowa City.

The times were different and so was the location; we lived in a college town sixty years later. Still, to many, we stuck out. Even if I put on Ben Davis overalls, Red Wing boots with pig shit caked on the soles, and drove a Chevy pickup, I'd still be a city boy, and everyone who took one look at me would know it. Save for some foreign students, I probably had the darkest, curliest hair in town, particularly against the sea of blond, chestnut, and redheaded kids. My first Iowa haircut, at Supercuts for six dollars, prompted so much apprehension in the nervous, young blond barber that, as she approached me, I think I heard the blades of the scissors in her hand clanking.

One Saturday morning we drove to the big city twenty-five miles north, Cedar Rapids, to check out the Linn County Pork Fair, where we tried pork sausages, pork wieners, pork fritters, pork pancakes, although we stopped short when it came to the pork ice cream. Mikey waved to Miss Pork, a svelte blue-eyed girl wearing an azure chiffon gown. From the fair, we walked to Smulekoff's, a furniture store with an entire floor filled with La-Z-Boy recliners. Iris still had a coupon from the Welcome Wagon lady for a free ring cleaning at the jewelry counter on the first floor. As soon as we approached, I sensed the jeweler, a white-haired man in his fifties, giving us the once-over. About the only thing he didn't do was put on his loupe and take an up-close look at the three of us.

"You from New York?" the jeweler started.

"No, we moved here from San Francisco."

"So, you're new to *the community*?"

"We don't live in Cedar Rapids. We're down the road, in Iowa City."

"You a doctor?"

"No, I teach journalism."

"At the university. Ah, a professor. What's your name?"

"Bloom."

Pay dirt. The jeweler stuck out his hand, then cranked his head my way, and whispered, "Have you met any *people* in Iowa City, yet?"

I wasn't a religious Jew, but all my life I had lived in cities with large Jewish populations. The grocery stores carried fresh matzos year-round, and the delis sold knishes and chubs. Here the local grocery store stocked pigs' ears that customers picked out of a big wooden crate. Wherever I had lived, even the gentiles peppered their speech with words like *shtik*, *schlock,* and *schmooze.* But it wasn't just the lack of Jews in Iowa; it was that there were so few ethnics, hardly any Italians, blacks, Hispanics, anyone who wasn't so blanched white. Many of the locals didn't quite know what to make of us.

One Labor Day weekend, we drove forty miles southwest to Washington, Iowa, to watch a parade. Parades in small Iowa towns are disappearing slices of Americana: homemade floats; John Deere tractors; fire engines; 4-H cows, heifers, and calves. Everyone on the floats throws candy to kids along the parade route, who scurry in hordes to grab the sweets. After the parade, we ate at Winga's, a family restaurant on the town square that has been serving meat loaf, mashed potatoes, gravy, and soggy greens ever since it opened its doors in 1928. Excited about the parade and buzzed by his cache of candy, Mikey was talking up a storm. Two elderly ladies in their Sunday finest sat nearby. They were as thin-lipped as the farmer's wife from *American Gothic.* They poked their forks in their roast-turkey-with-mashed-potatoes-and-green-beans special, each glaring our way, grimacing, whispering, then scrunching their noses into doughy twists. When we passed their table to leave, one lady looked up at me and asked in an Almira Gulch tone, "You're not from around here, are you?"

"We're from Iowa City," I said. "Why?"

The two ladies were speechless. Their cheeks turned the color of stewed beets, and when they hobbled away, they shook their heads. What they were driving at wasn't where we were from, but who we were, *what* we were: city folk, Jews, foreigners to these parts. Big-city people surely might have been as vinegary and as suspicious, but they wouldn't have been as forthright. Too many consequences, too many complications. And who cares in the big city, anyway?

Gradually, we became accustomed to the stares we got every once in a while. I either smiled as amiably as I could or just ignored the looks of surprise and chalked them up to the rural nature of Iowa.

A couple of weeks later, on a warm Sunday afternoon, Betty Nolan, the sixtyish daughter of ninety-two-year-old Margaret Nolan, walked up to our porch. I was rocking on our swing, nursing a Leinenkugel, as Iris was weeding the front lawn. The Nolans had lived across the street at 513 South Summit since 1941. Each year, the elderly Mrs. Nolan picked a family on Summit Street to host the Watermelon Social, a backyard event with a dozen or so watermelons, home-baked cookies, iced tea, and lemonade, never any beer, certainly no liquor. Margaret Nolan anted up twenty-five dollars to whoever was going to host the event. "I think it would be just wonderful if you folks hosted the Watermelon Social this year," Betty said to us, as Iris looked up from the grass.

We got started that afternoon. Iris drew shapes of watermelons on an invitation, and we copied the artwork onto red construction paper. With two weeks to spare, Mikey and I hand-delivered the invitations up and down Summit Street, ringing doorbells and stuffing postboxes. We rented two dozen chairs and six card tables, and picked lilies of the valley as centerpieces. I thumped watermelons at Hy-Vee Foods and found a dozen choice ones. A carrot-topped sixteen-year-old clerk named Eldon helped load the melons into the backseat of the car.

Sunday brought showers, which we thought might dampen the turnout, but the year before, there had been at least eighty people when the neighbors down the block hosted the event. With our long porch, we had good coverage should the downpour not let up, and we figured at least three dozen people could squeeze in.

But two o'clock came and went—and no one showed up. Iowans are prompt, so we were at a loss for where everyone was. By two-thirty, the couple from across the street, an English professor and his wife, straggled in, then a woman who was running for city council came by, along with three or four more people who sought refuge from the rain. By three, just as the showers abated, Margaret Nolan, in a cotton party dress, appeared, seemingly skipping up our walkway.

"Where *is* everyone?" she asked in her clear, honest Iowa voice.

Mrs. Nolan had a round face and ruddy complexion, a full head of white hair, and a nose that squiggled to the right when she smiled. For just a second, you could see disappointment in her limpid blue eyes. Her mouth concealed a frown.

"A little rain couldn't have scared off so many people." She shrugged, pausing. "Oh, well, at least, we'll be able to visit for a while."

We were more disappointed than we ever expected. We had looked forward to playing host to our new Iowa neighbors, but for some reason, they didn't want to participate.

Maybe the timing had been all wrong. Maybe people had errands to run. Or maybe it was anti-outsider, anti-city, an unconscious anti-Semitism that our neighbors didn't even recognize. Mikey and I sadly returned eleven uncut watermelons to the Hy-Vee.

There were other incidents that year that made us wonder how we would ever fit in. The longer we lived in Iowa, the more we realized how profoundly different we were. Iowa was a through-and-through white, Christian kingdom. Most Iowans were so accustomed to everyone else being Christian that they couldn't possibly imagine anyone not believing in Christ, or at least, reared to believe in Christ. They talked about church bazaars, Sunday school, Bible-study groups, Bible camps for their kids. They wore church T-shirts and their cars boasted church bumper stickers. Tiny gold crosses on necklaces seemed to be the jewelry of choice for many of my female students at the university. After one of my students got arrested at a local bar for underage drinking, she told me she got called home for a "Come-to-Jesus talk." I had visions of a large God-fearing farm family holding hands and kneeling in a prayer circle around a figurine of Christ. It turned out a "Come-to-Jesus talk" just meant a serious discussion; but the expression was vintage Iowa, invoking the name of Jesus as though everyone believed in the good Lord's son.

On Sundays, our back-door neighbor used to take out a white leather–covered, gilt-paged Bible and read it on his porch while swinging under a canvas canopy. Our first landlord, the track coach, made it a point to tell us the best corner in the living room to set up the Christmas tree. At Brennerman Seed & Pet Center, when a clerk in the tropical-fish department asked Mikey what Santa was going to bring him, Mikey said matter-of-factly, "We don't celebrate Christmas.

We're Jewish," which prompted the clerk to bag our two gold-fish quickly without further conversation. Later that week, bundled-up carolers stopped by our house, even though ours was one of the few homes in the neighborhood that didn't have Christmas lights. On Easter, the big-city paper, the Cedar Rapids *Gazette,* ran a banner headline:

HE HAS RISEN

Other than being offensive and irrelevant to non-Christians, the headline broke all the rules of news judgment that I preached to my students. The event was neither break-ing news nor could it be corroborated by two independent sources.

One of my few Jewish friends in Iowa worked part-time as a counselor in a rural mental health clinic. On Christmas Eve, he was leaving the clinic when two employees wished him a Merry Christmas. My friend thought for a moment, threw caution to the wind, and replied, "Thanks for the good wishes, but you know I'm Jewish." Without missing a beat, one of the women responded, "We know—we've been pray-ing for you."

Some well-meaning, good Iowa folks tried their best to make us feel at home. Whenever we got together with a couple I'll call Joe and Rita Williams, without fail, Rita would steer the conversation toward Judaism. The daughter of a minister, Rita seemed driven to bring up magazine articles, PBS television shows, newspaper editorials, books, lectures, anything about the Holocaust Memorial Museum in Wash-ington, D.C. Rita's other standby would be to launch into a prolonged appreciation of the movie *Schindler's List*. It was as though Rita needed to purge any latent guilt she still car-ried because of her fifth-generation German-Iowa heritage. It was akin to white people from Georgia socializing with blacks, feeling guilty about George Wallace, and dropping names like Harry Belafonte, Sidney Poitier, and Ella Fitzgerald. I preferred Joe's routine. Whenever Rita started in on her Aryan guilt, Joe piped up with the advice his mother back in Charles City, Iowa, had given him: If you want a good lawyer, always hire a Jew.

Every third Wednesday of the month, Mikey and I went to a Cub Scouts meeting held in the gym at Longfellow Elementary. It was a big deal to Mikey. For each meeting, Iris sewed one or two more cloth triangles on the sleeves, shoulders, and pockets of Mikey's blue uniform in what seemed like an endless array of badges ("Mom, PLEASE try to make them straight this time"). The meetings came with a mixed blessing. It was the only time Mikey on his own would tuck his shirt into his pants; the law of the pack demanded it. On the other hand, there was the mandatory Cub Scout prayer honoring God and Country that everyone recited at the beginning of each pack meeting. I felt a little squeamish joining the other parents and kids, but there was really nothing wrong with it. Jews believe in God and Country even though most are uncomfortable about announcing such a nexus in public.

At one meeting, the scoutmaster mentioned the theme of the evening—the Golden Rule. After a blond nine-year-old defined the Golden Rule, the scoutmaster said it was really very easy to remember. "All of us in this room have been taught to believe in God and Je—" and just as the scoutmaster was about to finish "sus," I stood up and arched my eyebrows into upside-down Vs. The scoutmaster caught my glare and skidded short. I was furious. Since when did the Cub Scouts believe in Jesus Christ? God was all right, but Jesus Christ?

The scoutmaster was a decent guy who volunteered his time to lecture boys on knots and the pinewood derby. The last thing I wanted to do was intervene and become a one-person Anti-Defamation League. I didn't want to make a scene. Part of Jewish assimilation in America, for better or worse, has been to shrug your shoulders at incidents like this.

But I needed no more proof that I was in an alien territory. I wasn't going to join nine other Jews to form a minyan at the local synagogue on Saturday mornings. My religion was the same as it had always been: private and personal, a reflection of my heritage. Iris, Mikey, and I continued to attend the woefully uninspirational High Holidays services at the synagogue; Mikey stuck through Sunday school each week, one of eight kids in his class. I grew accustomed to the hard, unsweetened doughnuts that passed for bagels at the local Bruegger's. Arranging for a seder at Passover was difficult, but we did our best with the sprinkling of Jews who shared our views of what it was to be Jewish.

More than ever in my life, especially with Mikey, it seemed essential to nurture our Jewish souls, the sense of who we are, how we think, where we come from. I was a Jew through and through, from my curly brown hair and robust nose to the synapses in my brain and the corpuscles of my blood. A day, an hour, didn't go by without my reflecting in some way on my culture and my religion. Religious culture and devotion to faith are two different things, and while I wasn't willing to become more attached to the organizational rigors of my faith, I wasn't about to let go of what I carried inside me every day.

One morning, while sipping a cup of Red Zinger tea, I opened a makeshift magazine published by a group of Iowa Jews who called themselves Lubavitchers. The magazine told of a fledgling settlement of ultra-orthodox Hasidic Jews who in the mid-1980s had moved from Brooklyn, New York, to a tiny northeast Iowa town called Postville. There, they opened a slaughterhouse that processed beef, lamb, and chicken so that it was *glatt* kosher, the strictest method of slaughtering for Orthodox Jews. Like the Lutheran frontiersmen who preceded them a century earlier, their first steps were to create a house of worship for their families. The Jewish community started with just three families, but as more Hasidim arrived, more followed, all in response to glowing accounts of life in rural Iowa. Soon, the town boasted more than 150 ultra-orthodox Jews. With three dozen Hasidic rabbis, Postville had more rabbis per capita than any other city in the United States, perhaps the world.

The Postville story fascinated me. It sounded like a Jackie Mason joke, a crack about the unlucky thirteenth tribe of Jews. Hasidic Jews, in their long black coats and black hats, in rural Iowa where pigs outnumber people by almost five to one? I knew a little about the sect of Jews that had settled in Postville. Lubavitchers are Hasidic Jews with a worldwide population of two hundred thousand; more than twenty-five thousand live near the group's world headquarters, in the Crown Heights section of Brooklyn—just fifty miles and two rivers from where I had grown up in suburban New Jersey. Their movement, one of the largest of some forty worldwide Hasidic groups that include Satmar, Ger, Bobov, and Belz Jews, began in the eighteenth century as a populist drive aimed at uniting alienated Jewish peasants in Eastern Europe. It spread through European *shtetlach* (villages) and centered on a circle of charismatic, mystical rabbis, *rebbes*. Lubavitchers' fundamentalist faith is anchored in the return of the Messiah, and unlike almost all other branches of Judaism, the Lubavitchers actively proselytize wayward Jews to return to the fold and learn the righteous ways of pure Judaism. Lubavitcher men have unclipped beards, the women don't practice birth control, and their families often number ten or twelve children. There were persistent myths surrounding the Hasidim, including one that everyone where I grew up seemed to know: When they engaged in intercourse, a sheet separated the man from the woman, and their union was made possible through an embroidered hole.

On trips to Manhattan, I used to stare at the men with their long beards, *payot* (curled sidelocks), and *tzitzit* (the tasseled edges of tunics worn under a shirt), shlepping old suitcases everywhere they went, their wives in tow several paces behind the men, the women wearing stiff *sheitels* that looked more like hats than wigs, riding far back on the crowns of their heads. To me, the Hasidim were a throwback to an antiquated world. While we were the same religion, they were strangers to me. These fervent sectarians I used to view from a distance were now in the middle of the *goyishe* heartland, just down a county road from us. I wanted to understand why they were here. Had they decided that they could find a clear path to salvation in Iowa? Did they leave the big city for reasons similar to my own?

My father had died during the fall of our first year in Iowa, and several years later, Iris's mother died. We felt landlocked, stranded in this vast middleland, surrounded by people whose multitudinous farm families went back for generations. I daydreamed that the Postville Jews would be long-lost relatives who had found us in this remote place in the center of America. The Postville Jews would become my own longlost *mishpocheh*, family. They, too, had curly hair, olive-colored skin. Perhaps I would find someone like my grandmother

Rose, who used to stand in her cluttered kitchen in New York, then Miami Beach, to mix matzo meal, eggs, and a dollop of *shmaltz* for her superb matzo-ball soup, all the while regaling me with stories about her grandparents from Riga. Maybe I'd find a counterpart to the singular legend in our family's lore— my grandfather's brother, Jack, who, seventy-five years ago, drove a convertible out west, became a cowboy, and ultimately died of tuberculosis in a Denver sanitarium.

An invisible force seemed to be grabbing me by my shoulders, pointing me toward northeast Iowa, and pushing me in the small of my back. While I knew the Lubavitchers to be fierce fundamentalists who proselytize other Jews the way Jehovah's Witnesses go after nonbelievers, I also realized the Hasidim in Postville were as close to family as Iris and I could muster in our new home state. They were reminders of where we had come from, of what our people had been like long ago. Even though we practiced our faith in very different ways, we were all Jews—an undeniable bond in Iowa. We were cut from the same cloth. I fantasized that the Hasidic enclave in Postville would be a hermitage of wise men. I imagined that they would brighten my soul with witty talk and warm my belly with nurturing food. I wasn't looking for a religious awakening. Maybe I just wanted someone to kibitz and nosh with.

CHAPTER 2

First Supper

Even though I am a Jew, I had no automatic entrée to the Postville Hasidim. The *macher* (leader) of the community was Sholom Rubashkin, a thirty-five-year-old Brooklyn-born Lubavitcher whose father had started the Postville slaughterhouse. When I called Sholom at the packinghouse called Agriprocessors, a harried-sounding secretary said she'd leave word for him to call me back. But Sholom never called. Over the next week, I phoned again, then again, six, seven, eight times, leaving more messages. I called the Postville synagogue, the shul. No one answered. I called Sholom's home and left a message with his wife. But Sholom never called back. I tried to contact other Jews in Postville, leaving messages on their answering machines, but none returned my calls.

I quickly realized I needed a go-between, someone who would introduce and vouch for me. I thought that Jeff Portman, the rabbi in Iowa City, might be helpful, but when I asked, he laughed. "I'm not your man. In the minds of Lubavitchers, I'm the enemy."

The Lubavitchers looked at Portman as a pretender, not fully committed to the rigors of his faith. A group of Lubavitchers from Des Moines had recently begun a letter-writing campaign to proselytize Jews in Iowa City and recruit them to the Lubavitch movement. Rabbi Portman responded swiftly in letters to members of the Iowa City synagogue, warning that these ultra-orthodox adherents were attempting to drive a wedge in the local Jewish community. A war of minor skirmishes was avoided when the Des Moines Hasidim backed off.

The Lubavitchers, though, could claim at least one recruit. Rabbi Portman gave me the name of a professor at the University of Iowa, in the department of statistics and actuarial science, who had recently moved with his wife and two children to Postville to join the Lubavitch community, commuting twice a week the 115 miles between Postville and Iowa City. In the small world of Iowa City, I learned that Martin Appel was originally from Milwaukee, had earned a Ph.D. from Johns Hopkins University, and had spent a year as a postdoctoral student at Cornell University. He had started teaching at Iowa in the fall of 1990. Martin was an expert in probability and stochastic processes, percolation theory, random graphs—a brand of statistics based on theoretical abstractions. He was married to a blue-eyed, blond woman from Lincoln, Nebraska, by the name of Beth, who had converted to Orthodox Judaism. When Martin interviewed for the job at the university, he looked like any other budding academic: tweedy, wire-rim glasses, closely cropped beard. But he wasn't a geek. At Cornell, Martin used to wear cowboy boots, ride an old bicycle everywhere, and play electric guitar in a rock band. After he moved to Iowa City, though, something changed. Martin started wearing the accoutrements of a Hasid: yarmulke, black baggy pants, *tzitzit,* the fringes readily visible under his shirt. His colleagues in the statistics department weren't certain whether Martin had hidden his religious zeal during the round of interviews or found it in between the time he accepted the job and after he moved to Iowa.

Once here, Martin's appetite for Orthodox Judaism grew voraciously. He joined the synagogue in Iowa City, but soon dropped out, complaining bitterly about the congregation's lack of commitment to the faith. He ordered kosher meat directly from a butcher in Des Moines and created in his home a kosher kitchen with two sinks and two sets of dishes—one for meat, one for dairy. Neighbors in the east-side neighborhood of Iowa City where Martin and his family lived remember the couple in the fall erected in their backyard a *sukkah,* an open-roof hut made with stalks and branches, decorated with fruit and flowers, to commemorate the harvest. The *sukkah* is the centerpiece of the Jewish holiday Sukkot, which starts on the fifth day after Yom Kippur and lasts eight days, ending with Simchat Torah, the most exuberant celebration of the year. Neighbors remember Martin entertaining Orthodox Jewish friends inside the *sukkah,* staying up past midnight, dancing and drinking. Martin and his friends waved *lulav, hadasim, aravot,* and *etrog,* green palm branches, shiny myrtle leaves, sprigs of willow, and citrons, as prescribed by Orthodox custom.

Sometime during his first year in Iowa, Martin started making trips to Postville to learn more about the Hasidic community. The trips turned into weekly pilgrimages, and eventually Martin bought a house in Postville. Back at the university, Martin was a stern, demanding teacher. One faculty member described Martin as "unbending, overly rigorous, almost Germanic in nature." Something else his colleagues noticed was that he never worked on a Jewish holiday, nor would he answer the phone on the Sabbath (Friday nights and Saturdays). Ultimately, when he came up for tenure at the university in the fall of 1996, his senior colleagues voted Martin down—an unusual action, considering his academic pedigree.

But for my purposes, Martin was ideal. In my mind, Martin bridged the secular world of Iowa City and religious cosmos of Postville. Martin and I were about the same age, as were our children. Our university offices were a couple of blocks away. We were two Jews, fellow travelers amid all the Christmas fanfare that erupted each year in Iowa. There had to be a natural kinship between us. In a land devoid of *Yiddishkeit*, what better person was there to usher me into the world of the Postville Hasidim?

I called Martin at his office and left a message. I called him at his Postville home and left another message. Over the next three weeks, I phoned Martin more than a dozen times. It was a replay of my trying to connect with Sholom Rubashkin. I couldn't fathom why a fellow Jew and faculty member in such a friendly, nonthreatening place as Iowa, where people go out of their way to help strangers, wouldn't return the call of a *landsman*. Iowans certainly weren't like that, so why should he be?

Finally, one morning Martin picked up the phone.

He seemed perturbed. "Why do you want to go to Postville?" Martin asked in a tone that sounded almost threatening.

"I want to meet the Jewish people there. I want to understand their lives in Iowa."

"But why? You teach journalism. Do you intend to write about the Lubavitchers?"

"Maybe," I said. "But what difference would that make?"

Martin's voice turned cold. "The Lubavitchers in Postville are very private people," he said, as though lecturing a farm kid who couldn't understand the difference between median and average. "They have absolutely no interest in publicity and they have no regard for the secular press. They have nothing to talk to you about. Do you understand what I am telling you?" Martin was practically yelling.

All I wanted to do was make a trip to Postville. Maybe I'd write something, maybe I wouldn't. I wanted to go to Postville to learn. I was curious, and I told Martin that. But Martin remained unconvinced, even suspicious.

"If you're interested for your *own* personal, religious reasons to learn more about the Lubavitcher way of life, then that's different. Some family in the community is always willing to host another Jew for *Shabbos* dinner. But don't bring any notebook, and don't go to write a story," Martin cautioned.

I thanked Martin, suggesting that we might run into each other either in Iowa City or Postville someday. It was a curt conversation, a harbinger of how wary the Postville Hasidim would be of anyone outside their following—even a Jew. Martin's parsimony underscored how difficult it would be to break into the Hasidic community. His icy reaction reminded me of the two ladies at Winga's, who after one look at Mikey, Iris, and me, turned up their noses at us, but Martin hadn't even met me.

In fact, the only person among the Postville Jewish community who would talk to me wasn't even Jewish. After striking out with Martin and Sholom and five other Lubavitchers,

I tried Don Hunt, the gentile operations manager at the slaughterhouse. Don took my call right away and said he would try to set up a meeting with Sholom whenever I planned to be in Postville. "Afternoons are good," he said. "Come by one Sunday afternoon. We'll be here. You don't have to make an appointment. Just stop by."

Before I left for Postville, I wanted to make contact with some of the locals, to get their reactions to the Hasidim who had settled there. They answered the phone, or got on quickly, and chatted me up like an old friend. "Come on up," Sharon Drahn, the editor of the *Postville Herald-Leader*, said, beckoning me in an unhurried, almost sweet tone. "I don't know many of the Jewish people, and they don't really like to talk to us, but come by so we can visit. I'm sure plenty of Postville folks will talk to you." After I hung up, I spoke to the mayor, the principal of the junior high school, two city councilmembers, a banker in town, and a woman who owned the local shoe store.

Within two days, I was on the road. It was the third Friday of May. The spring semester had just ended. No more classes, no more student papers to grade, no more faculty meetings. The afternoon was hot and humid. The radio weatherman was predicting heavy rains by evening, but that didn't matter. I was elated to get out of Iowa City for a couple of days, away from the unreality of Iowa life as seen from a university town. Just five minutes from Iowa City, newly tilled rows of cornfields were on all sides of me. The green plants had poked through the rich loessial Iowa earth, and were squiggly and ankle-high—the beginnings of corn.

In yards next to farmhouses, stiff cotton shirts and overalls flapped on clotheslines like cardboard cutouts. Fifty miles north of Iowa City, a motel advertised REFRIGERATED ROOMS with a burned-out neon sign. I drove past roadside bait-and-tackle shops (SPECIAL ON NIGHT CRAWLERS!), past grassy baseball diamonds outlined by white stripes of lime. When I got to the Postville turnoff in Elkader, a hand-scrawled note nailed to an oak tree read CLEAN FILL WANTED.

In a meadow of wild prairie indigo, the leaves of a willow tree fluttered like a gigantic grass skirt swaying in the breeze. Sun-bleached barns stood next to silver-topped Harvestore silos, close to whitewashed farmhouses with painted tin roofs. Some of the farms still had windmills, rusted and lopsided now, the spinning wheels missing most of their slats, a reminder of how people in these parts once tapped the earth for stone-cold clean water. Alongside the road, I saw a pair of teenagers riding sable-brown horses, manes and tails rising and falling to the cadence of a canter. In fenced pastures, two or three awkward colts stood uncertainly alongside mares, each tugging at the tall grass. Close in to the farms, near russet-colored milking parlors, crowing roosters strutted around barnyards like landlords waiting for the rent check.

If there is a door that opens onto heartland America, it is here in the northeast pocket of Iowa, near the Wisconsin-Minnesota state line, just off State Route 13. Many of the towns in the area had a motto lettered on a billboard at the city limits: Luana (population: 197): WORKING TOGETHER TO MAKE A GOOD TOWN BETTER; Gunder (population: 61): A LITTLE TOWN THAT KEEPS ON GOING; Elgin (population: 637): CAPITAL OF THE SWITZERLAND OF IOWA. A steeple, usually atop a redbrick Lutheran church, anchored each town. The church spires, with crosses atop their pinnacles, were visible for miles, designed so that farmers could see and sense they were in the presence of the Lord while working the fields.

From SR 13, I turned onto County Road X16, to B60, to W64, all pale, faint squiggles in my *Iowa Atlas & Gazetteer.* I drove along prairies, went past acres and acres of geometrically planted baby corn shimmying in the breeze. In addition to the corn crop, many of these farms were stocked with holstein and Guernsey cows, grazing in fields. An overwhelming mixture of pungent smells—fertilizer, ensilage, freshly turned soil, clover, and timothy hay—blew through the car's vents. I must have passed a pig farm because suddenly the smell changed to the sharp odor of manure. The scent was so ripe that the only place it could have come from was deep within the intestines of the animals that had just produced it. Iowa is the buckle of America's Swine Belt, and two-thirds of all hogs in the United States come from farms within two hundred miles of Des Moines. Many families in northeast Iowa raise Hampshires (black-bodied with a single white band) or Durocs (ruddy-colored), and as I drove that day, I could see squealing baby piglets poking their heads outside of miniature A-frame farrowing houses. To the locals, the smell of pig manure meant one thing—money—but to a city boy like me, it was a force that drew me deeper and deeper into a distant world that was not my own.

County Road W64 is a farm-to-market road with gravel pebbles that crunched when I drove on them. On W64, I passed a slow-moving John Deere tractor with oversized big-ribbed monster tires that came up to the driver's waist. I waved at the farmer on the tractor, and he nodded back at me: What in the world is a *car,* and one with out-of-county plates, doing in this land of pickups and tractors? What business could he possibly have with us?

A swirl of dust from a pickup ahead of me hung in the air

as I drove to a T-intersection. I made a left turn on Highway 18 and coasted a half mile to downtown Postville, a three-block-long strip of storefronts and businesses. At midday, I pulled into the driveway of Postville's finest: The Pines. The 1950s motel may once have been a roadside destination, but today its concrete swimming pool with varicose-vein cracks didn't look like it had been filled for decades. My T-shirt stuck to the back of the vinyl car seat and made a sound like tape ripping from a cardboard box as I stepped out. Inside my room, atop green shag carpeting, was a squeaky concave bed, and next to it, a nightstand with a matching green-cover Gideon Bible in its drawer. The room smelled of mildew and Lysol. But as I pushed aside the curtains hanging from a flimsy rod, my reward was immediate: a lush pasture, and not more than twenty yards away, a tan-and-white cow was lazily chewing grass. She looked up and seemed to give me a wink. I hurriedly changed my clothes, pulling out from an overnight bag a pair of jeans and a fresh University of Iowa T-shirt.

I had come primed, but nothing could have prepared me for what lay before my eyes that steamy May day. No matter what I knew about Hasidic Jews, I wasn't ready for what I saw. Bearded rabbis with long woolen waistcoats marched down the main street. They gestured with their hands, engrossed in conversations that sounded like a mishmash of Hebrew and Yiddish. Everyone seemed to be in a rush, a Hester Street of confusion. A half-dozen Jewish men, some still wearing blood-streaked white-cotton butcher coats and aprons, walked past me, seemingly oblivious to me and anyone else on the sidewalk. Jews in white shirts, black pants, and big fedora hats on their heads pumped gas at Home Oil, ducked into Moore's

IGA for a select list of groceries, or lined up at the post office to purchase money orders. In the front yards of three houses, next to overgrown beds of zinnias, Jewish kids played, yarmulkes pinned to the boys' heads. Flopping against their pale, white faces, the older boys had *payot,* long curled sidelocks. A pair of young Hasidic mothers, their heads covered with cotton scarves, hurriedly pushed old-fashioned prams. As I walked by the women, their eyes suddenly turned downward, but I could still hear the nasally singsong accent I knew to be only from Brooklyn. *And they seemed to be kvetching!*

Gradually, Lawler Street seemed to clear. The Jews had finished their tasks; all had seemingly disappeared into their homes, again restoring Postville to its natural order. Postville had two public schools (a high school and an elementary/ middle school), two coffee shops across the street from each other (Ginger's and Postville Bakery), a hardware store (John's), an appliance store (John's), a barbershop (Livingood's), five beauty parlors (Madonna's, Cheryl's Beauty Hut, Beauty Expo, Sandie's Hair Designers, and Possibilities), two plumbing-supply businesses (Larry's and Burnett's), a boarded-up antique store (Jim's), three gift shops (The Wishing Well, The Country Garden, The Millstone), and two taverns (Club 51 and the Horseshoe Lounge). Four veterinarians worked in the Postville Clinic downtown to treat, as a large wooden sign indicated, "large and small animals." There were three churches (Lutheran, Catholic, and Presbyterian), but St. Paul Lutheran dominated the other two houses of worship and, in fact, the entire town with its towering steeple. Outside the Postville Farmers Cooperative Society building, men wearing OshKosh overalls and muddy rubber boots complained about fertilizer and hog prices. Clean-cut teenagers wearing dungarees lounged in the Casey's parking lot. One man in a white shirt

and thin brown tie walked along the high city sidewalks, holding a plastic sheath filled with building plans and permits. A
man in a two-tone Ford pickup stopped at the town's four-way
stop at the corner of Lawler and Tilden Streets, and waved at
a woman crossing the street. This was the world I had grown
to expect from rural Iowa towns, and Postville delivered it in
spades.

By seven that evening, I got back in my car and headed
over to Moore's IGA to buy groceries for a makeshift dinner—
Italian salami, Swiss cheese, mustard, and squishy white-bread
rolls. Dusk stubbornly refused to turn into night, and there
was stillness in the air. I drove off Lawler onto Greene Street
and noticed neighbors rocking back and forth on their front
porches, their wooden swings moving in a cadence. The locals
were silently serenading the end of another day, the coming of
a weekend of rest and prayer. The quiet seemed overwhelming. Lightning bugs began to come out. Apart from the mur-
mur of voices that seemed far away, about the only thing I
could hear that evening was the clickety-clack of crickets.

I didn't want to return to the Pines on such a pretty
evening, so I ate my first supper in Postville in my car; windows rolled down, munching on my sandwich, I drove behind
St. Paul Church, next to the Lutheran cemetery, and parked
across the street from the white-shingle house, which had
been converted from a minister's home to the Hasidic shul.

Through the shul's windows, I saw two dozen men, all
with full, untrimmed beards. The shul's front door and windows were open to allow the evening's breeze inside. The
men were wearing black hats and *kapotes*, waistcoats, and
they were davening. In time, the crowd of men sat down
around long, rectangular tables, and I could hear their distinct, muted voices rising like vapor.

I put down my sandwich, got out of the car, and leaning against the door, I looked to the other side of the seventy-five-yard divide before me. I was eavesdropping on something sacred and private, yet I couldn't turn away. On this clear night, I was transfixed. As a Jew, I had participated in thousands of Jewish rituals, but what I was witnessing this night was something wholly different. These earnest Jews beseeching the Almighty were surrounded by nascent corn stalks in the middle of Christian Iowa, in a town few outside of a fifty-mile radius had ever heard of.

An hour must have passed, and then, as though on cue, a great roar of voices erupted from within the shul. The worship had ended and the men broke into raucous song. These liturgical melodies were booming and boisterous, each lasting twenty to thirty minutes. Soon, the singing was accompanied by banging. The men were pounding the metal tables with fists. They were stamping the shul's wooden floor with the heels of their shoes and boots. The collective sound signaled to me that the men must have been drunk (*shikker* was the word that came to mind, a throwback to my father long ago telling me jokes that mixed Yiddish and English). I was eavesdropping on some sort of loud, inebriated religious reverie. *Tummel* was the word my father would have used. The sounds shooting out from the shul's windows and front door were deafening on this otherwise serene Iowa night. If the beams of this once-elegant parsonage-turned-shul on the south end of Lawler Street could be raised by sound, then surely the roof by now would have been airborne.

Gradually, the singing and banging subsided. Men began to emerge from the shul, gathering in a knot at the front door. A milliner would have loved the sight: the men's hats were not limited to pedestrian yarmulkes (you can see them in almost *any* city) but included broad-brimmed Borsalinos, exotic *shtreimelech* (huge magnificent hats often with twelve fur tails, which, I was to learn, represented each of the ancient tribes of Israel), even *spodikem* (tall, majestic mink hats, a Jewish version of a top hat). As the men left, they headed toward downtown, walking two or three abreast, mixing Hebrew with English and Yiddish.

By now, twilight had turned to night, and the flickering shapes of stars on the blue-black sky had emerged. Brightened by a rising three-quarter moon, as the men reached Williams Street, they began to fade into silhouettes against a luminescent backdrop of corn in an endless maze of fields. Within seconds, the silhouettes turned into apparitions that seemed to float upward into the still night air.

CHAPTER 3

The Storm

By early morning, the Saturday sun already had risen high above the wide prairie horizon. I had planned to meet with Don Hunt and Sholom Rubashkin the next day at Agriprocessors, but before then, I wanted to poke around Postville. I stopped in the hardware store, the shoe store, the two coffee shops in town, the filling station, the police station. Most of the men I met that day were farmers, and if they weren't, they sold grain, insurance, seed, fertilizer, clothing, tractors, equipment, or silos to farmers. They were large, hulking men, and at Ginger's, I found out why. A typical breakfast included two eggs, four pork sausages, hash browns, cornflakes, toast and English muffins (with marmalade), coffee, and orange juice. Pork chops or cutlets were popular for supper, as were sweet pickles, tomatoes, or cucumbers canned last summer. Dessert was pink Jell-O mold, ice-cream cups, or a bowl of canned peaches. Potluck suppers always seemed to include a Crock-Pot full of Lit'l Smokies in barbecue sauce, fried chicken, fried pork tenderloins, and Corning Ware bowls of gooey hamburger or Tater Tots casseroles.

People in Postville swore by the sixteen-ounce hamburger

(garnished with grilled onions and mushrooms, peppers, lettuce, tomato, and cheese) known far and wide as the Gunderburger at the Shanti, owned by Jeff and Brenda Pfister, on County Road B60 in nearby Gunder. If you had a hankering for what owner Jane Willie billed as the "world's largest tenderloin sandwich," the Tap in St. Olaf was the place to go. The breaded, fried pork patty hung off the edges of the ten-inch plate it was served on and came with two hamburger buns.

Untouched by the vitality and vulgarity of America's urban sprawl, Postville had everything modern cities do not: innocence, tranquillity, cohesion, a sense of order. Almost everyone belonged to St. Paul Lutheran Church, and if they didn't, then they went to St. Bridget's, the Catholic church on West Williams Street or Community Presbyterian on South Reynolds Street. Apart from taverns, few places in small towns allow for outsiders, and when a stranger stepped into either Postville's Club 51 or the Horseshoe Lounge around the corner, word spread faster than a May hailstorm. Every resident was accommodated and accounted for in this closed society, and strangers were regarded with a mixture of curiosity and suspicion. The busiest the police chief, Mike Halse, ever got was when the Mexicans who worked at the nearby turkey plant drank too much and started throwing punches outside Club 51. The only case of vandalism anyone in Postville could recall wasn't even vandalism: One night last summer a carload of drunk kids from Minnesota sneaked onto a Postville farm and tipped one of the Jerseys that had gotten out of the barn. The poor cow couldn't get up until the next morning, and that was only after the farmer and his two teenage sons pushed her upright so she could stand again.

Postville was the kind of place where drivers automatically wave to each other and then think about who it was they just waved to. The farmers in their pickups had it down to a science: They barely lifted an index finger (if they still *had* an index finger) off the big steering wheel, and then nodded their head ever so slightly. No one used turn signals because everyone knew where everyone else was going. At Home Oil, you had two choices: You paid after you pumped, or Junior Porterfield wrote down in his dog-eared spiral notebook what you owed him, and you paid when *you* got paid. The red-and-white Phillips 66 pumps were the old-fashioned kind, with metal dials that clicked as they toted up. Inside, Junior and Mark Looney sat on a lumpy sofa and jawed about everything from the weather, to when the University of Iowa Hawkeyes were going to get some sense knocked into them and fire Hayden Fry's butt.

The last time any kind of official census was taken in Postville, the number stood at 1,465. Postville was fifty miles from the nearest freeway and thirty miles from the closest McDonald's. The nearest traffic light was the one in the county seat, Waukon, twelve miles north. On hot summer evenings, people left their car radios playing and their keys in the ignition whenever they ran into Casey's to buy an Icee. Every phone in Postville had the same prefix, 864, and if you dialed the wrong number, you ended up talking for ten minutes anyway. Older Postville people still answered by announcing their last names, a throwback to the days of party lines and local telephone operators.

Until she died a couple of years ago at age ninety-two, Hattie Rose, known as Postville's Pie Lady, was probably Postville's biggest celebrity. By her own count, Hattie had baked sixty-five thousand pies. Paul Harvey knew a good thing when he heard about it, and back when Hattie had finished her ten thousandth pie, he did a story on her. On Hattie Rose Pie Day (September 27, 1985), more than three hundred people turned out to honor Hattie's fifty thousandth pie, a sour-cream raisin concoction that fetched $960. The most pies Hattie ever made in one day was eighty-two for a local farmer's hog sale, which prompted the *Herald-Leader* to estimate that if all of Hattie's pies were lined up, they would stretch 7.1 miles.

Six months ago, a pesky black bear showed up in Steve Snitker's cornfield just north of town. Steve got out his camcorder and started shooting, which must have spooked the bear enough to make him climb up a tree, where the bear stayed for a month. The bear got Postville on the front page of the *Gazette,* and on the evening news in Waterloo and Cedar Rapids. That was probably the biggest local news story in years, second to the high school girls' softball team advancing to the state tournament in Fort Dodge, before losing a cliffhanger in the first round.

Postville had a full calendar of social events, and the job of covering all of it fell on Mabel Gullickson and Hazel Stee, the must-read correspondents for the *Herald-Leader.* "After having spent a week in the Ray Schara and Kathryn Waters homes, Tom and Sharon Waters left Saturday for Hackensack, Minn. to spend a week with the David Madsen family before returning to their home in Grand Coulee, Washington." Or, "Mabel Gullickson visited in the home of Ervin and Evelyn Johnson of West Union on Saturday afternoon." Or, "George Wander, Mrs. Evelyn Martin and Mrs. LaVerna Schopp had the birthday song sung for them. The afternoon closed with coffee and cookies. Mrs. Frances Harnack and Mrs. Ivanelle Kuhse were hostesses. Blue was the predominant color in the table decorations with small rail fences hung with strips of denim."

A popular feature in the *Herald-Leader* was the "Yard of

the Week" contest. Under a grainy black-and-white photograph, the caption read: "The Milo and Betty Helgerson residence on Murdock Street is the Park Board's selection for Yard of the Week. Here the Helgersons stand in their back yard. The entire property is beautifully landscaped with shrubs, perennials and annuals." Under the "Card-of-Thanks" column, Bud Swenson wrote: "A heartfelt thanks to the Postville ambulance for their quick response. Thanks to family and friends for the cards, food, visits, and most of all their prayers during my hospitalization at Waukon and St. Mary's Hospital. God Bless." In the classifieds, a single-family house "in good condition" was advertised for $19,000.

When editor Sharon Drahn turned fifty in March, the *Herald-Leader* ran a news story and invited people to celebrate with cake and punch at the newspaper office. More than sixty showed up with balloons, carnations, daisies, a corsage, even a couple of silk-flower arrangements.

Leo Riley, the thirty-eight-year-old priest at St. Bridget's, described to me the insular nature of Postville this way: "Unless your grandfather was born here and you've lived here for twenty years, you're considered an outsider." As in most small towns, there weren't too many secrets. If there was a divorce in the works, the locals were apt to get wind of it months before the unsuspecting spouse did. There were the unspoken truths that members of a small town like Postville accepted and shared. "You pick your nose here, and people know which nostril," Father Riley said. "You can't sneeze around here without forty people saying, 'God bless you!'"

As I made my rounds in Postville that day, the sky was turning dark and the humidity getting heavy. The radio weatherman had been right, but a day late. You could feel the moisture in the breeze, and you could smell the coming of a whopper of a rainstorm. Steam seemed to rise from the sidewalk. You could feel your pores open. In the fields, baby corn stalks bent and curled in a single, synchronized sway, a precursor to the storm the wet wind would bring.

"Here it comes," said Ruby Koenig, cashier at Moore's IGA, gazing out the plate-glass front windows at the sky, which had turned a dark, blackish gray. Ruby wasn't talking to anyone in particular. It was more a statement of fact. If you couldn't be friends with the Iowa weather, you at least knew what to expect from it. Through the automatic doors that kept opening and closing, shoppers hurried in to buy candles (should the power go out), and while they were at it, bags of ice, flashlight batteries, eggs, loaves of bread, gallon jugs of milk. "We sure need the rain, but not the wind. Oh, I hate that wind," Ruby said, shaking her head and wiggling her shoulders at the same time as though she had just gotten a shock of static electricity.

As I walked out of Moore's, the rain began to fall. The raindrops came down so hard and fast that when they hit your skin, it hurt. Jagged lines of lightning lit the horizon for a split second. Claps of thunder followed—so loud that the noise made you jump even though you were prepared for it. The temperature plunged eight, ten degrees in a couple of minutes. It felt like someone had just opened the door to a giant freezer on a hot night, and you were standing in front, dressed in your pajamas.

For the next three hours, I dodged the downpour. The locals surely must have thought I was crazy to be sprinting from place to place. My IOWA T-shirt was soaked. At Ginger's, I met a couple of farmers wearing overalls and feed caps. By then, the rain was coming down in sheets, and no one was going anywhere. Someone had turned on a television set, and six or seven people clustered around the screen, watching a Special Alert from Channel 7. The Doppler radar screen showed the eye of the storm, dense red and blue splotches, circling northeast Iowa, near Decorah. Craig Johnson, the usually cheerful weatherman, looked worried, and said northeast Iowa was "experiencing a severe thunderstorm." He counseled viewers to stay indoors. We looked at one another in Ginger's and nodded our heads. "And if you must go outside, please," the weatherman implored, "watch for downed power lines." Flash flooding, he said, was "likely."

But within an hour, the storm had apparently spent itself, suddenly veering off to the northwest, heading into the woods of Minnesota. A couple of leafy branches lay downed on the sidewalks and streets, but that was all. Whole shafts of late-afternoon sun, charged with rain-fresh ions, beamed down on Lawler Street. I saw several Hasidic men briskly walking between their homes and the shul on Lawler Street, but when I got near them, they hurriedly looked down, speeding by me.

When I stopped in to see Sharon at the *Herald-Leader,* she seemed as sincere as she had sounded on the phone. I felt a kinship to Sharon and the newspaper. No matter exactly why I was in Postville, I still felt like a journalist. When I told Sharon about my meeting Sunday with Don Hunt, her cinnamon-colored eyes lit up.

"You're going in*side*?" she asked, sounding almost awestruck.

As Sharon and I talked, more and more people came by the newspaper office. One by one, Leigh Rekow, Whitey Meyer, Beverly Schaeffer, Alicia Gustafson, Dawn Schmadeke, and Harold Schaufenbuel stopped in. When the topic turned to the Jews, Beverly, Alicia, Dawn, and Harold looked at each other. They weren't alarmed, but I could tell, they seemed skittish. It was only after I told them I wouldn't use their names that they began opening up, and soon I got the feeling I was in the middle of a coffee klatch. The paper didn't come out till Wednesday, and Sharon's deadline wasn't until Monday afternoon.

"*He's* going into the plant to meet Sho*lom* Rubashkin," Sharon announced.

"That'll be interesting," Leigh Rekow deadpanned.

"Good luck," Beverly Schaeffer counseled.

"Watch out," Harold Schaufenbuel warned.

"Why?" I asked.

"You'll see," Dawn Schmadeke replied, smiling broadly, as though she was the town keeper of secrets.

When the Jews first arrived in the mid-1980s, Postville was in the midst of a full-blown economic crisis. Banks were foreclosing on family farms throughout the state, and agricultural conglomerates, once considered the devil, were about the only saviors left, even though they lowballed anyone who thought twice about selling. A local grocery, a women's clothing store, and a haberdashery had just folded, with more retail stores on the chopping block. The local hospital boarded up its doors and windows. Like the occasional pickup that puttered by on Lawler Street, no one was in a hurry to do anything because to hurry meant to speed up the inevitable— Postville was turning into a town of empty storefronts. Any young people who hung around after high school or college probably didn't have much on the ball because if they did, why would they still be in Postville?

Just as the state was climbing out of the farm crisis, in 1987, Aaron Rubashkin, the Brooklyn butcher, came to town. Banker Jim Lage and a few other local businessmen helped raise $20,000 and offered it to Rubashkin to open the old Hy-grade slaughterhouse, just outside the city limits, which had lain defunct for almost a decade. Leigh Rekow recalled the first meeting between the locals and the Jews as probably the most positive town hall meeting ever held in Postville.

More than two hundred locals showed up to hear a Ha-sidic rabbi, Manis Friedman, as thin as a rail, sporting a fe-dora and a long black-gray beard. Depending on your point of view, Rabbi Friedman looked like either Merlin or a walk-on for a Marx Brothers movie. He talked funny. The words were English, but they came out strange, and he spoke way too fast for most of the locals to follow. Leigh remembered the joke that the rabbi tried as an icebreaker.

"Normally when you have two people, you have two opin-ions. But with Jews," Rabbi Friedman said pausing for effect, "when you have two people, you've got three opinions!"

Rabbi Friedman's raft of jokes, his mannerisms, like shrug-ging his shoulders, using his hands to talk, answering ques-tions with more questions, most of it had somehow worked. The locals had been painted into a corner. They needed the Jews. They figured that once the Jews came, the abandoned slaughterhouse would be reopened, and with more people moving into town, property values might stop nose-diving. That was important since most people in town were older than fifty, and they had all their assets tied up in the equity of their homes or land. The slaughterhouse meant home buyers, which meant increased demand on the housing stock in town and higher real-estate prices. By the time the evening ended, almost everyone at the town hall was smiling, even some of the tightest Iowans.

That was how it began, but at the *Herald-Leader*, the lo-cals spent two hours talking to me about the "Jewish Invasion"—at least that's how Harold put it each time he mentioned the Postville Hasidim. The way the locals in the newspaper office told it, their relationship with the Jews had turned into a marriage gone sour: The first months had been divine, but almost ten years after tying the knot, there had been deceit and deception. Some days both spouses wanted a divorce; other days neither could look at the other.

In the 124 years since Postville was incorporated, the locals had never seen newcomers quite like the Hasidic Jews. "They don't want to have anything to do with us," seventy-eight-year-old Harold said, shaking his head, the beginnings of a puffy blue vein appearing on his forehead. "We're invisible to them. They look right through us like we don't exist."

To the locals, though, the Jews were eye-openers. It wasn't just the woolen waistcoats they wore in the dog days of summer, or that during the frigid Iowa winters, they didn't know enough to turn off their outside water lines to protect their pipes from freezing and bursting. The Jews didn't know the first thing about driving. One Jew parked in the middle of Greene Street, another drove along the sidewalk, another roared down Lawler Street at fifty miles per hour. They made U-turns in the center of town, drove beat-up clunkers that needed mufflers, seldom bothered to get driver's licenses or register their cars with the Iowa Department of Transportation. At least once when police chief Mike Halse stopped a Hasid, the driver tried to bribe him. No one in Postville had ever done *that* before. Halse would shake his head as nicely as he could and tell the drivers to go on over to the post office, buy a money order, and send it to the Allamakee County Court House.

If the way they drove made Postville locals run for cover, the way they cared for their homes—at least the little anyone could see from the outside—made the locals shake their heads. When the Iowa spring comes round, Postville lawns are mowed like crew cuts—military cut, regulation length. In the winter, snowy front walks are often shoveled before the snowflakes stop falling. Order, routine, and neatness are next to godliness. But the Hasidim hardly ever raked the crinkly leaves that blanketed their front lawns every autumn. They certainly never followed the Iowa custom of getting all your tulip, gladiola, and crocus bulbs into the earth by Thanksgiving. Few probably even knew what a bulb looked like, so why would they ever think to plant one? Not many ever sprinkled seed in the bare spots on the lawns, or mowed the grass in the summer. Beverly, Whitey, Leigh, Alicia, and Dawn had a chuckle over that one. Everyone laughed except Harold, who was still smarting from the fall he nearly took last January. The Jews hardly ever shoveled or salted their front sidewalks, and Harold damn near fell and broke his other hip, the one that was still his, in front of one of their homes. To him, the Jews couldn't do anything right.

Postville people, by and large, were tolerant. They believed in the New Testament and what it preached about welcoming newcomers. Jesus, after all, was a spurned Jew, who had been spurned by strangers in town after town he traveled through. The Postville locals followed Jesus' gospel, to love thy neighbor, no matter who thy neighbor was. But these newcomers, well, Jesus himself would have a hard time with them. They were downright rude. They seemed to go out of their way to be obnoxious, especially when it came to business dealings. When they did their shopping, they bargained for the best prices, for everything from shoes and food to clothing and cars. Bargaining was a concept totally alien to rural

Iowans. Postville locals weren't wealthy by a long shot. Most worked hard and spent their hard-earned money wisely. When a price was quoted, that was the price. To bargain would imply that the price was unfair to start with, and to question it would be an insult to the seller, who was a friend of yours, and if he wasn't, he would be. Whenever some Jews hired local handymen, they strung out payments for months on end. Terry Szabo, who owned his own construction company, got so angry when he didn't get paid that he hauled one of the Postville Jews into the Allamakee County small-claims court, and got a judgment levied against the man. One elderly Postville merchant broke down in tears when a Jewish man started dickering for a lower price, and once the merchant agreed to an unheard-of price, the Jew refused to pay. "Can you imagine?" asked Dawn Schmadeke, shaking her head, her right hand on her hip.

"No way could they possibly treat their own people as poorly as they treat us," Beverly Schaeffer said, raising her pointy chin. "Hadn't their mothers taught them any manners?"

Reserved Iowans don't go out of their way to attract attention. The New Testament says, "God resisteth the proud and giveth grace to the humble," and "Whosoever shall exalt himself shall be abased; and he that humbleth himself shall be exalted." Most Postville people believed that down to their bones. Calling attention to yourself was poor upbringing. Yet last December, during Chanukah, one of the Jews, Yosi Gourarie, Sholom's brother-in-law, took the ten-foot-tall Agriprocessors' menorah (a candelabra used to celebrate the Jewish holiday) from its place next to the slaughterhouse gates, strapped it to a beat-up black Oldsmobile, and paraded up and down Postville streets for eight days. Yosi, the manager of live poultry at the plant, got a boom box, set up speakers, revved up the Olds, and cranked out Chanukah tunes at full blast. It was surreal. A dark-haired, full-bearded Jew with an ample belly, running his car on the snow-lined streets of Lutheran Postville a couple of weeks before Christmas, smiling, shouting, and waving to pedestrians like a Jewish version of Santa Claus.

The locals didn't quite know how to react. They winced, smiled uncomfortably, and shook their heads some more. What the hell was this blockhead doing? The locals weren't about to convert, and the Hasidic Jews knew everything there was to know about Chanukah. So, what was the point, except to embarrass anyone with any manners?

Yet Yosi's escapade, the Jews' clothes, their driving, even the way they walked with their shoulders hunched and their heads high—all of that ultimately turned out to be window dressing. These Hasidim were different from the locals, yes, but they also were different from newcomers anywhere. Generally, newcomers are eager to assimilate to a new culture. That's why they came in the first place. But instead of arriving at the lowest rung of the economic ladder, these Jews had arrived already on top. The Jews who settled in Postville came from cities, and many brought with them large sums of money. They renovated and transformed fine old Postville homes, adding bedrooms, remodeling kitchens, as per kosher requirements, with two sinks, two cupboards, two of everything so that meat and dairy products never mixed. Alicia Gustafson said that to accommodate his family, Sholom Rubashkin built an enormous house on Wilson Street in an area of Postville that the locals quickly labeled "Kosher Hill." Iowans were loathe to show such material wealth. "That Rubashkin home is a palace," Alicia said, and no one denied it.

Though the Hasidim were always on the lookout for men to work menial jobs at the kosher slaughterhouse, outside of the plant, they seemed to go out of their way to avoid the locals. At first, the locals welcomed the Jews, but even the simplest offer—a handshake, an invitation for afternoon tea— was spurned. The locals quickly discovered that the Jews wouldn't even look at them. They refused to acknowledge even the *presence* of anyone not Jewish. "If they mix with us, they think we'll contaminate them," said Dawn Schmadeke. "Like we have AIDS." Harold's vein popped out again.

To remain pure, the Jews would not allow their children to go to the Postville public schools, so the Hasidim rented space in the basement of what used to be the community hospital and turned it into a yeshiva, a Jewish school. Even though the Hasidic kids didn't attend public school, the school district gave them paper, pencils, supplies, even desks and chairs. The Hasidic Jews wouldn't permit their kids to swim in Postville's municipal pool. Leigh Rekow was worried that the Jews would force the city to establish a "Jewish swim hour," during which the locals wouldn't be allowed to use their own pool— not that the locals would want to use it if the Jews were obnoxious enough to ask for and get what they wanted. Dawn Schmadeke shook her head. She and everyone else at the *Herald-Leader* that afternoon were tired of the way the Jews went about almost everything.

An old idea about annexing the land where the slaughterhouse was located had gained more and more support. The slaughterhouse was on county land, three hundred feet outside the city limits. For almost forty years, going back to the 1950s, long before the Jews had arrived in town, people in Postville had talked about annexing land from the county, so that the city could grow. By 1990, the issue had come up again—this time with a vengeance. If the city could annex the land on which the slaughterhouse was located, it would increase control over the Jews. It would also create more tax revenue for the city. The mayor of Postville, John Hyman, the shop teacher at Dr. John R. Mott High, was swept into office in 1991 on a single campaign promise: Let the voters decide in a referendum whether to annex or not.

To say the Jews detested the plan is an understatement. "They've been kicking and screaming, saying all sorts of nasty things about us," said Leigh Rekow, a member of the Postville City Council. Annexation, the Jews said, would kill the kosher goose that had laid all of Postville's golden eggs. And if the people of Postville were foolhardy enough to annex the slaughterhouse property, then the Hasidim would pack up and vanish in a New York minute. But there was more: The Jews said that the drive to annex their land was pure and simple anti-Semitism, a reaction to all the wealth they had accumulated in Postville.

That only the Jews raised such a ruckus over the proposed annexation was typical of them and their tactics, said Leigh. None of the other large property owners in the proposed annexation area seemed to care whether their land was annexed or not. The owners of the local turkey plant and the plastics plant had even come out in favor of annexation. Whatever the vote was, it was the cost of doing business in these parts.

Annexation, it seemed, was a line in the Iowa soil that the Jews had drawn. Cross it, they said, and we'll pack up and leave. "If they want to leave," Leigh said. "That'll be fine with me and pretty much everyone else in town. We were here when they came, and we'll be here when they leave."

Though they might find their backs to the wall economically, everyone at the *Herald-Leader* except Harold seemed to take the Jews' threats in stride, even Leigh. They joked about the Jews, and still, after all woes, were curious about them. "I've heard the Jewish men make great husbands," Dawn Schmadeke said, her eyes widening. "I'd just love to nestle in one of their beards. But the first thing I'd want to ask would be 'How do you manage to keep that little beanie on your head all the time? Doesn't it ever fall off?'" Alice and Whitey Meyer laughed heartily. Leigh shook his head. Harold remained humorless, vacantly staring out the *Herald-Leader's* front window.

Was Dawn's comment an ugly slur on Jews, or just a naive question? Out of the blue, the incident at the newspaper office brought back a memory from when I was eight or nine. My family was about to eat at a crowded restaurant on the New Jersey shore. We had waited for more than an hour and had been seated by a tall, thin woman who held in her hand a metal clicker she used to alert the hostesses of empty tables. The hostess said something to our waitress, who, as she turned, looked at us and whispered under her breath, "Those Jews can wait." At least, that's what my father thought she said. Within seconds, he quickly roused my mother, sister, and me. My father said nothing to the waitress, as the four of us stormed out of the restaurant.

Was Dawn's comment as reprehensible as what my father had thought the waitress had said? Was it similar to what I had found lurking in Iowa City, something Mikey's Cub Scout leader might have said, or what the elderly ladies in Winga's may have been thinking? Didn't a righteous Jew have a moral imperative to stand up and challenge what Dawn had said? If the Hasidic Jews had heard it, they certainly would have.

But, as I did at the Cub Scout meeting, I said nothing. My role was to listen, not to challenge these people who seemed pleasant enough, and as I prepared to leave that afternoon, I thanked everyone. I sensed that they had been auditioning me, assessing whether I could be trusted to go deeper, to see more. That afternoon in Postville, I had somehow assumed the role of a confidant among the townspeople, at least among the half dozen at the newspaper. Whether it was because of the bond that people forge after the calm of a threatening storm, the novelty of an out-of-town visitor listening to their woes, the fact that I was a professor at the state university and therefore was neutral, or just that I had passed Sharon's muster, I had become their surrogate. Not for a minute did I think the locals figured me to be Jewish. Jews to them were the Hasidim, the men with the beards and the women with scarves. Tomorrow, just as everyone in Postville was getting out of church and about to eat Sunday dinner, I would get to see what the locals had never been allowed.

Outside the *Herald-Leader* door, Leigh Rekow took me by my right arm, and pulled me close to him. "Keep your eyes open," he whispered.

CHAPTER 4

Landsmen

Back inside my mildewy room at the Pines, I finished eating the last of the provisions I had bought at Moore's IGA, and prepared to head over to the slaughterhouse. It was to be my first opportunity to meet the Hasidim, and I was looking forward to it. I wanted to learn the Hasidic version of life in Iowa and in Postville. Did they, too, feel like strangers in a strange land? How did they cope with Christian Iowa? Was anti-Semitism really at the root of the locals' drive to annex their land?

I knew that killing and processing meat according to the strict rules of *kashrut* was a sacred obligation to Orthodox Jews. Labor was cheap, the livestock and poultry plentiful, and compared to New York prices, Postville real estate was a steal. Still, any Jew had to admit that Iowa was a curious place for a band of ultra-orthodox Jews. The state is synonymous with one animal: the pig. Pork reigns absolute. Iowans worship these squealing fattened animals; they are the engines that pull the state and its economy. Observant Jews, on the other hand, view pigs as the devil incarnate. They so thoroughly revile pigs that in Yiddish scores of expressions denote the pig's (*chozzer's*) lowly status: *chozzerai* means junk, trash, anything disgusting and repulsive; *Es past vi a chozzer* means "It's as suitable as a pig," something in the very worst taste; *Er hot azoy fil gelt vi a yid hot chozzerim* translates to "He has as much money as a Jew has pigs" (He's broke). The Jews' and Iowans' opposite views on pigs seemed to be at the symbolic center of a cultural war looming in Postville.

I also knew that Hasidim were loath to rely on anyone outside their *mishpocheh*, extended family. They were wary and suspicious of non-Jews, whom they routinely referred to as "goyim" and "eaters of *trayf*" (nonkosher food, and by extension, untrustworthy persons). Yet rural Iowans' second nature was to seek an ecclesiastic merging of soul, body, and spirit to survive. The hard Iowa farm life required a connectedness, a mutual support system among neighbors. Through the brutal Iowa winters, scorching summers, pesticide-thick springs, around-the-clock autumn harvests, a communal bond was crucial if the community was to survive. Maintaining this support system was the undergirding of rural life. Each year, if things went right, if the corn crops were good, if the hogs didn't get sick and die, if the market was decent for a change, if rain or drought didn't devastate your land, a sense of triumph over adversity emerged. A collective soul arose. Hope endured. Such an abiding sense of community embraced opposing agendas, factions, likes and dislikes, and had provided sustenance for these northeast Iowa farmers for more than a century.

If Harold and the rest of the coffee klatch at the *Herald-Leader* had been right, the Hasidim must have thought of their gentile neighbors as the cost of doing business in Iowa. The Yiddish expression, *Shlog mikh nit, un lek mikh nit*, probably summed up the Hasidim's feelings toward the locals: "Hit me not and lick me not," "Just leave me alone." How could the locals possibly get along with any newcomers who had become Postville's new power elite? Was envy part of the reason why the locals seemed to dislike the Hasidic Jews so much? Was it an ingrained discomfort with people different from them, as Iris, Mikey, and I had experienced in Iowa City?

As I backed out of the Pines, yesterday's rain had returned. Driving toward the silver water tower on the edge of town that had AGRIPROCESSORS stenciled on it in black letters, the raindrops sounded like marbles bouncing against the car roof. I crossed over the bumpy tracks of the Chicago, Milwaukee, St. Paul, and Pacific Railroad, and once on the slaughterhouse property, passed what appeared to be the giant menorah that Yosi Gourarie had strapped to his car last Chanukah. At a makeshift guard station, a middle-aged woman with a brunette ponytail motioned me with a cocked index finger to a parking lot a hundred yards away, fast turning into an enormous mud pit. Individual parking slots were identified with white wooden signs and black block lettering:

RABBI KLEIN

RABBI SHLOMO

RABBI S. GOTLIB

RABBI C. KEIN

C. MAIMAN

S. EIDLMAN

S. HOLTZBERG

M. HOLTZBERG

P. PERES

S. AMAR

M. GURKOV

G. BASS

A. KOKON

There were also two slots with signs that each read RABBI.

Then, just as I pulled into a stall next to one of the RABBI slots, it hit me: the sandwich I had just finished, the salami and cheese. My hands had touched pork! Worse, it was pork *and* cheese. For observant Jews, mixing any meat with a diary product was bad enough, but eating *chozzer* and cheese was a sin of unpardonable proportion. Such a meal was totally *trayf,* counter to all convention of Jewish dietary laws. The rabbis were liable to smell the *chozzerai* on my hands, and who knew what they'd do. I had driven all this way to talk with Hasidic Jews, and I smelled like pork. *"This* is smart?" I could hear Grandma Rose saying, shaking her head in the kitchen of her cramped Miami Beach apartment.

I laughed at my blunder as I pulled out a Wash'n' Dri from the car's glove compartment and rubbed my fingers and palms. I watched rabbis and workers dodging the rain, running past muddy potholes, going from one building to another. Most were dressed in white butcher coats, yellow rubber boots, and blue hard hats with yarmulkes barely visible underneath. You could see the fringes, the *tzitzit,* peeking out from under their shirts.

At the loading dock, chickens squawked, cramped four, five, six to a cage. The rain and mud splattered into the cages, matting the chickens' feathers, ticking them with brown spots. Even during the downpour, hard-hatted workers were unloading cattle from a long eighteen-wheel truck to holding pens adjacent to an enclosed area where sheep nuzzled against one another's woolly coats. The cattle were forced down a chute from the tractor trailer into narrow, confined spaces. Fifty yards ahead, the slaughterhouse pens were so crowded that the animals were positioned noses poking into rumps, jammed into pens diagonally, vertically, horizontally, eight to ten head per confinement area. Hooves scuffed the dirty concrete floor, and as the animals bellowed wails and grunts in unison, spectacular bolts of lightning illuminated the dark Iowa sky, followed by—one-Mississippi, two-Mississippi, three-Mississippi, four-Mississ—sharp claps of thunder. The stench from the animals almost overcame me—blood, fur, feathers, manure, and dirt. The uplifting scent of the fresh rainstorm had been subsumed into a nauseating sweet odor that momentarily took my breath away. It made the pure aroma of pig manure, which I had grown to like, smell like fresh-baked bread.

With my hands wiped as clean as a moist Towelette could make them, I climbed the stairs above the cattle queue to meet Don Hunt, a Cesar Romero lookalike with lizard-skin boots, a sporty mustache, and a quick smile. He greeted me with an outstretched hand, but said he had an emergency to take care of and couldn't talk to me.

"I'll try to arrange for you and Sholom Rubashkin to meet tonight, let's say, nine o'clock?"

"Nine? Tonight?"

He nodded and raised his right eyebrow slightly, as though to send me a signal whose meaning I wasn't sure I understood. It was the only time Sholom could see me, Hunt said, again raising his eyebrow.

I left the slaughterhouse, disappointed but also intrigued, and drove around Postville a couple of times. As I passed St. Paul Lutheran Church, I watched large families, the boys in clip-on ties and the girls wearing Sunday dresses, hurrying to minivans in the parking lot and heading for home. I drove back to the Pines to wait out the rainstorm.

At precisely nine that night, I again climbed the narrow, rickety stairs of the slaughterhouse and took a seat in the cramped business office above the pens of cattle and sheep. Despite the hour, the place was humming. A secretary typed. Phones rang. Hasidic Jews came and went, wearing white butcher coats, hard hats, and rubber boots. They talked in Yiddish and Hebrew, seldom saying anything in English. A man fresh off the killfloor, dressed in a white shirt and black waistcoat, who I later learned to be Lazar Kamzoil, scurried about, shaking his head, muttering. Even after I gave my name to the secretary, no one paid me any attention. No one said anything to me.

With the secretary busy, I left the waiting room and eyed a maze of narrow hallways. The linoleum floor was lopsided and uneven. I poked my head into Sholom Rubashkin's office, but he shooed me away with the back of his right hand. "Too busy," he said in English. "Wait outside."

Finally, at ten, Sholom called me to his office. He motioned me to take a seat as he continued talking on the phone. Sholom had a scraggly beard and deep dark circles under brown eyes. He looked as though he hadn't been in sunlight for years. Sholom pulled out a Marlboro Gold cigarette, lit it, and started sucking and then exhaling, all the while still talking on the phone in a mishmash of rapid-fire Hebrew and Yiddish. Cradling the phone between his right ear and shoulder, he was balancing his checkbook on an old-model computer. After he finished with the computer, he started making wild hand and arm gestures in response to what the caller on the phone was saying. When he wanted to make a point, his eyes narrowed into slits. Sholom got up, walked around in a small circle behind his desk, still cradling the phone and still smoking, all the while slapping the back of his right hand into the palm of his left.

"Sholom, line two. Sholom, line three," the secretary squawked through an office intercom.

"Who is it?" Sholom yelled out the door.

Through the intercom box came two names.

"Who's that?" he asked, shrugging his shoulders, now looking at me, leaning forward. "*You* know anyone with a name like that?"

"He wants to talk about the truckload. He's somewhere in Missouri," the secretary said.

"He's *meshugge.* Tell him to forget it. *Sheesh!*"

A red-bearded rabbi walked into the office, and soon Sholom was having a four-way conversation—with the caller on the phone, the rabbi, the secretary on the intercom, and sometimes with me. The rabbi raised his voice to Sholom, a barrage of Hebrew or Yiddish tumbling out of his mouth. Again Sholom slapped his left palm with the back of his right hand, which made a loud smacking sound. He went back to the caller, then back to the rabbi, then back to the phone, all the while raising his eyebrows to me.

The argument he was having with the rabbi had something to do with money. I distinctly heard the word *gelt,* and the rabbi counting in Hebrew. Sholom went back to the phone. Sholom swiveled his chair so that his back was facing the rabbi and me, and lowered his voice to whoever was on the phone. With Sholom's back turned, the rabbi pulled out three cigarettes from the pack of Marlboro Golds on Sholom's desk. The rabbi looked my way, put an index finger to his mouth, and whispered "*Shhhh!*" Then he left, muttering something in Hebrew directed at Sholom.

Finally, close to eleven, Sholom hung up the phone.

"Sholom. Line one."

"Take a message," Sholom shouted out the door.

We shook hands, two men sizing each other up. "You're Jewish," Sholom said, leaning forward again, peering at me intensely. "Don Hunt said nothing about you being Jewish." Sholom rose from his chair, tilted his head closer to me over the desk. "You *look* Jewish." It came out more as an admonition than an observation from an ultra-orthodox Jew dressed with yarmulke and *tzitzit* to a Reform Jew wearing T-shirt and jeans.

"How'd you know?" I asked, playing the straight man.

"With a nose like that, and you're not Jewish? Whaddaya take me for, a *shlemiel*?"

Welcome to Jewish Humor 101, where kibitzing was a finely honed art, mock aggressive and assertive in nature, totally alien to the deferential Iowans I had met yesterday. I was transported back to encounters with Stanley, the dry cleaner near my sister's house in Brooklyn ("You vant it vhen? Vhat, you a comedian? No vay! And I mean it! ... But maybe I could do it. But only this one time!"), and a salesman named Murray in my father's shoe store ("You're just a little *pisher*, what makes *you* think you can sell?").

"Where you from?" Sholom asked, cocking back his head, raising his bearded chin. "Where your people from?" Sholom didn't have to ask. He already knew, just as I already knew by taking one look at him where *his* people were from.

When I answered "Jersey," the division between us was merely for the record. Sholom and I may have been descendants of a single tribe centuries ago, perhaps even from the same father, but in the intervening years, that tribe had splintered into thousands of different families. I had grown up in a decidedly Reform Jewish family in northern New Jersey. I never had a bar mitzvah, the traditional ceremonial passage of boyhood to manhood that takes place on the thirteenth birthday. Instead, my Jewish parents opted to have me confirmed, a Reform Jewish practice borrowed, in part, from the Christian ceremony. Born in Sault Sainte Marie, Ontario, my mother was a Midwesterner, but my father was as East Coast as American Jews come—born in New York City. I grew up in the Jewish suburbs of Manhattan, in Essex County, where half my high school class was Jewish. Despite the preponderance of Jews, few of my friends learned Hebrew, few families lit candles at *Shabbos* dinner and few celebrated the Sabbath. Synagogue was called "temple," and most families attended only during the High Holidays, on Rosh Hashanah and Yom Kippur.

Yet despite the lack of Jewish worship and observance, and my family's total assimilation into everything American and secular, we were thoroughly Jewish. Our perspective was Jewish, as was our very essence. The world was split into two distinct halves: Jews and gentiles. Jews were always sought in business or social dealings over gentiles. A common expression used by Jews to describe a slow, dense person was—and still is—"He's got a *goyisher kop,*" which literally means "He's got a gentile head" but figuratively means "slow-witted." First question when I came home and boasted of making a new friend always was "Is he Jewish?" "God forbid!" (my father's expression) if I should ever go out with a gentile girl, and *"Oy vey!"* (which literally means "Oh pain!") if I ever got serious with her. All my parents' friends were Jews. They all shared the same role models: Sandy Koufax, Bernard Baruch, Bess Meyerson, Sam Levinson, Hank Greenberg, Arthur Goldberg, Golda Meir, Albert Einstein—these were people to be admired. And that poet with the beard, Allen Ginsberg, so smart, but the *faygeleh* (homosexual) business, such a waste!

There were two types of Jews. On one side were Jews like my parents for whom being Jewish meant keeping our Jewishness subordinate to our being American. On the other side were Orthodox Jews, notably Hasidic Jews, who retained their religion and the daily practice of it essential to their existence. Such ultra-orthodox Jews largely disassociated themselves from mainstream American culture, which they viewed as a threat to Jewish identity. The Lubavitchers and the Satmar, the two largest sects of Hasidic Jews, personified submersion into Jewish life.

To Sholom, I was simply a *Shabbes goy,* slang for a non-observant Jew, a sinner in the eyes of the Lord, but, as I was to learn, someone who could be saved. There was more kibitzing back and forth, and then Sholom launched into a lesson on the commerce of slaughtering. But even before I could register what he was saying, I was struck by the lilt of Sholom's speech. Apart from the two Hasidic mothers I had seen yesterday pushing the prams in Postville, I hadn't heard a New York accent so thick for years! And it wasn't just his accent, it was how Sholom carried on a conversation. Answers were never forthcoming; questions were answered with questions. Sholom's shoulders and hands seemed directly linked to what came out of his mouth. Seeing and hearing Sholom made me think I had suddenly stepped into the middle of a salesmen's roundtable at Ratners Delicatessen on New York's Lower East Side.

"It's a BUS-i-ness," Sholom lectured me. "Whaddaya THINK it is? We make money—or try to. Business is psychological. If it's not good today, it'll be good tomorrow. You have an industry that's making money. Right? I make money; you make money. That's the basis of making money. If there's a demand for something, it creates life. That's what we have done in Postville; we've given this place life. Why can't THEY un-der-STAND that? Is it *that* hard to figure out? We've cre-*ated* something here. We have the shul, the yeshiva, and two *mikvehs* [ritualistic, purifying bathhouses for men and women]. It's amazing what we've done here. In fact, it's more than amazing. It's un-be-liev-able. *Baruch Hashem!*" [Praised be the name]

Sholom soon shifted to annexation, the issue seemingly anathema to the Postville Jews. If the proposal ever got to the voting booth and passed, it would mean that the city would begin dipping its paws in the Agriprocessors' profits. At least, that's the way Sholom looked at the whole *goyishe* plan.

"They don't call it anti-Semitism, but that's what they're talking about," Sholom said leaning toward me, nearly screaming at me in a tone that reminded me of my conversation with Martin Appel. "They don't like Jews. You gotta be Einstein to figure that out? C'mon!"

"This annexation isn't logical," Sholom said, licking his lips, again edging forward. "I understand this city better than they think I do. They think they're dealing with a Jew who doesn't know them, who couldn't possibly understand how they think. But let me tell you something: Industry doesn't belong in a city. When did you ever hear of a packing plant located in a city? It don't make sense. It's *meshugge. You* know what that means."

Sholom was talking faster and faster, hands and arms moving in a blur. Annexation meant the goyim would be meddling in Sholom's business. They'd start sticking their little noses in the books and on the killfloor. And all of Sholom's life was dedicated to staying away from the *goyim.* He needed annexation like a hole in the head.

Sholom gestured with both palms cupped, then his fingers pointing. He got up from behind the desk. "We get absolutely zero if we get annexed. If annexation wouldn't hurt me, I'd say, 'sure.' But who invested in this place? Who stands to lose?

"Wake up, guys! Help *me.* 'What can *we* do to help *you*,' that's the question they need to be asking. Instead they want to put their hands into *our* pockets. No way it's going to happen."

Sholom pried open the plastic lid to a blue can of Planters salted peanuts, dug inside, and started tossing nuts into his mouth. He pointed the can toward me, but I shook my head. "If I'm welcomed in a place, then I want to stay there. If I'm not, I move. This isn't a personal decision. It's BUS-i-ness. It's like they're used to calling the shots, like they're the sheriff, and they're telling us, 'You betta listen to me!'" Sholom knocked back more peanuts, then lowered his voice. "Whadda-they tell you?"

The last thing I wanted was to be a conduit between the locals and the Jews. "How can you expect the Postville people to trust you when you don't let them into your lives?" I asked, suddenly startled by my own directness. "The Postville people I talked to say the Jews snub them."

"What's this, 'the *Jews*?' You're a Jew, and you think we snub them? C'mon!"

But before I could answer, Sholom had moved on to the topic that most Lubavitchers love to discuss, particularly with nonobservant Jews like me. "If you were a businessman, would you invest in Reform Judaism, with just a hundred or so years of history?" Shaking his head, the bridge of his nose down, the irises of his eyes stand-up alert, Sholom asked, "Wouldn't it make more sense to put your money in Orthodox Judaism, with more than five thousand years of history?"

Already he was starting in on me. Less than thirty minutes after I had met this man, and he was going after how I practiced my religion, what kind of Jew I was. Was this *chutzpah* or what?

"We *are* the Chosen People," Sholom bellowed. "That's what the Bible says, even the Bible *they* read. We have stayed on this planet longer than anyone because we believe our way is the right way. You start slipping, making changes here and there, and then you have nothing. We live by our own rules here, and they've got to understand that!"

The conversation continued, and quite frankly, I put down my pen and notebook, and just listened, exhausted by the crescendo of accusations, claims, threats. Sholom's one-upmanship was like a nervy kid in a religious-school playground, taunting, "I'm a better person than you are!" Two East Coast Jews in Iowa should have had something in common, but that was the same mistake I had made with Martin Appel. I had grown up just fifty miles from Sholom, but it could have been ten thousand. Sholom's people were more linked to Israel than to America, more to the Talmud than the *New York Times*. When my family ventured across the Hudson River to Manhattan in the 1950s, it was to see a Broadway play, the dinosaur bones at the Museum of Natural History, or take a tour of the United Nations. When Sholom's people traveled across the East River to Manhattan, it was to attend a benefit for Israel or to see *shmatte* salesmen on the Lower East Side to buy clothes for the whole family. If religion and geography didn't confer some kind of bond between Sholom and me, then what else would?

By half-past midnight, Sholom seemed positively invigorated. In between exhortations on annexation, the future of Judaism, and what religious training I intended to give my son, Sholom said he wanted me to take a tour of the plant tomorrow. "Ever been on a killfloor?" he asked, again pointing his bony index finger at me. "Tomorrow, you'll see what we made here in Postville. You'll see what the *goyim* want to take away from us."

CHAPTER 5

Tied Up

The weekend rains seemed to have transformed
Postville. The water-soaked soil began to resemble
the organic fields that would someday bear hardy, tall stalks of
corn. The sprouts along geometric rows of tilled earth looked
as though they had actually grown after yesterday's downpour.
Corn is known to farmers for its amazing symmetry. An ear
has fourteen, sixteen, or eighteen rows—always an even number—and depending on the number of rows, there are thirty-
five to forty kernels per row. In less than four months, corn
goes from a three-millimeter seed to a seedling, to a sprout,
to a seven-foot stalk with golden silk tassels. That rapid
growth has led farmers to swear something city folk can't
fathom: They insist you can actually hear corn growing. On a
quiet night in late spring to midsummer, in the middle of a
cornfield, there is an unmistakable popping, crunching sound.

The air on this Monday was no longer heavy and porten-
tous, but crisp and sharp. The sky, which yesterday was the
color of an iron skillet, today was a clear, almost translucent,
blue. People strode down Lawler Street and stopped to say

hello to one another. Their tone was unhurried, confident with purpose. Three men in overalls standing in the parking lot at Casey's nodded as another farmer got into a Chevy pickup and turned on the ignition. Beneath the shade of oaks and shagbark hickories along Greene Street, I saw a teenage girl in denim cutoffs flip a baton in the air, look up while holding her breath, and expertly catch the silvery staff as it glided back into the crook between her right thumb and index finger. The baton thrower's little sister, sitting on the front steps in shorts and bare feet, clapped her hands in delight.

Back at the slaughterhouse, the same woman with the ponytail, the sentry at the guardhouse, waved me through, today with a smile. Up the rickety stairs again, Don Hunt greeted me, and gave me a white butcher's coat, yellow hard hat, and black rubber boots. He pulled two pairs of goggles from a hook on the wall. "Better wear them to avoid the splatter," Don said. "You're going to see lots of blood."

The dilapidated kosher killfloor looked like a throwback to Upton Sinclair's days. I had imagined high-tech robotic devices that mechanically moved sides of beef as efficient teams of men surgically cut and carved. But there was nothing modern about what went on in this kosher abattoir. The slaughterhouse was divided into two halves: One side was the killfloor with the hot, sickening smell of hundreds of dead animals, their blood and guts spilled on the concrete floor; the other side was for processing, really a giant walk-in freezer, where the carcasses were wrapped, boxed, stored, and readied for market.

Still warm from life, the carcasses were very large—thirteen hundred pounds for a normal-sized steer. While workers killed, eviscerated, and disassembled the steers, the killfloor area was unbearably hot and humid. Steam rose from the cut-open animal carcasses. The stench of manure, cud, and entrails lingered in the air. I was afraid that if I thought too much about the smell and the sights before me, I would vomit.

The process was the exact opposite of the tried-and-true assembly-line concept that made America famous. Here, the raw product came into the plant whole, healthy, and intact. Once the animal was killed, it was *dis*assembled and repackaged into portions that transformed the animal's carcass to scores of sellable commodities. The workers were positioned at different stations: splitters guided the carcasses on platforms and then split the animals in half; deboners and trimmers worked with small knives, cutting inside the carcasses, drawing away fat and preparing the meat to be quartered and ultimately boxed. These workers could be gentiles; their jobs required no special religious training. But those who checked the lungs of the steers for lesions or imperfections (which would make the meat unsuitable since it would not be *glatt*) were specially trained and were all Jews.

In a small room where the cattle were being killed, there was no stun gun used; kosher-kill means to purge the animal as fast as possible of blood. In this killroom, three men stood in rubber boots knee-high in blood. Each steer was forced down a chute and loaded onto a giant vertical turntable. The animal slapped and wiggled back and forth in the mechanical vise, wailing against the inevitable. Once the steer was secured in the turntable slot, the apparatus lifted and spun, so that the animal was positioned upside down. A *shochet,* a Kosher slaughterer, in the pit, his apron soaked in blood, with his back toward the animal, took out a fifteen-inch-long blade and ran it quickly, in a single motion, across the steer's neck.

Blood spurted three or four feet from the severed neck in a pulsating, crescent-shaped arc that got larger and larger, and within ten seconds, ebbed to a trickle. The steer was then turned right side up again, mechanically pushed out of the slot, and hung ignominiously on a stainless steel hook, as another animal was loaded onto the turntable.

The only thing humane about the whole process seemed to be that the *shochet* shielded the shiny blade from the animal about to be slaughtered. One of the *shochtem* sloshing in blood saw me peering into the pit, eyes as large as saucers, and smiled amiably. "Come in! It's fun," he said in a Russian accent. "Vant to try?"

The *shochet,* whose name I later learned to be Moishe Tamarin, looked almost Amish, with a creamy complexion, a beard of thick straight auburn hair, and deep blue eyes set far apart. The eyes were difficult to forget. They were crossed, almost hypnotic as they drew me in. "Join me, I will watch out for you," his beguiling smile seemed to say.

I shook my head as Don Hunt grabbed my arm and led me to the chicken kill. Four rabbis, their beards confined by bluish, mesh nets, sat side by side, wearing white coats and goggles. Each held a small razor in his right hand, slitting the necks of chickens, 2,850 per hour. It was a sight—a flurry of squawking chickens all on death row. The neck of each chicken was forced into a metal brace, and as the cut-throat chickens moved past the rabbis' workstation, they still fluttered and bristled, advancing toward the next workstation, where feathers were removed in a chemical bath. The speed was amazing, 50 birds per minute.

Staggering out of the chicken kill with fresh poultry blood splattered on the coat I was wearing, I vowed to make good on a passing interest I had had to turn vegetarian. I made my way back to Sholom's office, and again, he was arguing with the red-bearded rabbi I had met last night. Sholom motioned for me to take a seat, and popped three Tums into his mouth. The rabbi took from his pocket a single cigarette and lit it. Their discussion seemed to be resolved.

"No problem?"

"No problem."

"You sure?"

"No problem."

"I don't want to have any problem."

"No problem!"

"You sure?"

"No problem!"

"Good!"

With that settled, the rabbi left, and Sholom went back to lecturing me on the sacred life righteous Jews ought to lead. For Hasidic Jews, there was good reason to remain apart from gentiles. To grow up Hasidic was to grow up in a nation within a nation. Hasidism carried its own deeply instilled history and myths, its indelible, almost-impossible-to-attain schema of how to lead the life of a *tzaddik*, a righteous, holy man. There were thousands of codes and rites to pass from generation to generation. For hundreds of years, Hasidim had dutifully explained to their children how Jews had been ex-pelled from country after country. Jews had been hunted, murdered, the victims of unspeakable pogroms. They had al-ways sought redemption as exiles, wandering from place to place. Because Hasids saw Jews assimilating all around them, being subsumed into the dominant Christian culture, Hasidic Jews were deadly serious when it came to carrying out the six hundred and thirteen commandments of the Torah with holy, fundamentalist zeal. These divine commandments, taken from the laws of Moses, controlled every facet of their lives, from the moment they awoke to the second they closed their eyes and drifted off to sleep.

Sholom suddenly looked up at me. He nodded almost imperceptibly. His dark eyes narrowed, turning into slits again. Sholom leaned forward, placed both palms atop old issues of *Meat & Poultry* magazine on his cluttered desk. "Have you done tefillin yet this morning?" he asked.

When I paused, Sholom asked, raising his voice, "You know what tefillin is? *Nu?*"

I had read about tefillin and had seen photos of Orthodox Jews wearing the leather straps and leather boxes, but had never used tefillin nor had ever seen a Jew wearing them. I knew that one box was to be strapped to the center of the forehead while the other was strapped onto the left arm through an elaborate system of wrapping and intertwining straps. The two boxes contain tiny parchments with Hebrew inscriptions from Exodus and Deuteronomy. Laying tefillin is essential in the execution of prayers for every Hasidic male past the age of thirteen, and tefillin are to be worn every day of the year other than six holidays and the Sabbath. I also had read somewhere that Lubavitchers believe that when a nonpracticing Jew lays tefillin it serves a special mitzvah. In fact, as I was to learn, Lubavitchers not only encourage, but vigorously exhort all Jewish men to observe the ritual. Lubavitchers with tefillin are like Jehovah's Witnesses on street corners holding up the *Watchtower.* Members of both faiths minister to all possible recruits through these tools.

Sholom's question to me wasn't really a question at all, but a requirement: Should I want to continue talking to him or other local Jews, I would have to submit to their rules. I played in my mind the reaction that shunning sacred tefillin would carry in the Postville Hasidic community. "He says he's a Jew? But he refuses to pray with tefillin? What kind of Jew is this?" I didn't want to wrap two yards of black leather around my arm and head, say a prayer that I didn't understand or believe in, as a way to assure Sholom that I was an upstanding Jew.

But why not? I had often mused about what it would be like to take a Communion wafer in my mouth. To kneel before a priest and have him place in my mouth a thin wafer was no more bizarre than wrapping an arm and forehead with leather straps and two square boxes. And this religious ritual came from *my* religion. It would be a way to get closer to the men I had seen from my car that first night in Postville, davening in the shul.

But it was more. It would be a way to separate myself from our Iowa City neighbors who had stiffed us at the Watermelon Social, from the scoutmaster who wanted to invoke Jesus' name, from Kurt Reynolds and his cache of guns. Isn't this why I had come to Postville in the first place? To commune with men like my ancestors, steeped in tradition and in religion?

Sholom got up from behind his desk, walked over to his office door, locked it, and then came at me. He gravely instructed me to remove my wristwatch and get up from the chair. He reached into a velvet pouch and pulled out the leather straps and two boxes, which he kissed. If I was going to be reborn an Orthodox Jew, it would be here, in the messy office of a slaughterhouse magnate, above the wails of cattle, sheep, and chickens about to be slaughtered in the middle of Iowa.

Sholom was quickly on me, first wrapping one strap around my left arm. The leather was smooth and warm. Sholom picked up my left arm, I was to learn much later, not simply because it is closer to the heart, but because the left hand is the weaker and feebler, more apt to be led astray. But like much in Orthodox Judaism, that, too, is unclear. It could have something to do with the prosaic reason that for most people, who are right-handed, wrapping the left arm with the right hand is just easier to do. Sholom wrapped my arm with the strap seven times, also cause for disagreement among Jews. Seven windings of the leather may be to recall the seven hand-maidens chosen to serve Queen Esther; or it may recall the seven angels: Michael, Gabriel, Raphael, Uriel, Tzadkiel, Yu-fiel, and Raziel; or it may conform to the seven benedictions recited at a Jewish wedding; or it may be because it took God seven days to create the world and rest. The way Sholom explained it as he busily tightened the strap up to my bicep, where he put the box on the inside of my upper arm two finger widths from the crook in my arm, was this: "Seven is a very special number to Jews."

In a slaughterhouse, being bound with black leather straps by a stranger, I couldn't keep a straight face.

"So seven is the number to bet on in Vegas?" I cracked.

Sholom's face allowed a brief smile. He pulled on the straps so that they were tighter, and then wrapped the leather to form a series of intricate loops and knots across my left palm and knuckles, ending on the second digit of my middle finger. The straps were looped to illustrate Hebrew letters. Sholom nodded his head and instructed me to repeat after him:

*Baruch atah adonai eloheynu melech haolam asher kidshanu
b'mitzvotav v'tzivanu l'haniach tefillin.*

(Blessed art Thou, Lord our God, King of the universe, who has
sanctified us with his commandments and commanded us to put on
tefillin.)

I repeated the words in Hebrew, which sounded vaguely
familiar, but at the time, I had no idea of their English meaning. In my mind, I tried to summon images that would connect me to generations of Jewish men in my family who years
before me must have performed the same holy ritual. I tried
to imagine the leather strap on my left arm as an electric wire
or antenna, the box on my forehead as a receiver picking up
signals from my father; Poppa Charles; or Jack, my great
uncle Jack, the Jewish cowboy. But all I got was static.

My attempt at cosmic ancestral reverie was interrupted
by a sharp knock at the door. "Sholom," came a shout. It was
the "No-Problem" rabbi again, who tried to jiggle the doorknob, found that it was locked, and yelled something in Hebrew to Sholom; but by now Sholom had severed himself
from the secular world of animal carcasses and smooth-lined
lungs. The rabbi continued knocking on the door, jiggling the
doorknob. Sholom ignored the knocks for five, ten, fifteen
seconds, and then finally he let forth a staccato string of Hebrew, including the word "tefillin," which prompted the rabbi
to back off immediately with a timid and final "No problem."

Just before Sholom tightened the leather box riding above
my forehead, he said three words at a time, and I dutifully
repeated:

*Baruch atah adonai eloheynu melech haolam asher kidshanu
b'mitzvotav v'tzivanu al mitzvat tefillin. Baruch shem k'vod malchuto
l'olam va'ed.*

(Blessed art Thou, Lord our God, King of the universe, who has
sanctified us with his commandments, and commanded us concerning
the mitzvah of tefillin. Blessed is the name of his Glorious Majesty forever and ever.)

Throughout the twenty-minute ritual, every several minutes, someone else knocked on the door, yelling for Sholom.
His phone rang, too, but Sholom was busy intoning Hebrew
prayers to a fallen Jew. As he finished unwrapping the leather
straps, he invoked the third prayer:

> Ve'eyrastich lee l'olam; ve'eyrastich lee b'tzedek u'v mishpat
> uv'chesed uv'rahamim; ve'eyrastich lee b'emunah—ve'yadaahta et
> adonai.

> (I will betroth you to me forever; I will betroth you to me in
> righteousness and justice, in kindness and mercy I will betroth you to
> me in faithfulness; and you shall know the Lord.)

And then we were done.

Sholom quickly wrapped up the leather boxes and smooth
straps, returned them to the velvet pouch, and placed the
sack atop a gray metal file cabinet. He took out a Marlboro
Gold from the pack on his desk and leaned back in his chair.
It was like afterglow; two people who had shared an intense
personal experience, now savoring their moment of union.
But within a minute, while Sholom exhaled plumes of smoke,
he began punching out checks, balancing his books on the
computer, alternately looking up at me.

"What *you* need to do is spend a *Shabbos* dinner with a
family here. That's what you need. I'll talk with Lazar Kamzoil
about your family staying with him for the Sabbath. You'll like
Lazar. He's a funny guy, maybe even a comedian. And who
knows? You might even learn something," Sholom said, shrugging his shoulders.

While looking over a ledger, Sholom told an allegory from the Rebbe Menachem Mendel Schneerson, the revered Lubavitcher leader who died in 1994. It was the kind of story to which I would grow accustomed in the company of Lubavitchers. "A businessman was having trouble with a competitor who was deceitful and dishonest.

"'Rebbe,' the businessman asks, 'how should I deal with this man? How can I cope with someone who doesn't practice in his everyday life the message of the Lord?'

"And the Rebbe asked, 'How old is this man, thirty-two, thirty-four? Give him time to learn the righteous way. He has a long way to go.'

"It takes time to learn," Sholom told me pointedly, again narrowing his eyes. "Don't be in a hurry. The way of the righteous takes time. You'll see. You'll learn the right way. Believe me."

CHAPTER 6

Ginger's

After I left Sholom and the slaughterhouse, I crawled into my lumpy bed at the Pines. It was late, and the tan-and-white cow outside my window had long ago clomped back to her barn. I missed Iris and Mikey and had a miserable night's sleep. Too many big rigs barreling down Highway 18 with their trailers packed full of sad-faced chickens, sheep, and cattle headed to Agriprocessors to be slaughtered, quartered, shrink-wrapped, and boxed. I started to count chickens and by the time I reached one hundred, I switched to sheep, then to big steers.

I felt shell-shocked by Sholom, and come morning, I realized my reasons for coming to Postville had begun to shift. Sholom and I weren't cut from the same cloth, not even from a remotely similar bolt of fabric. We might both have been exiles from the crowded coasts of America, two Jews by circumstance living in the middle of Iowa, but that was it. If I was expecting a cloister of wise and pious men, *tzaddikim,* in Postville, Sholom was not at its core. This slaughterhouse magnate was neither a link to my past nor a guide to my future. If blustery Sholom was indicative of the rest of the Postville Lubavitchers, the locals had their work cut out for them, especially if their move to annex Sholom's land ever gained steam.

The journalist in me had come out in full force. Martin Appel's suspicions about me, it turned out, had been right. I had barely scratched the surface, but clearly there was a culture clash of the strongest magnitude between two groups, both born-and-bred Americans, who rarely had the opportunity to clash. Here was a kind of experiment in the limits of diversity and community, the nature of community, the meaning of prejudice, even what it means to be an American. Postville seemed like a social laboratory, perhaps a metaphor for America.

Sholom had not chosen the rural heartland by coincidence. The economics of the region were important, but there was more. In the rural heartland, you could pretty much do whatever you wanted. No one told you what color to paint your house, how many benefits to provide your employees, whether you could build a second story to your factory. If anyone was looking over your shoulder, it was likely to pat you on the back for bringing economic improvement to a region long ignored by outsiders. There were two caveats—you couldn't break the law and you had to get along with everyone else. It was because Sholom and the Hasidim seemingly snubbed the Postville locals, not caring one whit about assimilating into or even acknowledging the local culture, that talk of annexation had resurfaced.

The problem for the Postville locals was that, by all accounts, Sholom and the Hasidim had succeeded handily. This vast expanse of fecund land, ignored or ridiculed by power elites of either coast, had been Sholom's frontier, and he and his minyan had taken it by storm. They wanted their piece of the American economic pie and they helped themselves to it, despite what the locals said or did. The Lubavitchers had become power brokers, and in doing so, had beaten the heartland gatekeepers at their own game.

My own interests turned to why Sholom (and the other Hasidim, I imagined) behaved the way they did. Why were they so difficult to get along with? Who died and made them rulers of the universe? To understand the Lubavitchers, I needed to plumb their community in Postville, but I also needed to learn about their antagonists—the Postville locals. These people were the guardians of generations of local tradition. Were they anti-Semitic, prejudiced, insular, or just plain envious? Were they building fences to keep out an America that represented change—or were they just desperately trying to hang on to a passing way of life being destroyed by a sudden influx of prosperity and arrogance?

Sharon Drahn, Beverly Schaeffer, Dawn Schmadeke, Whitey Meyer, and just about everyone I had talked to told me I absolutely had to meet Stanley Schroeder, "Postville's Unofficial Historian." Last year, Stanley had set up a display in the *Herald-Leader*'s windows, which included bathing suits (with bloomers), white lace-up corsets, long formal dresses with high collars, Easter bonnets, feather boas, and high-heeled button-up shoes. "If it happened in Postville, then Stanley knows about it *and he will tell you*," Sharon said, flashing a smile.

Under the Gideon Bible in the nightstand at the Pines, I pulled out the Northeast Iowa Regional Telephone Directory, thumbed the eighteen pages of residential listings, and found Stanley's name.

Stanley's wife, Marjorie, answered on the first ring, and as soon as Stanley got on the phone, I sensed he had been waiting for me to call ever since I had first arrived in Postville. Word had spread that the professor from the University of Iowa was asking questions about the Postville Jews, and Stanley was a natural to weigh in.

"Would you have any time over the next couple of days, so we might be able to visit?" I asked.

"Well, actually, you could come over now," Stanley replied. "That is, if you're not busy."

Within fifteen minutes, I was striding up Stanley's sidewalk to a stately, old redbrick house on East Williams Street. About halfway to the house, I noticed the lace curtains in the foyer flutter, as though someone had just let go of the lower right-hand corner while watching me approach. I rang the doorbell.

In his foyer, Stanley stood. He was in his mid-seventies, a solid, squat, square-shouldered man with thick glasses that were a little crooked. A cuckoo clock chirped, and we both smiled at the sound. Stanley asked me in, and as soon as I walked into the living room, I was greeted with teetering piles of papers all over, on tables and on chairs. "This all has to do with Postville history," Stanley said, waving his arm at the stacks of papers as though he was introducing me to a family member.

Stanley had lived in Postville his entire life. His father started Postville's general store, Schroeder and Schultz Co., in 1920, and when he retired, Stanley took over. Ever since 1955, Stanley had been typing just about every day, except Sunday, a thick single-spaced manuscript about Iowa, the nation, and the world as seen from Postville. He was the only person in the world with a complete set of the now defunct *Postville*

Review—1873 to 1920. There was so much in Stanley's house that it was hard to go from room to room without worrying about knocking over another stack of papers or books. You had to go sideways, squeezing between the TV trays, the lamps with pleated linen shades, the oak end tables. Stanley had so many papers, books, newspapers, pamphlets, and photo albums on Postville history that Marjorie insisted that he build an addition onto their house to keep it out of her way.

As he talked, I got the impression that Stanley was like a professor playing to an empty classroom. Stanley's life was devoted to telling Postville's history, and when someone, anyone, expressed even a passing interest in Postville's past, Stanley, on cue, would instantly be on the case, shuffling through folders and files, pulling out newspaper clippings, scrapbooks, pamphlets, purple mimeographed sheets that still smelled. He handed me original typewritten pages of his notes ("Just make a copy of it and mail it back to me whenever you want. No rush"). His eyes would bulge a bit, his speech quicken, and he'd insist that I sit right down, as he patted the sofa cushion next to his straight-backed chair.

Marjorie had heard all the stories before, yet she still smiled politely when Stanley launched into another one about Joel Post, the New Yorker who founded Postville in 1840, or about the twin Postville bars on Military Road, the two twelve-by-twelve-foot cabins called Sodom and Gomorrah that served as watering holes for fur traders, soldiers, and Indians during the Civil War. Sodom was owned by a drunk boxer named Taffy Jones; Gomorrah's owner was Graham Thorn, Postville's first dentist and physician, who took a Winnebago Indian maiden for a wife.

Most histories of backroads Iowa stop around World War

II, yet the recent entry of Hasidic Jews into Lutheran Post-ville augured the beginning of a new canon of history for Stanley. Stanley's business was the study of change, and the Jewish migration here was Postville's most dramatic change in a century. For Stanley, the Jews were a gold mine. How many historians could boast of so much raw, new material in their own backyard? As a man of history, Stanley could hardly wait to seek out these Jewish newcomers. He was an anthropologist about to meet a tribe of exotic strangers who had suddenly descended on his land. Their arrival was to be a gift to Stanley, a way for him to write the final chapter of his life-long work.

He said he'll never forget the exact moment when he saw the first Hasidic Jew set foot in Postville on a crisp fall day in 1987. Stanley was walking to the post office, as he always does in the midmorning. On this particular morning, heading straight toward him on Lawler Street, was a solitary man whose like Stanley had never encountered before. The man had long curly sidelocks and a black, very full beard. He wore a calf-length black frock, gabardine black pants, and an un-tucked white shirt with what looked like tasseled fringes coming out from under it. The man walked funny, hunched over, Stanley recalled. His hands were clasped behind his back, his eyes were cast down at the sidewalk, and he seemed to be muttering something to himself in a foreign language. Iowa farmers from another county were unusual enough in these parts, but a man who looked, walked, and mumbled like this guy pacing toward Stanley that day, well, Stanley didn't quite know what to think.

Who could the man possibly be? Where was he from? Why was he in Postville? How'd he even find this place?

Despite everything foreign about this foreigner, what struck Stanley most that day was what the man was wearing atop his head—a "little black beanie" is how Stanley described it. Stanley couldn't get the beanie out of his mind. Just as Dawn Schmadeke had been bewildered by Jewish skullcaps, Stanley, too, stood transfixed by the sheer physics of them. How in the devil did the man manage to keep that tiny round piece of material from taking off like a Frisbee? With sudden gusts of wind sweeping over the Iowa cornfields, billowing across the pastures, whipping through Postville streets, it was hard enough to open an umbrella without the damn thing collapsing, so how'd that beanie stay put?

That was the first time Stanley saw a Hasidic Jew, and after two or three more encounters from afar, Stanley decided it was time: He would approach one of them.

"I was walking down the street, and I decided to say 'good morning,' but this fellow wouldn't make eye contact with me. I wanted to invite him in for some cookies and Kool-Aid, but he didn't want to have anything to do with me. No, sirree."

Stanley had no idea how these newcomers would ever fit in, or even if they wanted to fit in. In the old days, when a Postville home burned down, the Volunteer Fire Department did its best to save what it could, and within four or five months, the men of Postville would have teamed up to rebuild the entire house. All the while the ladies in town would have cooked up dinners and given away half of what was in their armoires to clothe the family. It didn't make any difference whose house had burned down, how many kids they had, or what the husband did for a living.

Today, if a home of one of the Jews caught fire, Stanley

didn't know whether the Jews would even allow the locals to save it. But what bothered Stanley more was that for the first time in his life, he wasn't sure there'd be enough locals who'd come out and try to put out the flames.

There was an uneasy pause, and I could see Stanley felt guilty about it. The Jews had been a double disappointment to him. He couldn't get much if they wouldn't talk to him, but also, they seemed so different, so cantankerous. Stanley pushed himself off the straight-backed chair and shuffled around to the back of the living room, where he pulled out five large scrapbooks. Soon, he was launching into what he liked, Postville's golden years, the days when the Ringling Brothers, two Iowa boys, played their largest show to date under the big top in Postville, in 1912. By then, Postville had become a town made up almost exclusively of German Lutherans. So German a town was Postville that it wasn't until 1917 that the weekly newspaper *Iowa Volksblatt,* which was printed entirely in German, changed its name to the *Postville Herald* and began publishing in English.

For more than one hundred years, the epicenter of power and influence in Postville had been St. Paul Lutheran Church, the oldest and wealthiest house of worship in town. The monolithic church was the largest in physical size and number of congregants—thirteen hundred members, almost all of whom still proudly claim German heritage. From when St. Paul was founded in 1871 up until the mid-1950s, church services were conducted at least once a day in German. When completed in 1891, the church had 350 seats ("opera chairs" is how the early church records referred to them), but could accommodate six hundred parishioners. Stanley brought out an article written by W. N. Burdick, the editor of the *Postville*

Review, which described the church's dedication more than a century earlier:

> The erection of this church, more than any other cause, has tended to raise the price of land around Postville. It has brought large numbers of wealthy Germans here, and they all want a house within reach of this elegant house of worship, and they are willing to pay more than anybody else for lands in this vicinity. The result is that nearly every farm that is sold is sold to a German; and it will not be long before it will be a rarity to find an American born farmer in this section.

In fact, many Postville natives grew up learning English as a second language. Though German was officially banned during World War I, walking around Postville in the 1930s, Stanley said, you were more likely to hear German than English. Although Germans were spread throughout the state, their concentration was heaviest in the northeast, and the geographic capital for such German culture easily could have been Postville.

Postville's pecking order was thus set in motion for the next century. The German Lutherans were followed by the Scandinavian Lutherans, then the Irish Catholics, the Methodists, the Presbyterians. In the last couple of years, several Hispanics, even a Filipino family, had moved in—still there are no blacks.

When the Jews began arriving in the mid-1980s, Postville, as it had always been, was a closed, insulated, solidly Christian community—as much a *shtetl* as the Hasidim's ancestors had created in Eastern Europe, as much as the one the Lubavitchers had created in Crown Heights, Brooklyn. *Shtetlach* were incubators and fortresses of Jewish tradition where religious values were preserved and embellished. That's what

Postville had been for a century for the Lutherans, a kind of *goyishe shtetl.*

As in all of Iowa, Christianity has always been at the heart of Postville; in this town, though, the tradition goes deeper. The city's favorite son is still John Mott, the 1946 Nobel Peace Prize winner, who helped create the World Student Christian Federation. Mott's father, who ran a lumberyard, was the first mayor of Postville. A brochure on John Mott, written by Stanley Schroeder, put Mott's contribution in perspective: "For over half a century he riveted the minds of youth on the making of a Christian world." As a teenager, Mott "reached the decision to 'Give my whole life to Christian Service.'"

After an hour's history lesson, I must have passed a test of sorts. Stanley suggested I join him tomorrow at Ginger's, the coffee shop on Lawler, where he and two dozen old-timers had been meeting every morning (except Sunday) for as long as any of them could remember.

"But I want to let the men know first that you're coming," Stanley said, as he walked me to the door. "I'm sure they wouldn't mind. You could come unannounced, but I better let the fellas know beforehand. That way we all can have a nice visit. *Don't-cha-think?*"

Even though Stanley had been born in Postville, as were his parents, he still hadn't given up his drawl. And at the very moment I heard Stanley's *"Don't-cha-think?"* something ridiculous dawned on me. The sentiment and intonation were exactly the same as when Sholom yesterday had asked me, *"Nu?"* just before wrapping me with tefillin and intoning the canon of Hebrew prayers. *"Don't-cha-think?"* and *"Nu?"* meant the same thing.

At nine sharp the next morning, Stanley saw me through the front window of Ginger's and hurriedly put down his coffee mug. "There he is," I heard Stanley say as I entered, as much to himself as to the men around the table. Stanley pushed himself off his chair, and as he walked toward me, he straightened out his back every few feet so by the time he greeted me at the door, he was upright. Fifteen heads, all but one wearing caps emblazoned with logos from John Deere, International Harvester, Pioneer, an array of pesticide manufacturers, drywall businesses, and feed companies looked up in unison. I nodded as amiably as I could. Stanley cupped my left elbow with his right hand and steered me toward four worn Formica tables pushed together at the far end of the restaurant. I noticed a sign taped to the back of the cash register, and written on it in a black-ink scrawl was TODAY'S DESERT SPECIAL: DING-DONG CAKE.

Stanley's manner was meant to be reassuring, and it was. None of the regulars was actually eating breakfast, but all had in front of them thick coffee cups that could have doubled for shaving mugs. The youngest around the table was about forty-five. The oldest, in his mid-eighties, was a man who squinted when he talked and had the habit of holding his earlobe between his thumb and index finger and shaking it vigorously when anyone said anything.

If the shul down the block was the temple for Postville's Hasidic men, then Ginger's was the sanctuary for these guys. They were the backbone of Postville. Like the tens of thousands of rows of corn surrounding Postville, these men, too, lived in abiding order. They, their grandfathers, fathers, sons, and grandsons had made Postville work for more than a hundred years. Through the go-go years of the 1970s, when righteous corn crops made local farmers' revenue swell the vaults at Postville State Bank and Citizens State Bank, to the Farm Crisis of the 1980s, when the same banks foreclosed on these once-bountiful farms, the men at Ginger's had given Postville its continuity and its sustenance. They teased and joked as befitted men who had grown up together. They knew each other's parents, wives, daughters and sons, and aunts and uncles. If they hadn't been born in Postville, they hadn't been born far away.

At first, these men didn't say much more than a couple of "yeps" and "nopes." I could see in their eyes the same quizzical look—"Who's this stranger and why'd he come all the way from Iowa City to talk to *us*?" But under Stanley's beatific gaze, they began to warm. I had had similar experiences on the first day of classes: Iowa students weren't nearly as forthcoming as their West Coast counterparts, but by the end of the semester, the Iowa kids would be as engaging, friendly, and curious as the most loquacious Californians.

Stanley introduced me with a wink. I was a PRO-fessor from the University of Iowa. And as such, I had to know Hayden Fry, the winningest football coach in Hawkeye history, an icon in these parts like none other, save Nile Kinnick, the All-American who died when his fighter plane crashed during World War II, and after whom the football stadium was named.

"Hayden and I get along just fine," I joked, even though Fry and I had never met and the closest we'd come was through binoculars from my seat, high in the north end zone of Kinnick Stadium. "Though he sure didn't listen to me when we played Northwestern last fall. Boy, was that ever a mess!"

The icebreaker generated a tableful of guffaws and nods. I had done Stanley right, and as I looked over to my left, Stanley was smiling.

If the Iowans back home in Iowa City thought of me as a city boy, I wasn't quite sure what these guys in rural Iowa made of me. Currency here is counted in bushels of corn and in hog lots; status is the kind of pickup truck you drive and how many bullheads you could pull out of a river. One thing I was certain about, though, was that none suspected me of being Jewish, simply because Jews, to the men before me, were one kind of people: the funny-looking guys traipsing around town with beanies on the top of their heads. Besides, the Jews stuck to themselves. The Jews would never ask questions of the locals. They'd certainly never walk into Ginger's. And to sit down with us? No way.

Stanley had done his job. These men soon spoke up without any prompting. Their comments came out at first in isolated notes, then built to a chorus. I was struck by how bitter they were and how fast their rage tumbled out.

"They're all about the dollars," one man said slowly, shaking his head. "They do what they please whenever they want, and everyone else be damned!"

A man to my left: "A letter comes from the city clerk, telling this Jewish lady who lives next to me that she can't keep her sheep in her yard. So, she goes to the city clerk up at city hall, and the clerk tells her, 'You've got to move to the country to have animals in your backyard.' And the lady says, 'But I *am* in the country.'

"This Jewish woman, she thinks she can do anything she darn well pleases. It doesn't make any difference what you talk to them about. The Jewish lady thinks she lives in the country, so why can't she have these sheep as pets? Can you imagine, *sheep as pets*? She'll probably want to name them!"

That was a good one, and just about everyone at the table

had a hearty laugh over it. When the hoots died down, the men seemed to shake their heads in unison, caps and bills going right to left, then left to right, in a free-flowing natural choreography.

Then it struck me why Dawn, Stanley, and all the locals seemed so mesmerized by the Jews' yarmulkes. Both farmer and Jew would never go anywhere without their heads covered. The skullcaps were something like what the farmers wore on their heads. Yarmulkes were symbolic badges of honor, a constant reminder that the wearer pays homage to the Lord's continual presence. The farmers' caps shielded them from the scorching sun or from the rain when the heavens opened up and let loose a downpour. In a sense, the caps, too, were homages to the power of nature, the power of the Lord. No one needed any protection against the sun, heat, or rain in the middle of Ginger's this morning. These men wore hats because they were supposed to wear hats. As with the Jews, hats were an essential part of their uniform; both groups felt naked without them. Neither would ever think of going anywhere without wearing a head covering, whether it was a hand-stitched yarmulke or a cap with John Deere green colors.

Some of the men at Ginger's were smiling tightly, others frowning, but all expressed the same emotion, somewhere between frustration and exasperation. One man in bib overalls inhaled deeply and let out a sort of snort, a reaction to which everyone in Ginger's could relate. There was a built-in, natural bias that folks around these parts had against city people, whether they came from Des Moines, Cedar Rapids, or New York. That bias could have been code for anti-Semitism, but how many Jews were there in Des Moines or Cedar Rapids? The locals wouldn't trust anyone from those places, no matter what religion they were, even if they were Iowa-bred and Evangelical Lutheran. But maybe I was being too easy on the men sitting before me.

From down at the other end of the table: "Every time you say something to them, they threaten to pull out. From Day One, they've done what they've wanted. To expand their slaughterhouse anyone knows you have to go to the county with plans, but they don't listen. They don't want to be bothered."

The mood at the table was turning gloomy. These men, the elders of Postville, had never dealt with people like these Hasidic Jews. In their darkest nightmares, they couldn't fathom how different and difficult newcomers could be. One man, a retired farmer, laughed. "You can't retaliate against someone who ignores you. They look the other way when they see us coming. They don't pay no attention to anyone but their own."

Another man, this one younger, about fifty: "If they say, 'Annex us and we'll leave,' then I'd say, 'Hallelujah, praise the Lord! Tell me when you're gonna pack up and I'll help put all your suitcases in your car. I'll even buy the first tank of gas.' These people don't belong here, not the way they act."

Someone else: "They hire an attorney, and they make sure they pay him real good—I'm sure their attorney doesn't argue with the money they pay him. And this attorney draws up papers for this and papers for that. They stall, file more papers, and all the while they do whatever they damn well wanna do. And you know what? There ain't a damn thing we can do, not a damn thing."

"Except watch them get away with murder," said the man to my left, which, after my harrowing stroll through the slaughterhouse, I thought is exactly what the Jews do at the packing house.

The bills of the caps around the table went up and down in agreement. For a split second, as I sat looking at these guys, their heads bobbing in unison, it appeared as though they were all davening, just like the Hasidim they disliked and mistrusted. This was a Lutheran daven, not from the waist, but from the neck up.

The retired farmer: "The Jewish people say they're so good for local businesses, but they're bringing in all these heavy appliances on trucks from New York. Do they think that we don't know what they're doing? They think we're *that* dumb? They've set up their households, they put in whole new kitchens, but they don't buy any of their appliances from the local merchants."

The lament was heartfelt and sincere, but at the same time, what the locals were describing was so...well, Jewish. Hearing their complaint, I repeated to myself the old Jewish refrain: "What, and pay retail?"

I wondered whether these local men knew how much more they were spending by buying local. They could save a bundle by shopping at the Wal-Mart in Decorah or Prairie du Chien. Or—better yet—by talking to the Jews and finding out the Lubavitcher source for all the refrigerators, washing machines, and dishwashers coming in on the big trucks from New York.

I was feeling more comfortable with the men at Ginger's, and I thought I'd try. "Have any of you guys approached the Jews and asked them about where all this stuff is coming from, and how much they're paying for it?"

My suggestion was greeted with fifteen cold stares, followed by stony silence.

I compounded my mistake. "Well, at least you could talk to them and ask," I said. More silence.

No one here cared about saving a couple of bucks if it meant not buying from the neighborhood grocery, shoe store, gift store. If *we* don't support one another, who else is going to? It was hard enough to make ends meet *with* the locals' help. Sure, some shopped at the chain stores, but for goodness' sake, they didn't talk about it! Maybe for tires or Pampers, they might drive the distance. But to pick up a box of Easter candy at Wal-Mart, knowing full well that Moore's IGA on West Tilden or that the Health Mart Pharmacy on West Greene has all the chocolate-covered eggs and marshmallow bunnies anyone could possibly want, would make most Postville people feel as though they had committed some sort of crime.

Stanley adroitly brought me back to groupthink. "Heck, they don't even talk to us. I don't think anyone would feel comfortable enough even to ask them about their personal business." That sounded very Iowa—mind your manners, for heaven's sake.

"Let me tell you something," Stanley said to illustrate his point. "The other day I was handing out flyers for Ag/Industrial Days, and I see one of the Jewish ladies, so I thought, 'What the heck? She lives in town, she might want to go.' So I go up to her, she's on her porch, and I start to hand the flyer to her, and she stops me right there. She points with her finger to the porch railing and nods. Not a word out of her mouth. I put the flyer on the railing and then I walked away. She didn't even want to touch the flyer because it came from me! How can you go against that?" Stanley's eyes were bulging.

The old-timer halfway down the table had heard enough. He laid his leathery palms on the table and looked at everyone. "They'll take whatever they can get. The Jews, as long as they have their hands in someone else's pocket, then they'll stay. That's their history—to take as much as they can."

The old-timer's comments were like a punch to my solar plexus. As a journalist, I was accustomed to hearing outrageous things and doing nothing about them, except for writing them down and letting others judge for themselves. But this guy had launched a frontal attack on my own faith, and no one at the table had budged an inch. If they talked this way in front of a stranger, I could only imagine what they said when they were alone. Sholom was right.

Some of the men nodded; others tipped back their thick mugs to finish off the rest of their sugary coffee. Two men at the far end of the table began talking about corn prices, and the hefty cattleman, who looked as big and as ornery as the steers he raised, grunted about beef prices going down. Again. There was a collective settling of fact: The Jews were here, and they were here for as long as they wanted to stay. Nothing the locals could do would get them to leave. Maybe the annexation plan that John Hyman and Leigh Rekow had cooked up might work, but it was so damn complicated and took so long to get on the ballot, that no one put any stock in it. And even if it did pass, did anyone really think the Jews were going to pack up and leave?

I broke up the lull by asking what the men thought of the *mikveh*, the bathhouse the Jews had converted from a two-car garage next to Eldo Kugel's house on Williams Street. But as soon as the words tumbled out of my mouth, the men seemed dumbstruck.

"A bathhouse? For men and women?"

"What do they need *that* for?"

"It's just for women," I said. "From what I understand,

Orthodox Jewish women need to purify themselves each month."

Well, you could have heard a pin drop in Ginger's at that moment.

All fifteen men looked back at me with blank stares. They didn't have a clue what I was talking about.

"You know, when they go through their monthly"—I paused—"time, they have to take a special ceremonial bath. So," I said slowly, "they've built a communal bathhouse for the women, down the block, a couple of doors in from Lawler."

It took several seconds for the words to register. Perhaps some of the men were conjuring up images of Jewesses disrobing and submerging in cleansing, pure biblical waters. Maybe some were picturing their own wives taking baths. Maybe their thoughts were of memories past of their wives and daughters.

"And where's this bathhouse located again?" asked one man.

I realized that I had hit these guys with a double whammy. Not only did they not know why in the good Lord's name the Jewish women would have to take this special kind of bath once a month, but they had no idea that the Jews had built a bathhouse in Postville. In this town—where everybody knew everyone else and everything anyone did, said, or thought—that the Jews had managed to convert an old garage to a brand-new bathhouse by extending underground plumbing lines, remodeling the inside and outside, and building a tub into the ground, right under the noses of the locals without their knowing it, well, this was too much for the oldtimers at Ginger's. The Jews had slipped another fast one by everyone. And for an outsider to let them in on the secret!

I had a hard time believing that no one at the table knew about the *mikveh*. At least, no one let on that he knew.

Stanley finally spoke up and confessed to knowing a little about the bathhouse for ladies. "Whether it's legal or not, I don't know," he said, his eyes widening. "The point is, it never was addressed. That's the point. That's how they do things. They don't ask any questions—they build it, and they don't ever let on what they're doing."

Just as I was about to bring up the coda from *Field of Dreams*—"If you build it, they will come"—the oldest man at the table, who thus far had been biding his time, spoke in a pitched strained voice: "When they first bought the plant, I thought, well, now we're going to be Israel in Postville. And that's what Postville has become! Little Israel."

Another man at the table: "I've dealt with Jews for a long, long time. And every time, they set out to fleece you. You can see it in their eyes. They're users, and they've always been users. That's their way."

Again, I felt the wind go out of me, but just as I was about to say something, anything, Stanley jumped in. "Wait a minute," he said, raising his voice, steering the discussion from turning nasty. "These are the *ultra-radical* kind of Jews. Not *all* Jews are like that."

At least one man, in a blue-and-white cap and tan Carhartts, wasn't buying. "Look what happened to the pair of Jews that robbed that P-n-P in Decorah. They almost killed that poor woman, and all one of them got was a slap on his wrist just because his daddy's rich. The Jews just laughed in that lady's face."

I didn't know what the man was talking about. I wasn't even sure what a P-n-P was, but Hasidic Jews robbing a store and shooting a woman? Before I could get in a word, another man, taking off his feed cap, shook his head. "Why are they always picking on poor old [former Cincinnati Reds owner] Marge Schott. Just because she said Hitler did some good things in the beginning. Well, he did, damn it! He made that country work again, but gosh, today you say anything positive about Hitler, and they say you hate the Jews!"

Whether that kind of talk was just plain crazy, or whether it was plain crazy *because* a stranger was there, or whether it was that the roundtable just naturally broke up at about eleven, a couple of men pushed back their chairs, and the coffee klatch was over. "Ouff dah," one man said, as he got up and straightened his back. As I prepared to leave, one of the men I guessed to be in his early sixties, wearing Ben Davis overalls, Red Wing boots, and a Pioneer seed cap, nodded at me and touched the bill of his cap. He reached out to shake my hand. My soft flesh betrayed me as a city boy. This man had an enormous hand with fingers that were as rough and stubby as carrots just pulled from the ground.

"You be fair," he said, nodding. He touched the bill of his cap, turned his back, and walked out of Ginger's.

I came to believe the farmer's admonition wasn't a warning, but a reminder of how farmers do business, at least how farmers ought to do business. It was an endorsement of sorts, a pact that said, "We're willing to trust you, but don't disappoint us."

CHAPTER 7

Backfire

I mulled over the farmer's words as I bounced along the gravel road to Leigh Rekow's 240-acre farm, five miles outside of the Postville city limits. As a city councilman and Postville *Herald-Leader* columnist, Leigh was the point man for the regulars at Ginger's. More than anyone in this town, Leigh was the one who led the battle against the Jews. His immediate goal was to petition the state to allow for the local annexation referendum. Once within the city limits, Leigh promised, the city would have control—at least, some—over Agriprocessors and the Jews. Annexation would allow Postville to impose taxes and levies on the slaughterhouse, as well as approve and monitor any expansion. And if the Jews wanted to move once the slaughterhouse land was annexed, then that was their decision. No one could ever say the locals pushed them out.

If slaughterhouse maven Sholom Rubashkin was on one side, then on the other side was Leigh Rekow. They were bitter enemies, each other's nemesis. When I had mentioned Leigh's name to Sholom at the slaughterhouse, he practically spit and called Rekow "an anti-Semite." One was defending his business, the other was protecting his town's legacy, but each fought the other so that his own heritage would prevail. And, as I was to learn, both shared an agenda: to convert me to believing their way was the right way.

As the white door to the Rekow farmhouse swung open, Leigh's daughter, thirty-five-year-old Brenda Bernhard, greeted me. She was wearing an apron—right out of a 1950s Frigidaire commercial. The last time I saw a woman wearing an apron, I think, was when my mother served my sister and me TV dinners. Brenda poured me a glass of iced tea as we waited for Leigh to get home. Brenda and her husband, Stan, farmed the land, but Leigh was there almost every day to help in the fields. "It's a hard life, but we wouldn't give it up for anything," said Brenda, a handsome, big-boned strong woman with raven-colored hair who looked more at home in a pickup than a car. She pointed to the red barn a hundred feet away. "You've got to milk those cows seven days a week; we go on twelve-hour intervals. On the farm, there's always something to be done, and as soon as you get that done, there's something else. It never stops."

To supplement their income, Brenda explained that she and Stan occasionally host city folks from Chicago for a weekend to get, as Brenda laughed, "a real farm experience." The first thing these weekend farmers want to do, of course, is milk the cows. So Brenda and Stan take them to the barn, sit them down on a three-legged stool, and show them how to pull on a Jersey's fleshy teats. Usually they just get a dribble of milk, so Brenda takes over, and like a combination of Annie Oakley and Aunt Bea, she aims a continuous stream of milk into the center of the aluminum pail, which makes a sound like a rapid-fire BB gun. Bubbly, foamy, still warm, this milk isn't even white the way it is in the grocery store, but more like the amber color of the coat of the cow that produced it.

The cow milking is Brenda's warm-up act. Next, she gets the weekend farmers to chase down a Rhode Island Red. She picks the rooster with the brightest red comb, one with floppy, wrinkled wattles. Of course, no one can possibly catch the rooster as he struts and clucks and runs around in circles, sneering at the humans who are laughing and running after him. Stan casually reaches with one hand, grabs the imperial cock by his neck and places it, feathers flying, on a wooden block and chops the head off, one, two, three. Anyone who's been around chickens knows what happens next: "We let the poor thing run wild, back and forth, and these city folks just can't believe their eyes," said Brenda. "They think they've died and gone to heaven!"

Next come the rides on the tractor and on the horses. The horses don't take kindly to strangers riding them, and as these city folks approach, their tails begin to swing. Brenda shares her secret: rubbing their noses. These city folks can't believe how soft a horse's nose is. After the rides, it's time for an old-fashioned cookout—baked beans, steaks, corn picked that afternoon, fresh-baked pies—and a bonfire that Leigh lights in the evening, which illuminates the green and golden fields of crackling corn. At the least, the country routine gives the city folks something to talk about around the water cooler when they get back to work Monday.

"I'm just a country bumpkin," Brenda said. "I don't like cities, and if you ask me, you can have 'em all. When we're driving up towards La Crosse or down to Cedar Rapids and you've got four lanes, I get real nervous. But not as bad as Stan. He won't even drive anywhere near a city. That weenie!"

When I brought up the subject of the Postville Jews, Brenda's reaction was a kind of awe. "I wave at them, and sometimes the ladies smile back, but that's really about it. I think the kids are so cute, walking hand in hand. They're so nicely dressed.

"But, of course, there's no way to get to know them," Brenda said, shaking her head, pursing her lips. "They can't have us in their homes, you know. It's against their religion. And you know what? I'd give anything to go into one of their homes. What an experience that would be." Brenda drummed her finger on the kitchen table, pausing to imagine what she'd find inside.

Her reverie was cut short by Leigh's arrival. I heard him come into the mudroom, scrape his boots clean, and then pull them off. When Leigh appeared in the living room, I reacted the way the locals probably had upon meeting their first Jew; but instead of "Now, *that's* a Jew," my take on Leigh was *"This* is a farmer." Dusty Carhartts, fertilizer cap, squash-sized biceps, lilting speech, periwinkle blue eyes. If anyone had Postville soil in his veins, it was sixty-two-year-old Leigh Rekow. Seeing his thick, lined skin made me think that the history of this land was etched in the faces of the farmers who tilled it.

"Just got back from playing cow pasture pool," Leigh announced in a boyish way, and when I looked quizzical, he smiled. "Golf. That's what we call golf around here."

As Sholom had done two nights earlier, Leigh tried to size me up. I got the feeling he was amused by the whole experience of a city slicker interviewing him. I stacked Leigh up against Sholom and I could imagine no greater difference possible. Their appearance, speech, body language, thinking, mannerisms, the way they sat in a chair—all of it was different. Neither of these men would talk to the other, although each seemed content to confide in me.

"I started in a country school, just one room for all eight grades. It was in a German neighborhood in a tiny community called Ludlow, a little north of Postville. All the kids spoke German. My wife was a year ahead of me in Postville High, and we were married in 1953, downtown at St. Paul Lutheran.

"I always wanted to be a farmer. I spent two years in the military. I had an opportunity to go to college, but what I really wanted to do was farm. I had to save some money first, so I got a job with the electric company. Then I worked for my father-in-law and bought my first farm in 1955, one hundred and twenty acres. In 1961, I bought this land. When President Kennedy talked about the Peace Corps back in the sixties, that dream became my dream. By 1985, I had done a lot of farming, the children were grown, Africa was having a famine, and the Peace Corps was advertising for agricultural volunteers. It was my turn.

"So at the age of fifty, I found myself in Tanzania, West Africa. It was something I wanted to do. While in the army, I was never sent overseas to kill anyone, so here I was overseas now, trying to help people grow things and stay alive. Was I ever in for a big surprise! I ended living in an abandoned kibbutz that the Israelis had set up in Tanzania. I had a cement house with a tin roof. They threw a dead cow on the floor, and every day, the tribespeople, along with the cat, ripped off a piece of it. I didn't hear a telephone for a year, had no electric lights. I climbed Mount Kilimanjaro, but I damn near froze off my left index finger.

"Here, take a look," he said, wiggling a fleshy finger in front of my nose.

"A year later, I signed up for Volunteers in Overseas Co-operative Assistance. That time, we lived in a palace—a marble hotel as guests of the president of the Ivory Coast. Another time, I spent six weeks in Haiti with my wife, planting corn. Other times, we went to Czechoslovakia, the Ukraine, Lithuania, and last time I was sent to Kiev."

Leigh was in his second term on the Postville City Council. "I speak up. You need to put your name on the line. If you don't, what good are you?" His complaints about the Hasidim echoed those of the men at Ginger's. Leigh estimated that if the slaughterhouse were annexed by the city, Sholom's tax increase would be $13,000 to $15,000 a year, "not a heck of a lot compared to their annual gross, but that's not the issue. They don't want us poking our noses into their business. Personally, I'd like control over them. You talk to the average man on the street in Postville, and he'd tell them, 'Get the hell out!'

"They need to follow the same rules we follow. If they don't like the rules, let 'em go and change 'em. We can't have two sets of rules. A local woman wanted to have a beauty parlor in her house and we said no. But then the Jewish people go ahead and start a bakery. No permit, no application—nothing. We send out a zoning person to the bakery, and when we finally get an answer a couple of months later, they tell us they aren't selling but *giving* bread away. If we say anything, they say it's anti-Semitic. They can use anti-Semitic all they want. If they need a Jewish bakery, why not do it legally? Why not rent a storefront downtown and open it up to the public? Why should they be allowed to do what someone else isn't?

"It's strange, though. One of the Jewish families bought a refrigerator from a Decorah store, and they tipped the deliveryman twenty dollars! Can you imagine that? Everyone in town heard about that one. The delivery guy couldn't believe it. For one of their holidays, one of the Jews needed a couple of branches for his Thanksgiving hut, so I chopped down some limbs from a tree on my property. And guess what? The man insisted that he pay me thirty dollars. I said no, but he wouldn't take no for any answer. I thought it was pretty silly to pay me for a couple of branches.

"The complaint I hear most is that they need to live by the same rules as all of us. That's only fair, isn't it? It's not such a great religion if they don't want to be a part of the community, is it?"

Leigh Rekow sounded eminently reasonable. His speech was not hurried, anxious, not really even very vindictive. He could give elocution lessons to Sholom. Leigh seemed to be responding the way farmers deal with trouble, whether it was insects eating up the grain in their bins or a late-spring frost threatening the corn crop. You make provisions. You tinker, you talk to other farmers, you make do, you solve the problem as best you can. You never eliminate adversity, but you control what little you can. When asked how things are going, Iowa farmers, on cue, all have the same rote answer: "Could be worse."

The way Leigh and other Iowa farmers went about their business was a lesson in farm economics. It made no difference whom they fed—fellow Iowans or the people on the other side of the globe. It was an almost antiquated view: Farmers considered it a privilege to produce food, sustenance for all mankind. Sholom Rubashkin and his family held to a totally dissimilar vow in creating the *glatt* slaughterhouse. The Rubashkins' obligation was not to mankind, but to a tiny sliver of it: Lubavitchers and other Jews who eat meat killed and processed by exacting biblical standards and rules.

If Sholom and the rest of the Postville Hasidim had their

way, they would have absolutely nothing to do with the locals, for fear of contamination, assimilation, control. This kind of insular mentality seemed not particular to Postville. The Postville Hasidim personified self-interest and factionalism—"What's in it for *me*; what's in it for *my* people?" That's what Sholom professed to care about and nothing else. Such a mind-set has become commonplace in America. Everyone seems to belong to a personal interest group, which could be as broad a niche as race and religion, or as narrow as whether members eat meat, smoke, or have been through therapy (if so, which kind). Affiliation with your own people had taken precedence over being a part of a larger, world-wide community of humanity.

Had Leigh seduced me with his farmer shtik and his unexpected raft of stories of far-off places and public service? I needed to get a larger sampling of Postville opinion than just the gang's at Ginger's or from Leigh Rekow or Brenda Bernhard, so over the next several weeks I canvassed everyone I could, which wasn't too hard in a place like Postville. I walked the streets, poking my head into practically every Postville merchant's store. I set up interviews with people who had written letters—pro and con about the Lubavitchers—to the *Herald-Leader.* As I interviewed more and more locals, I got more names: "This has been a nice little visit, but if you *really* want to do your story right, you ought to talk to Joe or Tad or Butch or Myrtle. *They'll* tell you what you want to know." By the time I got to talk to yet another Postville local, the response usually was "I was wondering when you'd ever get around to me!" There was so much meat to the story that in 1996, I wrote an article for the *Chicago Tribune Magazine* about what was happening in Postville.

People wanted to be counted, and they wanted to be

counted right. The collective reaction to the Jews, I discovered, was to scratch your head and wonder what in the good Lord's name was happening here in Postville. Oh, some locals welcomed the Jews and went out of their way to help them. Some thought the Jews were bringing a welcomed dose of the big city to small-town Iowa ("Isn't this what they mean by *diversity?*" Sharon Drahn asked me). Many were merchants whose business had doubled and tripled because of the Jews. But overwhelmingly, the response to the Jews was the same as the morning coffee klatchers' at Ginger's.

In fact, two distinct camps had emerged in Postville, and each had created its own safe haven. Ginger's had become the sanctuary for the anti-Hasidim, and directly across Lawler Street, the Postville Bakery had turned into a refuge for the pro-Hasidim. Two restaurants in town, across the street from each other, and each had its own philosophical requirements for jawing with fellow diners. Every morning, the Ginger's coffee klatch gathered and bad-mouthed the Jews, while at the same time, three or four locals tipped back their coffee mugs at the Postville Bakery, shaking their heads in dismay at how those men across the street were behaving.

A bellwether to the storm was Rosalyn Krambeer, a feisty woman in her seventies with fine, straight fingers. Rosalyn wasn't some fettered, stuffy town matron. For twenty-five years, she had been a nurse at the hospital in nearby Waukon. With her boyfriend, Oren, whose elaborate bouffant hair would put Wayne Newton to shame ("I get a lot more compliments now that it's white," Oren said), Rosalyn travels throughout northeast Iowa as often as possible to go ballroom dancing. Born in Luana, a speck of a town just outside of Postville, Rosalyn still had a twang to her voice, and like Stanley Schroeder, often ended her sentences with *"don't-cha-know?"*

"You betcha I'm going to vote for annexation if it ever gets on the ballot," she told me. "And don't go thinking it's because I don't like the Jews. That just isn't true. It's for a simple reason: They don't clean up their yards. Keeping up our property—that's important to us. I'm not asking that they landscape their yards. I'd just settle for mowing the grass once in a while.

"I guess there's a problem with their culture. The women don't do this kind of outside work. It's the men, and the men just don't know how. They're busy working in the meatpacking plant or reading their Bible, or doing whatever it is they do." Rosalyn shook her head, with the same frown I saw on the men at Ginger's. "If they'd only just ask us, we'd love to help them."

For as long as Rosalyn could remember, Postville has had a lingering reputation as being a snooty town, and as a child, Rosalyn was the victim of a condescending attitude that she said can suffocate outsiders who move here. "Oh, I remember what it's like to be different and to try to break into the right circles here. Yes, I remember," she said with no small amount of stored-up rancor. "If you weren't born here—and remember, I was born just down the road a couple of miles—they just didn't take to you. Mind you, I wasn't from Decorah or Cedar Rapids or Des Moines, but from a Lutheran small town less than five miles away, and they still wouldn't take to you! People from the farm were considered hayseeds. I never finished high school until I was an adult, and they didn't like someone coming in here who wasn't a high school graduate. It wasn't just that, either. The Catholics walked on one side of the street and the Lutherans walked on the other. And if you were Presbyterian, well, I guess you didn't walk at all!" Rosalyn laughed a hearty laugh, but it was laced with a bitterness that even sixty years couldn't conceal.

So, when it came to the Hasidic Jews, another set of outsiders to Postville, I hoped Rosalyn would be charitable. But the single and sole positive attribute Rosalyn allowed about the Postville Jews was this: "Well, I suppose you don't feel unsafe around them."

Word of my snooping around got quickly to Marie Schlee, a widow in her sixties, who let people know that she wanted to give me a piece of her mind. When I talked to Marie, she immediately attacked the *Tribune* article I had written. "Your story was just good publicity for the Jews. They'll read that and more will move into Postville. That's what's gonna happen, and you can count yourself responsible." Marie said that I had made Postville locals "seem like backwards people, carrying on like we keep heifers as pets." The entire article from the first to last word was a pack of lies, a complete disgrace. "You ought to be ashamed of yourself!"

Like Rosalyn, Marie's chief complaint against the Jews was their untidiness, but her problems with the Jews cut deeper. "I'm very proud of my land, five acres, and two of those acres are grass, which—by the way—takes me four and a half hours to mow. The Jews are dirty. They leave their windows open, with the curtains flying out and the bugs flying in. And they're buying up all the homes in town. On Saturday, they're all over town after sunset. They walk five, six abreast on the sidewalk, and you have to get out of *their* way. Can you imagine! When they go to the swimming pool, they want *our* kids to clear out. It's the way they do things. I don't dislike the Jews, and don't you go making me out to be someone who does. I dislike what they're doing to this town."

Marie was just getting going. If they allowed women at the morning coffee klatch at Ginger's, she would be at the head of the table, right next to the regulars who thought Marge Schott was a saint. She kept railing against "the Jews," even more strident in tone, and as I scribbled in my notebook, she dropped something that made my ears perk up.

"I was born in Elgin. There was a Jewish doctor there, Doc Wolf, but he didn't flaunt it. He practiced for fifty years, and you know what? Those who knew he was Jewish didn't care one bit."

A country doctor who was Jewish in these Lutheran parts of northeast Iowa (Elgin was 12 miles from Postville)? A Jewish physician who practiced for fifty years here? Someone who delivered half of the town, who set kids' broken arms, who saved the fingers ripped off farmers' maimed hands—few rumors, aspersions, secrets would have slipped by him. I scribbled down Doc Wolf's name in my notebook and circled it.

But before I could get to Doc Wolf, I had a long list of locals ready to unload on me. As I walked from Military Road, up Maple, to Tilden, past the post office, I looked across the street and saw three Hasidic men get into a beat-up Buick with a dent in the passenger door. So, here was the enemy, the men Marie Schlee, Rosalyn Krambeer, Leigh Rekow, and all the others had in mind.

These Hasidim looked to be in their early twenties. They were in shirtsleeves, wearing *tzitzit*, black pants, and hard-soled leather shoes. They weren't wearing yarmulkes, but instead, black broad-brimmed fedoras that dwarfed their sallow, angular faces. These hats made a statement. Even to me, these guys looked menacing.

Everything was wrong with the picture. On this lazy summer Iowa afternoon, these young men were dressed in black and they were in a rush. They were jabbering away in what sounded like Hebrew, pointing to one another, shouting out orders. They kept glancing over their shoulders. They didn't seem to be in sleepy Postville, but double-parked on a busy street in Jerusalem or Crown Heights. No one else around them mattered. The men were loud and seemingly unaware of the singular commotion they were creating. The Buick had mud splattered on the hood, roof, and fenders. The car's sagging front bumper was held in place by black electrical tape. Where'd these guys even find a car like that?

Everyone on Tilden was looking at the Hasidic trio from afar, from the corners of their eyes. It was like being at the state fair, when you see a couple of men acting strange on the midway, maybe they've had too much to drink or they're just showing off in front of their girlfriends. Everyone keeps an eye on them, but you don't quite know what to do except keep your distance. The locals on Tilden this afternoon were watching these three Jewish men in the same way, but you couldn't put down your bag of groceries on the sidewalk, fold your arms, and just stand there gawking.

When the driver turned the ignition key to the Buick, a plume of sooty black smoke shot out from the car's muffler, and then suddenly, the car backfired. The explosion made a loud, piercing noise that sounded like a shot from a revolver. Within an instant, the noise silenced Tilden Street. Everything stopped. Ruby Koenig shot Whitey Meyer a glance. Junior Porterfield, who happened to be in the post office, must have whispered something to Mark Looney, because they both shook their heads, then chuckled.

The Hasidic men, meanwhile, seemed oblivious to the hubbub they had just caused. The Buick lurched forward, grinding gears, and continued to sputter puffs of smoke as the trio took a right at the corner and drove to where Lawler Street ends and where the shul stands.

From a fractured moment of discomfort, back to the clear afternoon sun, the incident was suddenly over. Things went back to normal—at least, until another happenstance involving the Hasidim reared its embarrassing head. I imagined what the locals must have been thinking. The Jews *were* out of sync with the natural symmetry I was growing to understand. There was an unspoken order to Postville. Not only did the Jews not care about it, I doubted whether they were aware that such an order even existed.

CHAPTER 8

Coon on a Hound's Back

I left Tilden Street and walked to the Postville Bakery to meet Forest Kelly, a real-estate broker who had sold more than two dozen Postville homes to the Jews. Toey, as everyone called him, was dressed in powder blue Sansabelt pants, a bright green shirt, beige patent leather shoes, and a white belt with a brass buckle that read SMITH & WESSON. He wore black glasses like Buddy Holly's. Toey's hair was combed in an exaggerated pompadour that firmly placed him in the Wayne Newton school of hair design.

I was momentarily taken aback. Was this guy for real?

Toey realized the power of his presence. He smiled and paused, allowing me time to savor the visual aberration before me. There were several seconds of silence, and Toey seemed to be enjoying them. These weren't awkward moments, but moments to take in all that was there. Then, as though on cue, Toey stuck out his right hand to shake mine. His grip was like a vise, and as he pumped my hand up and down, he nearly wrung my arm from the shoulder socket. As I was recovering, Toey presented me with a gold-embossed business card. In red ink was Toey's motto: I WOULD RATHER MISS A SALE, THAN MISREPRESENT ONE.

Toey got down to business fast. He sat in one of the bakery's straight-backed chairs in front of a china mug of coffee and angled his chin toward Ginger's across the street. "Too many people in this town have closed minds. You ask me, and I'll tell you something: I don't give a diddly damn who owns it [the slaughterhouse], this town's better with the plant opened than closed. Any damn fool knows that!

"I had a house for sale and the seller asked me, 'You gonna sell to the goddamn Jews?' And, you know what I said? I told him, 'I'll sell to anyone who wants to buy, because that's the law, and if you don't agree with me, then you and I are going to be in one big heap of trouble.'"

Toey had a sheen of pride on his face. Of course, he was making a killing—between 3 and 5 percent commission per house adds up. Until the Jews came, being a real-estate agent in Postville was at the bottom of the job heap, below being Postville's funeral director, who happened to be Stanley Schroeder's brother-in-law. Actually, though, when you looked at it, selling houses had been even worse than burying people because the funeral business was one of the few local businesses booming. Before the Jews came to town, most Postville people over thirty stayed put until they died. Where were they going to go? There was no reason to sell your house, unless your health was nose-diving, and then you had to move into the Good Samaritan Center, but who'd buy your house if there was no way to pay for it?

It was talk of annexation that worried Toey the most. If the old coots who run this town got that annexation issue on the ballot, and enough of the locals turned into sheep and voted to redraw the city limits so that the slaughterhouse was inside, then Toey might as well say good-bye to all the manna that had been falling into his lap these days. "I've played enough poker in my life to know that the man over there might not be bluffing. They might leave; they might not. But I don't want to give them any reasons to pack up. It'd be a damn shame, that's what it'd be."

Toey was sick with the way Postville people were fussing over the Jews. It was an embarrassment, that's what it was. "Every couple of days, someone will come up to me and ask, 'So, how you getting along with the Jews, Toey? How many houses did you sell to the Jews this month?'" Toey scrunched up his long face and shook his head. "Aw, it's disgusting."

Toey glanced at his gold wristwatch and said he had to show a house to a buyer. As Toey rose from his seat, I wasn't looking forward to saying good-bye. But Toey took my hand anyway and shook it to the bones. All I could do was smile like an idiot and hope the handshake wouldn't last long. My lasting image of Toey was his lurching across Lawler Street, loping like an awkward antelope, jiggling change with those big hands in the pockets of his blue pants.

With another couple of hours left in the day, I walked through downtown to meet Glenda Bodensteiner, the manager at Tindell Shoes. I especially wanted to visit Tindell's because my father had owned a family shoe store in northern New Jersey—Townley Shoes, he called it—and from the outside, both Tindell's and Townley looked eerily similar. Stepping into Tindell's was like stepping back thirty years in my own life—the smell of leather, Kiwi polish, and rubber cement (to glue innersoles) still tickled the insides of my nostrils. Like my father's store, Tindell's had upholstered green vinyl chairs, metal Braddock foot sizers, displays of handbags and socks, floor-to-ceiling walls of wooden shelves filled with shoes that went from 5B to 12EEE, an antique cash register, and a pair of slanted mirrors that made your feet look smaller than they really were.

Like my father, Glenda didn't just know the names of all of her customers, she knew their shoe sizes. She, too, allowed her good customers to run up a tab. Just as my father used to do, during prom season, Glenda brought out a spiral-bound chart with hundreds of color swatches, so that girls could match the exact color of their new shoes to the exact color of their long dresses. Glenda asked the girls to leave a swatch from their gowns, since the dyes usually came out darker, and she would then hand-dye peau de soie pumps. "Haven't had one come back yet," Glenda said, sounding like a female version of my father.

These days, Glenda's memory of shoe sizes was getting taxed, and that was good. With such large families, it wasn't unusual for the Hasidim to drop $350 at her store in a single day. Imagine! And they didn't buy sneakers and sandals. They bought shoes, the old-fashioned kind, the ones made with leather and arches, lace-up shoes that gave your feet good support. The Jews wanted Glenda to fit each and every kid's foot, to check the length and the width, to pinch the toe box to make sure there was just enough room to grow but not so much that the kid would trip. The Postville Jews were a shoe merchant's dream. Glenda said her business had jumped by more than 20 percent since they arrived. And it wasn't just shoes she sold to the Hasidim. Glenda handcrafted more than a hundred velvet-lined leather knife sheaths every year for the butchers at the slaughterhouse.

"The original owner of Tindell's, Clarence Tindell, who owned Tindell's for more than sixty years, told me right before he retired, 'The Jews are your future,' and he was right.

"A lot of the Jewish people come in here, and they're young, and they have what seems like millions of dollars. Some of them come in with a thick roll of bills. It's envy; that's what it is. Postville people are envious; that's all it is. That's why people around here don't like them. Plain and simple: They're jealous."

About six months ago, when a Lubavitcher family was in Tindell's, Glenda's thirteen-year-old son, Jarrod, started playing in the store with the boy, Chaim Jenkelowitz, also thirteen. "They got along great, and soon Jarrod started asking whether he could play with Chaim after school, and I thought, 'Well, why not?' So Chaim came over to our house, and Jarrod went over to the Jenkelowitz house. Jarrod showed Chaim how to play football, and one day, Jarrod asked Chaim if he wanted to go fishing with us. And you should have seen Chaim's eyes. He said, 'Yes, I'd love to go!' So, we all went to the Mississippi and we had a great time."

It was starting to sound like a made-for-TV movie. Especially considering what Glenda said next. "The Jenkelowitz family gets ten phone calls a week, and when they answer, the caller just hangs up. Last March, Chaim was riding his bike and a couple of local kids saw him, and they headed him off the road. Can you imagine? Postville kids did that. Chaim fell off his bike and had to get stitches. It was Saturday, and they couldn't drive on account it was their Sabbath, so we took Chaim and his mother to a clinic outside of Postville, and by gosh, you should have seen how they treated Chaim. They looked at him funny, and they made him wait for two hours! I was furious!"

That's not the only example of anti-Semitism Glenda had seen. Like Toey Kelly, Glenda got cold stares because she did business with the Jews. Perhaps it had something to do with the delicate fact that Glenda actually *touched* the Jews' feet when she slipped shoes on. Once while Glenda was fitting Chaim's father, Jacob, two elderly women came into the store. "I was already waiting on the Jenkelowitzes, and these ladies just looked at me, and then they started staring at me, and one of them, her eyes got real mean, said to me, 'If you're going to wait on them first, then we'll take our business elsewhere.' The Jenkelowitzes apologized, but why should I drop everything when they were here first?"

One thing that Glenda wasn't prepared for—none of the merchants were—was the bargaining. "Sometimes they come in and try to bargain, but I just say no," said Glenda. "I stop them in their tracks before they get started. You have to be firm about it. The owner of the variety store around the corner said the Jews would come in and hassle him all the time about prices, and he asked me how I handled it. He just didn't know what to do. I told him you just have to say no. That's all. Be firm, and they will listen, but if you waver, then that opens the door to their custom of bargaining. And once you start giving in to them, then there's no going back."

The bargaining was a minor detraction. Bargaining or no bargaining, the Jews had brought truckloads of money, and Glenda and the other merchants in town were supremely thankful for it. "It's the discount centers in Decorah and Prairie du Chien, that's what people who care about Postville should hate, not the Jews. Wal-Mart is a swear word in our family. That's what's closing down Postville. The Jews have brought us jobs and with the jobs come salaries and the ability to buy things. Wal-Mart has taken jobs and money out of our pockets. If you're angry, get angry at those places, not at the Jews. That doesn't make any sense." My father and Glenda were fellow foot soldiers when it came to such David and Goliath battles. He, too, used to rail about the "highway stores," and how they would eventually put him out of business.

Across Greene Street, inside hot and steamy Home Town Cleaners, Roberta Dreier also looked at the Jews as saviors. "My biggest business is right before their holidays," Roberta said, hanging a pressed shirt on a serpentine rotating track that had handwritten numbers and letters above each slot. "Right before Passover, we get swamped. Totals that come to seventy, eighty dollars are not unusual. Can you imagine someone from Postville paying that much for dry cleaning?" Roberta was amazed that *anyone* would pay that much for dry cleaning.

The temperature outside was 95 degrees, and inside Home Town, it must have been close to 110. The smell of dry-cleaning chemicals and steam from the press made me wince, as though Roberta had twisted and split a gauze tube of smelling salts under my nose. Roberta had bought Home Town five years earlier, and the Jews had been a bonanza for her. Even in the dog days of Iowa summers, when the mercury shot past a hundred degrees by noon, every week she cleaned the Lubavitcher men's black coats, linen prayer shawls, broad-brimmed Borsalinos, *shtreimelech,* and even *spodikem.* Roberta said the most frequent stains were from red wine on white shirts. She irons every shirt by hand, twenty-seven in an hour. "Some Postville people go to church in jeans," she said, shaking her head. "Maybe we can learn something from the Jews."

Long before the Jews arrived, Postville had been split on a host of matters, even where local people put their money. There were two choices. Citizens State Bank was the Lutheran bank in town, while Postville State Bank, across the street, was known as the Catholic bank. For generations, that's how it's been. The Lutherans banked at Citizens and the Catholics at Postville State, a chasm never to be bridged, never to be challenged, not unlike the parting of Lawler Street between Ginger's and the Postville Bakery.

Jim Lage, the president of Citizens Bank, looked the part of a small-town Midwestern banker: compact, white shirt, glasses, striped tie sitting atop the protrusion of an ample belly. He leaned back in his cushioned executive chair, in his glass-walled office at the back of the bank on Lawler Street, next door to the *Herald-Leader.* The lenses of his thick glasses reflected a row of fluorescent lights, and when he lowered his gaze toward me, I could see the reflected images of the tellers behind me, Linda Langerman, Kay Ruckdaschel, and Terri Downing, working the three windows in the lobby.

Of all the businesses in town, Citizens Bank had the most to gain from the Jews' arrival. Agriprocessors helped double Citizens' assets from $23 million in 1982 to $42 million in 1996, during a time when scores of family farms had been lost and not just a few banks had closed. No wonder Jim Lage told me, "Heavens no! I wouldn't want Agri to leave. Everyone benefits from their being here. Everyone. Every dollar in Postville gets spent seven times. You pay someone for a product, and that money gets circulated to pay the labor, the utilities, the taxes. If they were to leave, we'd have a glut of houses for sale. We could have thirty homes for sale. That would collapse our housing market." Not only did Agriprocessors draw its payroll checks on accounts held at Citizens, the Rubashkins drew checks from Citizens for spin-off businesses the family had incorporated, including Nevel Properties, which owned more than two dozen homes and apartments in town.

Yet, even with all of the Rubashkin business, Lage had problems with how the family went about running the slaughterhouse, and he wasn't bashful when it came to talking about it. Sholom *kvetched* about the ribbons of red tape the state and feds required for Agriprocessors to qualify for reduced-interest or interest-free loans and outright grants, but Jim Lage said not a dime would ever go to the slaughterhouse because the Rubashkins refused to open up their financial records to anyone. "The government isn't going to give away free money without demonstrating a need, yet the Rubashkins don't want to disclose figures. So they complain a lot, but they seem to *like* to do that," Lage said, allowing for a thin smile. "That's the way they are. You get used to it."

Jim and his wife, Arlene, had been invited to Aaron Rubashkin's daughter's wedding in Brooklyn a couple of years back, and on a lark, they made the trip. The Lages were two gentiles in a room of 750 Jews. "What I really remember was when they put the bride up on a chair and walked her around the room, high in the air, with everyone singing and shouting. I had never seen anything quite like that before. It was something."

To show his appreciation for the Rubashkin family and for the gold mine the Jews had brought to his bank, during Chanukah, Jim had a customer-appreciation day. Leah Rubashkin, her sister-in-law Basia, and some of the other Jewish ladies set up a table in the bank foyer with a big spread of Jewish pastries on it. "I tell people to take some of the food, it's good, but many customers don't want to touch anything. I think they're afraid to sample the food; they're afraid something's going to happen to them—and that's a shame because it tastes so good," Lage said as he patted his stomach.

Sonny Thomas was the first local person Aaron Rubashkin

hired when he bought the slaughterhouse in 1987. Sonny painted the entire plant by hand, but first he had to contend with a menagerie of rodents and vermin. "Hygrade [the former owners] just left the place to rot. When I first saw it, I didn't want the job. To paint the whole place took me seven and a half months, working by myself. Before I started, I had to hire a crew to get rid of all the damn raccoons."

Sonny, a native Tennessean, was a tall, rail-thin guy with greased-back hair in his sixties who played the bass and drums for a local country and western band, and had a penchant for More cigarettes, which he chain-smoked. I imagined Sonny could blow perfect smoke rings. "Mr. Rubashkin used to call me Rembrandt. I'm talking about the father, Aaron. I never did get along with his sons, but Aaron, he was very nice to me. When I was painting once, I fell down and sprained my ankle. And the next day Mr. Rubashkin, he came to see me. He helped me up and down the ladder all day long. It was nice, but to tell you the truth, he was sort of a nuisance, hanging out there and looking at my work, day in and day out. Though, I can tell you this: I never met a nicer, finer person. He was the nicest person you'd ever meet, that Mr. Rubashkin.

"When word started circulating that I was working for them, people would call me 'Jew lover.' They'd say, 'You work for the Jews! How can you do that?' They'd tell me that to my face, they'd yell it from their cars. You wonder what they said behind my back. To tell you the truth, I got a little pissed by it all."

Sonny broke for a cigarette. He exhaled and out came a cloud of dense smoke. "I had my share of confrontations. A few kids spray-painted swastikas on the side of buildings and telephone poles. Sometimes, the kids would salute me and yell out, 'Heil, Hitler!' But it didn't make no difference to me. Mr. Rubashkin was good to me. I don't give a damn if they were black, Jewish, or Chinese. They treated me good. I know people who when the Jews came to town, they changed their locks. They thought the Jews would come in and steal from them. Can you imagine?"

If Sonny was a sheep painted black by the community, then many of the locals must have wanted to dip Cliff and Ida Mae Olson head first in a vat of coal-black tar. Cliff and Ida Mae, who have been married fifty years, along with Sonny, were among the first to break away from the local xenophobia and work for the Rubashkins. For almost a decade, Cliff, a retired car salesman, has been the Jews' personal chauffeur, or as some of the locals referred to him, the "Jews' errand boy."

"It all started when I was waiting to pick up a passenger at the La Crosse Airport. I had some time on my hands, and I saw a man dressed in black with a big bushy beard, and I struck up a conversation with him. To tell you the truth, this man really looked like a fish out of water, and I'd always been curious about the Jewish people. This happened when the Jews were first coming here to look at the plant, even before they bought it."

Soon, the Jews were using Cliff for all their rides to and from La Crosse Airport, which is seventy miles away from Postville. Since he started in 1987, Cliff figured he's made as many as five hundred trips to the airport in his Oldsmobile 88, mostly transporting slaughterhouse employees, but also picking up mechanical parts for the plant. Cliff charges fifty dollars one way, but pointed out, with gas, and wear and tear on the car, "You don't make anything from it, but you do learn a lot."

Ida Mae filled in for Cliff, but only for special occasions.

Before the Postville *mikveh* on Greene Street was opened, Ida Mae once drove a Jewish woman all the way to Madison, Wisconsin, for a *mikveh*. "They asked especially for me," Ida Mae said, nodding her head up and down. "Yes, sirree. They wouldn't have Cliff in a car with a woman alone. No, sir!" So Ida Mae drove the woman without asking any questions and waited an hour in front of the Madison house with the *mikveh* in the basement.

Cliff, who was wearing a green jumpsuit with a white vinyl pocket protector full of pens and pencils, is a third-generation American, but his first language was Norwegian. "When I was growing up here, the northeastern part of Iowa really was segregated. Postville was where the German Lutherans settled, in Elgin you had your Swiss Apostolates, and in Clermont and Gunder, the Norwegian Lutherans settled. In high school, you just didn't date the Catholic girls. It just wasn't done.

"A lot of people here don't want to accept the Jews because they think they're going to take over. They're reliving the war. Some actually don't believe there was a Holocaust. They say, 'The Jews invited their troubles,' that's how they put it. I sold cars for twelve years, and over and over again, I used to hear the expression 'Jew you down.'"

Then Ida Mae, sitting quietly at the kitchen table with us, cleared her throat. She had something on her mind, and she looked me straight in the eye. Her tone wasn't nearly as vinegary as that of the lady from Winga's who had asked me where we were from, but Ida Mae's question nonetheless caught me by surprise.

"Are you Jewish?

Cliff grimaced, shook his head, and looked at his lap. "I

hope you don't mind my asking," Ida Mae said, "but that's just the kind of person I am. I like to ask questions. A lot of people around here don't like me for it, but that's just too bad. They just keep quiet and just assume things, which is probably how all the gossip around here gets spread. They just want to believe what they think is true, but they never go out of their way to find out the truth. When I want to know something, I ask it straight out. So, are you? And please don't take umbrage at my question."

"Why shouldn't he?" Cliff said, sounding exasperated.

I got the feeling that Ida Mae was the one in this relationship who asked all the questions, and that Cliff and Ida Mae had arguments all the time about it.

"If he's Jewish, he'll tell you," Cliff said. "He's got nothing to hide. If it's his religion, he'll tell you."

"Shush up, Cliff. How's he gonna tell anyone anything if you keep on talking?"

In all my time hanging out in Postville, talking to farmers, merchants, anyone who wanted to visit with me, no one had ever bothered to ask me about my own religion. In a crowd of fifty people in any metropolitan city, I'd be among the first picked out as Jewish: my olive skin, curly hair, ample nose. Here, though, whether it was small-town provincialism or just good manners, my own background had never come up. At least, no one had ever brought it up, except Sholom as soon as he saw me. This was a moment of truth of sorts.

"Yes, I am," I said, but with a caveat that came out fast. "There are lots of different kinds of Jews, different orders, branches, affiliations, not unlike Christianity. And I'm about as far away from the Hasidic Jews as you can get and still be called Jewish."

"But you *are* Jewish, right?" Ida Mae persisted, not letting any fancy footwork deter her.

"I sure am," I said finally, trying not to betray any equivocation.

"Then what do *you* think about what they're doing to the Jews? You've got to have an opinion."

Until Ida Mae had pointed her finger at me, I had merrily gone on my appointed rounds, playing an Iowan when I was with the Iowans and a Jew when I had been with Sholom Rubashkin. But here was Ida Mae asking me to take sides. This was a complicated question, and I wasn't sure where I stood.

"I think there's some anti-Semitism here," I replied, and I wasn't referring to just Postville but to all of Iowa. I flashed on the Watermelon Social, Mikey's Cub Scout leader, the time when the Iowa ladies told my Jewish friend they were praying for him. "Then again, maybe it's fear of people who are just plain different, people who didn't grow up here, people from the city. I'm not so sure."

Cliff wasn't so charitable and jumped in right away. "You bet you're not so sure. It's all over this place. They don't like these people for one reason: It's because they are Jewish. You can say whatever you want, but that's the bald-faced truth."

And then Cliff brought up the same tantalizing tidbit that Marie Schlee had mentioned: the Jewish doctor down the road, in Elgin—Henry Wolf.

"Doc Wolf must have delivered twenty-five hundred babies and when he was dying, he put in a request for the Postville rabbis to pay him a visit. So, someone ran down to the slaughterhouse and got a bunch of the rabbis, and they came to Doc Wolf's bedside and said a whole bunch of Hebrew prayers over him. People in Elgin knew he was Jewish, but a lot of younger folks in Postville didn't. And within an hour, word got out real fast that Dr. Wolf was Jewish, and 'Oh, my God!' was the reaction. You should have heard them! It just turned my stomach.

"Here's a question for you: What would they have done if they had known Doc Wolf was Jewish while he was operating to take out their appendix or to deliver their baby?"

"Cliff," Ida Mae said, as though warning him about eating too many tomatoes, "calm down."

But it was now Cliff's turn to shush Ida Mae. "There isn't a business in town that's been hurt by the Jews being here. Why be down on something you're not up on? They don't know ANYTHING about the Jews. And they don't *want* to know anything about them. The first words you hear are 'Those damn foreigners!' They're *not* foreigners. The last time I checked, Brooklyn, New York, where the Rubashkin family is from, was part of the good ol' U-NI-TED STATES of AMER-ICA. But the locals don't want to believe that. They don't want to get to know them. They think the Jews are like a coon on a hound's back. Once they're here, they'll never let go."

As soon as Cliff said "coon on a hound's back," I was mes-merized. I figured Cliff was talking about raccoons and dogs, and when I asked, he smiled in an almost sweet way, then laughed. "You *are* a city slicker!"

Clift leaned forward, his elbows on the Formica table. "When a raccoon is chased by a dog, the coon generally heads for one of three places," Cliff explained. "The coon can burrow in a hole in the ground, he can climb a tree, or he can head for water. If the coon goes for a river or a lake, the dog mostly likely will chase him there, getting in the water. Lots of coons will climb on the dog's back while in the water, and their weight will drown the dog. The coons know what they're doing, and they'll kill that poor dog."

If the locals saw the Jews as coons, then they saw themselves as the dogs, struggling to breathe, about to go under, and Cliff, dammit, wasn't doing anything to help. At least, that's what many of the locals told him.

"All the time, I hear 'em saying, 'Oh, here comes Cliff, again. He's the Jews' friend.' And, you know what? I'm sick and tired of hearing that. Oh, I can take it; that's not it. It's that my neighbors, the people I have lived with in the town for seventy years, some of them are a bunch of closed-minded bigots!"

Through it all, Ida Mae nodded in agreement. Her lips formed a tight straight line, and I noticed a slight bulge in both her checks as though she had exhaled and was holding her breath. Cliff said that all the reasons the locals gave for not liking the Jews, what Rosalyn Krambeer, Marie Schlee, Leigh Rekow had said, well, all of it was a bunch of hooey. "These people say they don't like the Jews because they don't mow their lawns, because they don't shovel their front walks. Well, that's plain crazy. I'll take you to a home that's a mess— and it'll be local Postville people, but you never hear the locals picking on them.

"I'll tell you what I think the Jews should do here. Instead of that sign on the way in to town that says Postville is the place where Dr. John Mott was born, they should take that sign down—that was more than a hundred years ago!—and they should replace it with another sign that says Postville is the home of the largest kosher meatpacking plant run by Lubavitcher Jews in the world. That's what it should say. Postville should be proud of what the Jews have brought here!"

Ida Mae nodded.

"Yes, sirree," she said. "Instead, we try to hide it. It's about the only thing Postville's got going for it."

Fat chance, I thought. John Mott was Postville's singular hero. No one was going to take down a billboard about a crusading Christian and replace it with one about a band of bearded Jews who slaughter animals.

Just as I was at the door, I asked Cliff and Ida Mae what had been lurking in the back of my mind all day—about the two Hasidim, Stillman and Lew, the pair I had heard about in Ginger's. "Now, why you wanna go looking into *that* for?" Cliff asked, looking at me, his chin tucked under his neck. "Bunch of rotten apples. That's what they are. Those boys don't represent the Jews. You find out about Doc Wolf. That'll tell you everything you need to know."

Before I could learn more about Doc Wolf or track down Stillman and Lew, I had promised to meet Dwight Bacon, the manager at Postville Farmers Cooperative Society, which sells pretty much everything farmers need: grain, seed, tools, material, clothing, equipment, diesel fuel. The Rubashkins buy five thousand to seven thousand gallons of diesel fuel a month, making Agriprocessors the co-op's largest single purchaser of fuel. It was a touch of irony—a kosher slaughterhouse doing business with a man by the name of Bacon.

For a vacation in 1995, the Bacon family—Dwight, Lisa, Stephani, and Staci—decided to do something totally different: They got on a plane and headed to New York City. On the second day, Dwight coaxed Lisa and the girls into a taxicab and told the driver to head over to Brooklyn. So, over the Brooklyn Bridge they went "just to see what it looked like and how the Jews lived," said Dwight. "We were in New York, so why not?" Dwight had an address in his pocket, and he gave it to the driver. The taxi took them to the kosher restaurant in Borough Park that Aaron Rubashkin owned and his wife ran.

The trip the Bacon family took to Brooklyn was good tonic. It was the same medicine the Jews had swallowed when they first got to Postville. "We walked up and down the streets, four people from Iowa, and everyone was staring at us, like, 'Who are *you*? What planet are *you* from?' We couldn't believe we were still in the United States. My girls were very uncomfortable, they wanted to leave. We did, but not before we all learned an amazing lesson of what *they're* going through *here*.

"No one can deny that the Jews are here and that they're here to stay. They're part of the backbone of this community. That's a fact, and people around here better get used to it— no matter how hard that is to take."

CHAPTER 9

Between the Cracks

Actually, not many of the Postville locals worked in the slaughterhouse. The low-level, menial jobs at Agriprocessors, which paid six dollars an hour, were at the bottom rung of the Postville economic ladder and were usually filled by newly arrived non-English-speaking immigrants from Eastern Europe. These workers, who were all gentiles, had to have strong backs for lifting and sliding the giant carcasses along the factory killfloor and for hauling the heavy boxes of cut-up beef and chicken parts onto refrigerated trucks. They had to tolerate sickening sights and putrid odors and be willing to work in the packinghouse's near-freezing temperatures for eight, ten hours a day. Most were men, but a surprising number were women—young, divorced, or single mothers hellbent on making it in America.

Not many of the Postville locals were so down and out that they were forced to work in the grimy packinghouse. Wal-Mart was always hiring, and those jobs paid more, were easier, some even said pleasant, and they came with a 10 percent employee discount. The few locals who worked at Agriprocessors rarely stayed long, usually opting to move on to higher paying, safer jobs after several weeks or months at the slaughterhouse.

Almost three-quarters of the three hundred or so workers at Agriprocessors were foreigners. At least, that's what the employees I spoke with figured the percentages to be. The work required no English, and the plant was a haven for immigrants who spoke just a smattering of English or none at all. Flouting the law, Agriprocessors didn't require its employees to supply work permits or proof of U.S. citizenship, employees told me. And at any given time, they said, probably as much as 60 percent of the slaughterhouse workforce was illegally employed. In the first years of operation, the Rubashkins helped some workers get green cards, and even paid their rent. But as more workers came to Postville, that practice ceased. The plant was the only large-scale beef slaughterhouse in the state that wasn't unionized. The regional meatcutters' union passed out leaflets to workers at the plant in 1993, but after the Rubashkins went out to the gate and told the organizers to leave, union activity ceased.

The immigrant workers at Agriprocessors fell between the cracks: Neither Jews nor locals, they were Russians, Ukrainians, Kazakhstanians, Poles. They lived in trailer courts on the outskirts of town or in small apartments that five or six workers rented together. Many would hang out at the Club 51, the tavern on Lawler, which cashed workers' paychecks and carried a wide assortment of Russian vodkas. When I walked in one Friday evening at about eight, the cigarette smoke was so dense that I couldn't see from one end of the bar to the other. I could make out a card game going on in the center of the tavern, and through the haze saw *Wheel of Fortune* playing on the TV behind the bar. Weary Russian and Ukrainian men, chatting in their native tongue, stopped in for

quick shots of vodka, even though some had unopened pints
sticking out from their pants' pockets. A vending machine
that offered five different kinds of state lottery tickets was
sold out. At the Spice-n-Ice Redemption Center down the
block, there was an astonishing array of vodka: twenty-four
brands and types, vodkas from Russia, Denmark, Sweden,
Finland, even Belize, double and triple distilled. For a moment, I felt I wasn't in Postville at all, but in a working-class
Eastern European village just as the factory whistle had blown.
These gentile immigrants were a third element to Postville
society, a rerun of the classic American story: Newly arrived
in the land of plenty, working in the lowliest of jobs, between
shots of anesthetic to deaden the pain of their labors, they
scrimped and saved, sending money to their wives and children back home.

A friend of mine who taught English at the local junior
college had arranged a meeting for me with twenty-five Russian and Ukrainian workers at Community Presbyterian
church on South Reynolds Street. In the church basement,
we sat around four rectangular wooden tables pushed together; in the middle, I had put two coffee urns, cups, paper
plates, and a box of two dozen gooey or powdery doughnuts I
had bought at the Casey's on West Tilden. An exchange student from Belarus volunteered to be a translator.

"Remember, he's not an INS agent," my friend, Gay, told
the translator, who repeated the words in broken Ukrainian.
Everyone looked doubtful.

"No, really, he's not." There was a pause for translation.
"He's a college professor. He wants to learn about the work in
the slaughterhouse and what's it's like to live in Postville."

Several shrugs; two men across from me looked unconvinced as they whispered to each other. "Where do you come

from?" I tried, as the translator turned my question into Ukrainian, directing it to everyone.

Sitting across from me was a woman, who looked to be in her early thirties, wearing a hand-knitted red sweater, baggy Chic jeans, aviator glasses, and chipped pink nail polish. "My mother, I guess," she replied.

Whether it was a well-timed riposte, a linguistic happenstance, or faulty translation from the student volunteer, the girl's response cracked everyone up, including me.

As had happened at Ginger's, the people around the table opened up. I discovered that the men were all meatcutters or deboners; the women packed boxes or worked on the chicken assembly line. Most earned a straight six dollars an hour with nothing taken out, and if they worked overtime, the pay was time and a half. Everyone's constant complaint was how cold the slaughterhouse was and how heavy the boxes and crates were to lift.

Still, even these low-level jobs at the slaughterhouse were prized, sought-after employment compared to what workers earned in their homeland after the fall of the Soviet Union. Meager wages weren't the only factor in their exodus to Postville. Many workers talked about the emergence of a Mafia in the Ukraine and in Russia. Stories about strong-arm tactics, about broken legs and execution-style gangland murders, abounded. There seemed palpable fear from the Ukrainians and Russians in the room when they mentioned the word *Mafia*. The men and women shot one another glances and shook their heads. None wanted me to use their real names, based not on modesty, but fear of reprisal.

"If anyone reads that we are in America and working, they'll think we're living in palaces and rolling in cash," said one meatcutter. "They'll try to extort money from our relatives back home, or they'll steal the letters we send them because they'll know they contain money orders."

As the evening progressed, there were other issues on which everyone agreed, and one was that the Rubashkin family had gone out of its way to provide opportunities for them. The working conditions in the slaughterhouse were miserable, the pay paltry, and the jobs mind-numbing and monotonous. But the Rubashkins paid a lot more than any of these workers could earn back home. One single mother from the Ukraine was living in New York for three years with her son when she heard about the Rubashkins' operations in Postville. She took the subway to visit Aaron Rubashkin's butcher shop in the Borough Park section of Brooklyn. Rubashkin offered her a job on the spot, flew her to Chicago, and then transported her to Postville. She traveled with five other Ukrainians, all of whom started working the day they arrived in Postville. "Rubashkin is wonderful, but the labor is very, very hard," she said. The woman developed headaches, then fell ill, and was sent to the regional hospital. Rubashkin didn't pay the bills—but she didn't expect him to pay. Some said that they had signed documents when they started working that stipulated if they were injured on the job, the employee—not the employer—would be liable for all financial responsibility.

"The reason we work here," said a killfloor deveiner, speaking for the entire group, "is that you don't have to be legal. The business is flourishing because of that. Rubashkin has lots of profit from cheap labor and illegal labor. People here work harder. They push you to work hard. It really is crazy now. There is too much pressure. The bosses are very demanding. You cannot slow down. And it's freezing inside.

Sometimes we get no breaks. It's just work, work, work. But, still, we are grateful to Rubashkin for hiring us." Everyone nodded.

The woman in the Chic jeans: "I lived in New York when I first got to America. The traffic, the noise, so many people—it was driving me crazy. The conditions were terrible, too many people living in the apartment we had in Borough Park. It was so tiny that my brother slept with me and my husband in the same bed." The immigrants sitting around the table laughed, and several people nodded their heads knowingly.

A woman in her mid-twenties: "The managers are incredibly rude. One manager fired me because I wouldn't go to bed with him." The translator used the word "manager," but the woman was most likely speaking of one of her supervisors, who would have been a Christian. "If the manager wants to sleep with you and you do, you get a raise. If you don't, he makes your life miserable. Girls have no choice." No one disputed what the woman said.

A man in his early forties: "Rubashkin offers to find us apartments. At first, they put you in a trailer, with two or four people. That costs thirty-five dollars a week, and they take it out of your paycheck. Then they help you find an apartment, but they won't pay for it. I pay three hundred a month for a two-room apartment for me and a friend. Rent is two-twenty, plus another eighty in bills."

Another worker, whom I'll call Uri, an engineer, said his neighbor in the Ukraine used to work for Agriprocessors. With that shred of a job lead, Uri flew to Baltimore, where his sister-in-law lives, and then made his way to Chicago. There he met a friend, and the two drove to the packinghouse, where they started working the next day.

Pasha, also from the Ukraine, with two earrings in his left ear and a punker's haircut, arrived with his father in Postville two years ago. Their first stop in America was New York, where they found out about Aaron Rubashkin's butcher shop in Borough Park. Rubashkin gave Pasha and his father plane tickets, and when they arrived in Minneapolis, they were met by Cliff Olson and driven to the slaughterhouse, where they started working the next day.

"I like it here," twenty-one-year-old Pasha said. "I have freedom. What I want to do I can do. I'm not afraid like I was back home. I really have everything I want. We've got bars. I'm learning Tae Kwon Do. I just got my first apartment. Why would I ever want to go back to the Ukraine? I love America."

Another émigré, Dmitri, also from the Ukraine, who looked like Jesus Christ with a well-trimmed beard, piercing eyes, and two gold-capped front teeth, worked several months in the slaughterhouse but got fed up with the low wages. In two months, he planned to travel to Kodiak, Alaska, leaving his wife and nine-year-old son in Postville. "I hire myself out on a fishing boat for four months in the Bering Sea. It's cold and dangerous, but the money's good. You make anywhere from a thousand to five thousand a month. It's five- or six-day trips, but if the fishing is good, we stay out for as long as fifteen days at sea, four men to a boat."

It was getting late, and many of the workers had to get up to make their 5:00 A.M. shift at the slaughterhouse. Pasha and Dmitri took with them the last three doughnuts. My friend, Gay, had told me that she had set up a time for me to meet another worker by the name of Leonid tomorrow at the Postville Bakery. As the meeting broke up, the Ukrainian women strolled arm in arm, chatting and laughing under the streetlights on Reynolds Street. The men seemed to stride with a purpose, walking briskly.

At nine the next morning, as I glanced over the *Herald-Leader* while sticking my fork into the two eggs sunny-side up and the hash browns waitress Tari LeBrec had placed in front of me, a pudgy hand suddenly appeared in front of my face. It belonged to Leonid, who resembled a squat Little League umpire, his barrel chest so large that he looked as though he were wearing a chest protector under his shirt. Leonid sat down, and when I asked him if he wanted breakfast, he waved his right hand, dismissing the mundane thought of food. Leonid had a story to tell about his plans to get into American politics. In his accented English, he talked fast.

"I went to a vocational school in western Ukraine and opened up a small business repairing VCRs and TVs. But I always was scared by Mafia. One day they came to my place and said they wanted thirty-five percent of whatever I took in or they'd break my neck. They weren't kidding. Then and there, I knew I had to get out. At about this time, I read an article in the state newspaper about five Ukrainians who had just returned from Postville.

"It was a dream I always had to come here. I had taken English classes in school and loved American movies. My favorite still is *Once Upon a Time in America*. So I got together with two other guys who also wanted to come to America. They didn't speak any English, and they were scared. I took eight hundred dollars with me, and we all landed at Kennedy Airport in May 1992. In a couple of days, we found a *berze* [a street-corner hiring pool of laborers], in Borough Park, Brooklyn. But it was a very bad way to get a job. Some of the men were very well educated in the Ukraine or Russia, and they were selling themselves out to be busboys. If you were lucky you might be able to get a job for a couple of days as a carpenter or an electrician. Anyway, so we are in Borough Park, and the *berze* is totally for the birds—that's what you say, right? So we walked and walked and walked, and we knocked on every door in the neighborhood. We went from store to store, and in each store we asked, 'Do you have job? Can you help us find work?' Well, this *berze* was two blocks from Aaron Rubashkin's store. So we go into Rubashkin's place and the clerk tells us to come back when Rubashkin returns.

"We were really excited because this was the first place that said come back. We must have walked around the block a hundred times. We practiced what we were going to say. We finally met Rubashkin, and it was a relief because he spoke Russian. He told me and my friends that he could give us three jobs in Iowa. We couldn't believe our luck! We had been in the United States two days, and here was this guy who didn't know us, and he was offering us work. He bought three airplane tickets for us, from New York to Chicago, and then at the airport, a company car brought us down to Postville. The driver even brought us Pepsis and doughnuts. We couldn't believe our great fortune.

"The driver took us directly to Agriprocessors, and they hired us on the spot for two hundred and forty a week. Rubashkin eventually was able to get me a green card, and so I also got Social Security card. Sholom paid the rent of the apartment and the bills for the first year. I couldn't believe my luck. At first I was a meatcutter, and I stayed at Agri for four years. When I wasn't working, I studied English with cassette and books from library. I wanted to buy a car, and six months after I got here, I passed DMV test, and got Chevy Cavalier 1987. I paid three thousand dollars for it.

"So now, when I'm not working, I like to go fishing in the Mississippi. Catch big fish. I spend time at Celebration, a dance place in Decorah. I can do all the dances—polka, rock and roll, country, macarena, lambada, whatever you want. It's very hard for me to find a good dance partner. I met a girlfriend in the Horseshoe Bar in town, and we stayed together for four months. Then I got another girlfriend, and when that didn't work out, I got another. I bought my own house in town and paid eighteen thousand dollars, and I put forty percent down payment. Each month I pay one hundred and thirty-two dollar to bank, plus bills. Two-bedroom house. It's mine. I own it.

"When I was working at Agri, what bothered me was that every day was the same. It was boring. What kept me going was that I knew I was going to college. So I quit Agri in the summer and now am my own boss working for Amway and going to school full-time at North Iowa Community College. Then I want to go to Upper Iowa University to get a B.A., and after that, I go to the University of Iowa for an M.B.A, and then get my J.D. degree and become a lawyer."

All this had come out in a blizzard of words, all within five or ten minutes. There was a pause. "What do you eventually want to do in America?" I asked.

"Be president of the United States."

"But you have to be born in the United States to be president," I said.

There was a moment of silence. "OK, then vice president."

"But you still have to be born in the United States to be vice president," I said, reluctantly taking the role of a spoiler.

"OK, maybe senator, but I'm not too sure about that."

"About wanting to be senator or about whether you have to be born in the United States to be president or vice president?"

"I want to be president, that's all."

"Why?" I asked.

"Because I love this place. My favorite things about the United States are money, my car, and Eskimo Pies. I love them. They don't have Eskimo Pies in the Ukraine, just in Moscow."

I suggested that Leonid manufacture something like an Eskimo Pie in the Ukraine and make a lot of money, but he said, "No, that is no good. Mafia would be behind it, and that is bad. No way to make any money in Ukraine without Mafia. Very bad idea."

When it was time to leave the bakery, I pulled out three dollars to pay Tari for my breakfast. Leonid glanced at the plastic cards in my wallet and said, "I have no credit cards."

"Very un-American," I countered.

"Who need credit card? Why buy something I can't afford?"

CHAPTER 10

Kosher Hill

"What do you *do* up there, anyway, Dad?" Mikey quizzed me on one of my trips back home from Postville.

"I ask questions and people give me their answers."

"But about *what*?"

"About a lot of things," I said. In the ridiculous logic of a father unwilling to treat his seven-year-old like a seven-year-old, I described the tensions between the Jews and the Postville locals—the unmowed lawns, bad driving, name-calling. I didn't go into much detail, but I wanted Mikey to understand some of it, since the next weekend, he and I were planning on staying with a Hasidic family in Postville.

"Daddy, one question: Who are the good guys and who are the bad guys?"

My response was straight out of *Mr. Rogers' Neighborhood.* "Well, I don't think either side is good or bad. They're just different."

"But there are *always* good guys and bad guys," Mikey pressed, a casualty of too much Saturday-morning television.

Back in Postville, the next Monday, as I made my way

down Lawler Street, I thought about Mikey's good-guy, bad-guy world, and how the black-and-white truth of what was happening in Postville, once so stark, was fading. There were no absolute truths to Postville, and if there were, I wasn't quite sure I knew what they were. Neither tidy vision—the "Jewish invasion," as Leigh Rekow and Ginger's coffee klatchers saw it, or the "miraculous rebirth of a dying heartland community," as banker Jim Lage, Glenda Bodensteiner, and Cliff and Ida Mae Olson saw it—really explained what was taking place in Postville. There was a cultural war going on in this tiny hamlet. Tensions ebbed and flowed, escalated and dissipated. Sharon Drahn, the editor of the Postville *Herald-Leader*, told me when I first met her that the locals felt threatened, that their reactions didn't have as much to do with the newcomers being Jews as with their being outsiders. "The same kind of thing would have happened if the newcomers had been atheists, a bunch of Buddhists, or a colony of French people." I wasn't sure that was true. In part, the locals' resentment had to do with the Jews being outsiders, but it also had to do with their unwillingness to become members of the Postville community. Increasingly, though, I realized that, for some of the locals, their resentment was based on just who these outsiders were—Jews.

Going deeper and deeper into the story was like piecing together a three-dimensional jigsaw puzzle. Just when you thought you were finished, you'd look in the corner of the box and discover yet another piece. And when you finished connecting that piece to the puzzle, another piece would magically appear.

One of the missing pieces I found was Reverend Chuck Miller, a friendly, jovial man who resembled the actor Wilford Brimley. When the Hasidim first started arriving in Postville,

Miller, who presided over St. Paul Lutheran Church, said more than a few parishioners came up to him and asked him to "do something about the Jews taking over this God-fearing town." And Miller replied in kind—his own kind. Every Sunday sermon Miller delivered stressed humility and tolerance. Miller, whose hobby was the fine art of sauerkraut-making, was a natural supporter of the Jews. He liked the fact that finally some diversity was coming to white, Christian Postville. As pastor of the largest church in town, he appreciated the economic turnaround the Hasidim and their slaughterhouse had brought to Postville. A stagnant local economy makes it hard for people to embrace the Lord's will.

But ultimately, Reverend Miller got stiffed. The Jews showed him no respect. Perhaps even worse for a man of the cloth, they never even acknowledged that he existed. None of the Hasidic rabbis in Postville ever called on Reverend Miller. None deigned to introduce himself. That was just common courtesy, Reverend Miller thought. A clergyman new to town always pays a courtesy call to the local pastor. But Reverend Miller wasn't petty, so one Thanksgiving, he and the clergymen from Postville's other two churches invited the Jews to an ecumenical service. Reverend Miller proposed holding the service at the high school gymnasium, a neutral place, since he figured the Hasidic Jews wouldn't set foot in a church. The three men of the cloth set the place and time, but through an intermediary Miller got word that as long as the service wasn't going to be held in a church sanctuary, it could be held at St. Paul's. So, Miller shifted the Thanksgiving service to the Fellowship Hall, a sort of catchall room adjacent to the sanctuary that neighborhood groups used all the time. Reverend Miller had typed up a program and had arranged for refreshments. But on the day of the service, word got to him that

146

none of the Jews would attend. They gave no reason. It was like the Pilgrims planning a Thanksgiving shindig—going out of their way to be civil—only to be slighted at the last minute by the Indians, who figured there had to be something up the Pilgrims' sleeves.

"The Jewish community always had a reason not to come," Reverend Miller told me when I visited him in St. Paul's vestry. "What they were really saying was, 'We aren't interested.' But that's who they are. They maintain their identity by keeping their walls up."

"The Jews are lambs surrounded by seventy wolves," Rabbi Moshe Feller, the Lubavitcher rabbi, explained to me over the phone one night. "We've got to stick close to each other and to the shepherd at all times. If we don't, we might get eaten." That attitude held whether the wolves were Leigh Rekow or the old-timer at Ginger's who extolled Hitler. The Hasidim kept their guard up so high that they couldn't see the difference. And by keeping that guard so high, they encouraged—perhaps even created—wolves like some of the coffee klatchers at Ginger's.

Hasidic Jews would never enter a church or even get close to one. When I was ten, on a Sunday afternoon, my family drove the twenty-five miles from our suburban split-level home through the Lincoln Tunnel into Manhattan to see Hayley Mills in *The Parent Trap* and the high-kicking Rockettes at Radio City Music Hall. After the show, we strolled around the corner of Rockefeller Center, and there in front of us, on Fifth Avenue and East Fiftieth Street, was the most beautiful building I had ever seen: St. Patrick's Cathedral. The place was like a dream. Its elaborate facade must have been designed by believers with a direct line to God. I looked up, a small boy gazing toward the heavens from the sidewalk, and I followed every inch of the ornate twin spires as they soared and finally pierced the afternoon sky. I didn't care what the building was; I wanted to go inside.

I excitedly asked my parents whether we could. As hypnotized as I was with this great building, I was equally struck by my parents' faces. They didn't know what to do. My mother whispered something to my father, back and forth they went, until the eventual answer: No. My parents shook their heads in unison. I protested. There were further sub-rosa discussions, with my father raising his voice to my mother, something I had seldom seen or heard. My mother must have presented all the arguments for multiculturalism four decades before the word became popular. After further negotiation, my parents reached a compromise: I could go inside St. Patrick's, but I would be accompanied by my mother and sister. My father would not enter the building. I still recall my father's scowl upon losing his son, wife, and daughter to the pope, Catholicism, and the Holy Trinity as we gingerly pushed open the giant great wooden door to the church.

Certainly if such distrust flourished when it came to my thoroughly Americanized Jewish family, deeply righteous Jews like the Lubavitchers inhaled it with each breath they took. But you couldn't blame the Postville Lutherans for trying to bring the Jews into their civic fold. The problem was that the Lutherans were no more capable of accepting what the Hasidim stood for than the Jews were capable of celebrating Easter. When the Hasidim rebuffed the locals so resolutely, the Lutherans didn't turn the other cheek, some turned away angrily.

While traipsing around Postville I met two locals who flatly refused to let me use their names. They had axes to grind, but everyone had some kind of ax to grind or they wouldn't be talking to me. These men told me that if anyone found out that they were talking to me, the pair would be hounded out of Postville. One, whom I'll call Ralph Gustafson, held a responsible job in Postville and had much to lose if he went public with some of his feelings about the town. He had been a Postville resident for only a few years, but as a God-fearing native Iowan, he believed he knew small-town Iowa well. "Postville is a town that will simply not accept the Jews, and no amount of coaxing, persuading, cajoling, is going to change that basic fact."

Gustafson said he had an inside track on why Reverend Miller had suddenly left his post at St. Paul in late 1995 and put in for a transfer to a smaller parish in rural Wisconsin. Reverend Miller had been an essential cog in Postville's social structure, as well as throughout northeastern Iowa. He paid weekly pastoral visits to the old folks at Veterans Memorial, Winneshiek Memorial, Guttenberg Municipal, Gundersen Lutheran, Central Community; performed all the requisite funerals, weddings, and christenings; was in his church study to give counseling every day; and delivered a rousing sermon every Sunday. But it was the Sunday sermons that got him in trouble, at least according to Gustafson.

"This is the land of Luther," Gustafson said. Ninety percent of the population of the northeastern corner of Iowa is Lutheran; out of the sixty-one tiny towns in the area, places like Froelich, Nordness, Osterdock, St. Olaf, and Volga, there were fifty-seven Lutheran churches. "The Lutherans run the show, and if their minister isn't in sync with them, he quietly leaves," Gustafson said one morning, over a breakfast of sausage, eggs over easy, and hash browns at the

Postville Bakery. "Chuck left because his parishioners didn't take a fancy to his viewpoints on the Jews. He tried out his social agenda too much. If in every third or fourth sermon he talked about what he liked to call 'inclusiveness,' then he wasn't relying enough on the gospel for these folks. He wore out his welcome. He was condescending. Chuck had his causes: civil rights, welfare, easing migration and naturalization requirements. He was way out of kilter with this community. The folks around here didn't like that one bit."

Later, when I interviewed Reverend Miller after his departure, all he would say was that he left for personal reasons, and he wouldn't elaborate, but he said that any disharmony about his sermons and his message of tolerance had nothing to do with his decision to leave Postville. Personally, he said, he was frustrated by the Jews. He had gone out of his way to be friendly but felt continually snubbed.

Gustafson popped half a sausage into his mouth. The Jews were the lightning rod for years of pent-up frustration the Postville locals harbored. "The Jews are scapegoats. What really is happening here is that the benchmarks of this community are folding up. The locals see people on the street, and—Oh my God!—they don't speak English! They see their children moving away. But why would young people ever *want* to settle in Postville? And what would they do here? Debone cattle for six dollars an hour?

"The older folks see their hometown changing right before their eyes. They say they fear Postville is turning into a packinghouse slum town. That might be some of their concern, but what they're really scared about is that outsiders are taking over. They can't stand it. But can you blame them?"

Gustafson prided himself on being able to read the tea

leaves of small-town Iowa. "In a place like Postville, they will forgive you anything but one thing—success. If someone in Postville is taking a vacation, they won't say where they're going. Oh, they might say to Florida, but not the cruise, the cruise ship, the expensive stateroom they've booked. That would be in very poor form. To Iowans, conspicuous consumption is frowned upon. Take a look at the houses—nothing gaudy, nothing showy, all very modest. The locals' feeling is, if the bank president drives a ten-year-old pickup, then that's good enough for everyone else. But the Jews don't buy that Midwestern ethic at all. They work hard and want to reap the rewards. Look at Sholom's house, up on Kosher Hill. Iowans won't live like that. Ever."

Gustafson suggested I contact Bill Erickson, a deeply religious man, who left Postville three years ago. "I can't tell you how often I heard the phrase 'the goddamn Jews,'" Erickson told me. "It used to turn my stomach. I mean these were supposedly God-fearing people, and they had in their gut an odious feeling whenever they saw or thought about the Jewish people. If I was feeling testy, I'd shoot right back at them and say, 'Better be careful what you say about the Jews. Remember, Jesus was a Jew!' They'd look at me sort of strange and just walk away. In many ways, the people of Postville are close-minded, obtuse, thickheaded, stubborn, unwilling to bend.

"But they may have met their match, because these Hasidic Jews are not an easy lot, either. The Hasidim in New York will drive down a one-way street the wrong way, get into an accident, and then blame the other driver for the crash."

The day was getting late. Gustafson and Erickson had given me more to mull over. I wanted to follow up on Doc

Wolf and Stillman and Lew, but I had agreed to meet Sholom Rubashkin at his house, the palace on Kosher Hill, and I was late.

As I drove past the sign for Highway 18, the main thoroughfare that goes through Postville, I realized something that had eluded me during all my previous trips to Postville: Eighteen! Highway 18 was one of three ways into Postville, the entry point from the east or the south. Hasidic Jews solemnly believe in numerology, and of all numbers, they believe eighteen is the luckiest, even luckier than seven. Before inflation, eighteen dollars was the present of choice for weddings, bar and bat mitzvahs, *brises.* The numerical value of the two Hebrew letters that spell the Hebrew word for life, *chai,* totals eighteen. What better place than a town that starts and ends with Highway 18 could there be for Hasidic Jews?

If the Rubashkins and the cadre of Jews who came with them to Postville in 1987 felt like gefilte fish out of brine jelly, it had only been for a fleeting moment—when they weren't working fifteen-hour days, when they weren't praying or poring over the Talmud, when they weren't sitting around the *Shabbos* dinner table, when they weren't reading Hebrew nursery rhymes to their prodigiously large families. Fact is, many of the Jews who came to Postville came to make money, lots of it. Their succeeding beyond anyone's wildest dreams overshadowed their being surrounded by so many gentiles and their being so far away from the corner kosher restaurant that served up matzo-ball soup and flanken. The money was hardship pay, and any involvement in the larger Postville community for most of them was irrelevant. I got the impression that the *goyim* were window dressing, a necessary evil.

Even with the necessities in place, one would think that the culture shock for the newly arrived Jews would have been severe. Postville and Brooklyn were poles apart. Public transportation in Postville meant hopping in the back of your neighbor's pickup. To take in a movie, you drove thirty miles to either the three-plex in Decorah or the six-plex in Prairie du Chien unless you wanted to go to the single-screen Main Feature twelve miles down the road in Waukon. But all that *goyishe* stuff meant nothing to the Postville Hasidim. Strict Hasidim seldom read secular books or go to movies. Wherever these Hasidic Jews settled ultimately didn't make much of a difference, as long as they maintained their faith. Like Mormons or Jehovah's Witnesses, Lubavitchers were sent from their headquarters in Crown Heights out to the world's most remote outposts to spread the gospel of the Rebbe. The Lubavitchers' daily commandments were to wage holy war against assimilation, a Jewish trend the Lubavitchers likened to "the spiritual holocaust." In Postville, the Lubavitchers were on the same mission they were on in their fifteen hundred outposts worldwide: To establish a separate, self-sustaining community. Those who had come to this remote expanse of no-man's-land were Hasidic pioneers, lighting out to the rural territories to provide their fellow Jews worldwide with the purest, most sacred kosher meat and chicken available anywhere. Lucky Highway 18 threaded their dreams.

By the time I drove to Sholom's place, it was close to midnight. I hesitated, but Sholom had insisted that no matter when I finished talking to the locals, I should plan on stopping by his house.

The two-story home would have looked modest in a place like Miami Beach, but in Postville it was indeed a mansion. At midnight, it shone from the inside; every light seemed to be on. I thought momentarily that the house was lit up like a Christmas tree, and then laughed.

I parked in front, and Roza, Sholom's thirteen-year-old daughter, the oldest of the Rubashkins' seven children, answered the door and showed me in. Sholom was on a portable phone, talking half in Yiddish, half in Hebrew, wheeling and dealing. He motioned me to come in, and as I stood in a vestibule, I saw more than a dozen people in the living room, hallway, and dining room, all seemingly involved in deep conversations. Some were standing; others were seated. Some were whispering; others were having heated arguments, pointing fingers at one another's chests, raising their voices. People were constantly coming and going, dickering, arguing, cajoling.

Just as Sholom finished one conversation on the black portable phone he was cradling between his ear and shoulder, the phone would ring again. In the forty minutes I waited to talk to him, the phone rang eleven times. All the while, more Jews in long black coats and broad-brimmed hats arrived, talking to Sholom, whispering to him, pleading with him. About what, I wasn't sure since I understood neither the Yiddish nor the Hebrew, and only a few English words and phrases like "OK," "Lez go," "Too much," "Gotta cigarette?" were tossed into the mix. Some of the men brought their wives, who amiably chatted with Leah Rubashkin, Sholom's wife. The voices were muffled, but occasionally two Hasidic men in the living room would raise their voices; all the while, Sholom was on the phone, cupping the receiver, carrying on two, sometimes three conversations at the same time. Occasionally, Sholom segued into English from Yiddish to pepper the dialogue. "So, you vant me to do that? How'm I gonna do

THAT? YOU tell me? That's impossible! Vhada you think? I'm *meshugge*?" It was machine-gun delivery, one conversation after another.

Between calls, Sholom motioned me to sit down at the dining-room table. Leah and Roza joined me.

"We have gefilte fish, some rolls, some soda. You must be hungry, no?"

I shook my head, but my protestations went unheeded. Leah brought out a tray of cookies, macaroons, rugelach.

"Take," she said, waving her right hand over the sweets.

I begged off the food and focused on Leah, who beamed a smile my way. Leah, thirty-four, was different from the ascetic, downcast, almost downtrodden visages that I had come to expect from the Postville Hasidic women I had seen on the sidewalks walking in pairs behind the baby carriages. She was a firecracker, a dynamo. Even with her obvious *sheitel,* she was a knockout. Given a few minor adjustments, she would look like Demi Moore. Throw out Moore's pouty lower lip, and throw in some yenta laugh lines, and you'd get Leah Rubashkin. In another setting Leah could have been an attorney, a physician, even a television news anchor (if she could ditch her Brooklyn accent).

Dressed in a starched, tailored blue-and-white striped shirt with gold appliqués of palm trees, she had small gold earrings that dangled in opposite directions when she shook or nodded her head. She talked to the men in the room and looked me square in the eye. I was tempted to reach out to see if she would shake my hand, but that, I thought, would be going too far.

Out of the blue, Leah brought up the *mikveh.* During menstruation and for seven days afterward, a wife and husband are forbidden from touching, even passing a plate, until the wife purifies herself in a ceremonial bath. This is a basic and fundamental tenet of Jewish Orthodoxy, and when a Hasidic community is established, the creation of the *mikveh* is one of the first projects undertaken.

"You should have Sholom take you there," and when I looked at Leah quizzically, she laughed, "Not when any of the women are there, silly! It is a beau-ti-ful facility. You should see it. We used to have to drive all the way to Rochester [Minnesota] every month, and in the winter, with all the snow and ice—*Oy*! Was that ever a problem!"

As I started taking notes, Roza leaned over my shoulder and began reading from my notebook. "You wanna be a journalist?" I asked.

Then it dawned on me that Roza indeed may have wanted to be a journalist, but chances were slim that she'd ever become one, unless it was for a Lubavitcher publication like *The Jewish Homemaker, Beis Moshiach,* or *Chabad.* Her job was predestined by Lubavitchers: She would be a wife and mother. Few Hasidic women who are ardent about the religion work outside of the home. They may volunteer, they may write newsletters, prepare food for the shul, visit the homes of sick, help out in the family business. Some may go to Hasidic colleges for women, but few carry on a profession other than that of homemaker, wife, and mother of many children.

"How do you write so fast, and why are you writing down what my mother said?" Roza asked.

I didn't get a chance to answer. Sholom was off the phone, and he had latched onto his favorite topic: the damnation of the city of Postville for trying to annex Agriprocessors. "If the city annexes the property, you get a silent partner, and they

won't be very silent for long," Sholom said, scrunching his
face, stroking his patchy mahogany beard and then shaking his
head like a guy who knows that he is absolutely, infallibly
right. He went on and on, raising his voice, even pounding on
the dining-room table with the heel of his hand to make a
point.

The conversation turned to me, and Sholom wanted to
know how I got into journalism. "For a Jew, that's unusual,
isn't it, to work for a newspaper? There aren't many Jews who
do that. And working for someone else? If they have a choice,
Jews don't do that. They work for themselves or their family,
but not the *goyim.*

"But you don't do that anymore, right? You're with the
university. You make any money in that? Your father—whad-
da-he do for a living?—and whad-da-he think of this journalism?"

Before I could answer, Sholom's phone rang again. He
shot up from the table and began schmoozing, *kvetching,*
krechtzing, ignoring me.

Could I possibly have come up with a better example of
chutzpah? Sholom had trashed my livelihood, demanded to
know what my father did for a living, and asked that I define
my relationship with my father. It indeed was a world of
difference from the deference and modesty of Stanley
Schroeder or Leigh Rekow or all the local Postville people I
had met.

When Sholom got back to the table, he had seemingly
forgotten our conversation. "Eat a little," he intoned. "You
should eat!"

He pulled out the business card I had given him, peered
at it, and said, "So, you're a TEACH-a!" But what was really

on Sholom's mind was my days of interviewing the Postville locals. "So what did that anti-Semite Rekow say?"

"So, Mr. College Professor, what would YOU do about this annexation thing? The gentiles want to take away everything I've worked for. What would YOU do?"

"Why ask me? Ask them."

"*Nu?*"

"You want to know what *I* would do?"

"Why not? Who better to hear it from? You've talked to all these people—the old-timers, the merchants, the banker, the anti-Semites. I've been checking up on you. So I'm asking, What do YOU think we should do? YOU know how they think. They talk to you; they trust you. Whadda they tell *you?*"

I was curious that Sholom knew I had talked to so many locals. Postville was just as small a town for the locals as it was for the Jews, but how'd Sholom know the locals trusted me? Who was talking to him? Or was it all bluster, Sholom's trying to sandbag me?

"You need to allow them to get to know you," I said. "You might not be able to go to their houses to eat and mingle, but there's nothing that prevents *you* from having them in your home. Then you put on the *charm!*"

I was being sarcastic about the charm, but Leah bought it.

"Let's have a bar-be-cue!" she said excitedly, clapping her hands.

"You certainly have enough meat," I deadpanned.

"We'll have to put in for a special order," said Leah, suddenly talking like a Jewish Martha Stewart. "We can start inviting people over to the house and hold a party in the backyard. On a Sunday afternoon. It'll be fun!"

Leah would cater the party! She'd get all the ladies together and assign them different tasks: the invitations, the music, the chairs, the centerpieces, the decorations. But who'd sit where? There was no way to know how many would show up. A buffet line! Paper plates, plastic utensils. It would be WONDERFUL!

"But," I cautioned Sholom. "You can't have this party a couple of weeks before the annexation vote. Then, it'll back-fire. The locals will say, 'The Jews are at it again, too little, too late. They're trying to buy our votes.' So you should start now—which already is probably too late."

Sholom stroked his beard, then the phone rang, and the slaughterhouse maven became engrossed in another long conversation, alternating between Yiddish and Hebrew, twirl-ing the curly hairs of his beard around his index finger. Roza was nodding off at the table (it was 1:30 A.M.). I knew it would be another long wait till he was finished. When I said good-bye, Sholom barely seemed to notice.

During my drive back to the Pines, I thought about the evening at Kosher Hill. Why did Sholom get under my skin so much? What was it about him that irked me so? His shtik was all too familiar. The mock-aggressive tone, the lowered eye-brows, using guilt as a tool to try to get what he wanted. No matter how assimilated I was, or wanted to be, remnants of that culture were still a part of me. Bits of Sholom reminded me of my own father. The Iowans' complaints about the Jews were complaints I had heard many times before—complaints about cheapness, bargaining, the unilateral bending of rules to conform to their own standards. It was an undeniable part of my own culture that I did not embrace. But whenever anyone raised even a meek voice against this behavior, the questioner was automatically turned into an anti-Semite. A reciprocal question also nagged me: Why did I have so much patience with the Iowans? Was it because they were fresh and different? Was it because the Postville locals offered me an excuse to examine and ultimately judge the motives of the Hasidim, people with whom I shared a common heritage? In a way, the locals had become a lens to view my own heritage and my own self—and confirmed what I had implicitly known the first day I had set foot in Postville—that I'd have to choose which side I wanted to be on.

CHAPTER 11

Invitation

My only contact with the Postville Jews thus far had been the wrestling match on the phone with Professor Appel, my late-night encounter at the abattoir with Sholom, the next-day's tefillin-wrapping, my visit to Kosher Hill, and an afternoon I spent talking with the half-dozen Hasidic men who lived upstairs at the shul. I still didn't know much about the Hasidim in Postville. Who exactly were these people, able to engender such extreme emotion in the non-threatening Iowans? Was Sholom and his shtik just bravado, New York moxie gone awry in the cornfields? Was it posturing, a Brooklyn guy full of talk? I could see how the locals thought the Jews were obnoxious and imperial, but unlike the locals, my Jewish background had given me preparation for what I was to encounter. They had none.

Sholom had asked me to spend a *Shabbos* weekend with a Lubavitcher family, an experience I hoped would deepen my understanding of the Hasidim, both as a Jew and now as an Iowan, the two personas that underscored why I had set out for Postville in the first place. The specter of a tableful of Jewish food, as well as witty, fast conversation, appealed to me, but I was skittish about what Martin Appel had implied: that Lubavitchers open their homes to nonobservant Jews for one reason—to proselytize them.

Lubavitcher homes around the globe are open to Jewish guests for the twenty-four hours of the Sabbath, from sunset Friday to sunset Saturday. Like the Mormons or the Jehovah's Witnesses, the Lubavitchers send emissaries to remote corners of the planet to bring secular Jews back to the fold. The Shluchim International boasts hundreds of Lubavitcher outposts—Anchorage to Zurich. For anyone in between, the Lubavitchers are available twenty-four hours a day in cyberspace through Chabad-Lubavitch Online. They try to reach potential *baalei teshuvah*, "returnees to faith," through newspaper advertisements, billboards, bumper stickers ("The *Moshiach* Is Coming!"), 1-800 numbers, thousands of books, videos, magazines, worldwide cable hookups, and Mitzvah Tanks— roving vans outfitted with loudspeakers. But the best way to awaken a secular Jew's interest in Judaism is to share a Lubavitcher *Shabbos* dinner.

Ultimately, though, what led me to Postville for a weekend with the Lubavitchers was Mikey.

By now, Iris, Mikey, and I had entered our third year of living in Iowa. We had grown to accept the state's natural underpinnings of Christianity—the church bazaars, manger scenes, caroling, the Christmas lights promptly strung up the weekend after Thanksgiving. Mikey had gone on several Easter-egg hunts and was none the worse because of them. But the Christian trappings had made for an uneasy truce. Iris and I had complained to the regional Boy Scout office after the troop leader announced the December activity would be making Christmas-tree ornaments. When Mikey's best friend,

Nick, invited him to spend a long weekend at his grandparents' home in Onawa in western Iowa, Mikey's first question to us was: "What happens if they go to church on Sunday?

"What should I do?" he asked anxiously, a rewind with an edit of my experiences when I was nine in front of St. Patrick's Cathedral.

Our answer was that he should go to church with Nick and his family. Look at it as a school field trip, like an adventure with Miss Frizzle and the Magic School Bus. Don't do anything that would make you feel uncomfortable. Other people practice their own religions, and it's good to learn about how they view God. We'll tell Nick's parents and grandparents that you're Jewish.

But Mikey didn't buy the idea. He was ecstatic about the weekend but terrified of Sunday morning. "If they know I'm Jewish, they'll stop me at the church door. And if they don't, what happens if they make me kneel down and pray?"

Mikey eventually made the trip to Onawa and had a blast. Onawa is best known as the home of Christian Nelson, the high school chemistry teacher who in 1922 stuck a stick in a bar of chocolate-covered ice cream and called it an Eskimo Pie. (I made a mental note to tell Leonid about Onawa.) Mikey and Nick saw the original Eskimo Pie Dipping Machine, housed in a museum, and snapped a photograph of it. Crisis was averted when Nick's family chose not to attend church that Sunday, I think, more out of deference to Mikey than anything else.

But the Onawa encounter, as well as our daily lives in Iowa, pointed out the need to give Mikey a thoroughly Jewish experience, and what better place would there be to do that than in Postville? The Hasidim were extreme, and I knew their version of religion might scare Mikey, but how many chances would he ever get, especially in Iowa, to participate in such an intense Jewish adventure? Any heavy-handed prose-lytizing would be a small price to pay for the experience.

So with that goal in mind I began arranging a trip to Postville for just Mikey and me. Iris was in her second year in law school, communing daily with thick blue books about con-stitutional law, criminal procedure, and the First Amend-ment. She looked forward to having the house to herself for the weekend. Sholom had suggested we spend the week-end with the thirty-nine-year-old computer guru for Agri-processors, whom I'll call Lazar Kamzoil. Born in Toronto, Lazar was a fifth-generation Lubavitcher rabbi. He and his wife, Bielke, had seven children, and had lived in Postville for three years.

I had met Lazar one morning in Postville a week before Mikey and I were to make our trip. Up the creaky steps of the slaughterhouse, the harried secretary wordlessly pointed me to a door to her left. When I peeked in, pushing the door open a crack, I wasn't even sure whether Lazar was there until a sheepish man with a bemused smile poked his head up from the back of an ailing computer. He was surrounded by tangled wires, a half-dozen junked computers with their gray metal cases opened and green circuit boards exposed, four or five computer manuals spread out on their spines, computer boxes of varying shapes and sizes, Styrofoam packing mate-rial, electronic components, and diagnostic computer tools strewn all over. The room was air-conditioned, but reeked of cigarette smoke. Lazar was dressed in a long-sleeved white shirt, *tzitzit* underneath, black pants, black wing tips, and black yarmulke. He was tall, maybe six foot one or two, with a budding paunch.

We shook hands, and I again noticed the difference between an Iowan and a Jew. Lazar's hand was like mine—soft and fleshy, but his handshake was barely a handshake. He hardly squeezed my four fingers, the way an elderly woman might shake the hand of a lady friend. Lazar looked anemic in comparison to the sunbaked leathery Iowans I had met. On his cheeks and around his eyes, Lazar's skin was like a baby's, soft and pliable. The ruddy, weathered skin tone of the Iowans was anathema to the Hasidim. Observant Orthodox Jews spend their time inside, not outdoors: that was for *goys* who raked leaves or tinkered with cars on cement blocks in their driveways—or for Reform Jews, who went to the beach or played golf. Hasidic men worked at their jobs under a roof, presided over *Shabbos* dinner at home with their family, or prayed inside the shul, poring over sacred tomes, for God's sake.

"So, you must be Mr. Bloom? Sholom has told me a lot about you. A lot."

"I hope it was all good."

"Good and bad, but mostly good, although, to be perfectly frank, there was some bad, but who's to worry about that?" Lazar said, shrugging his shoulders. "Sholom tells me your family will be having *Shabbos* dinner with my family. This is right?"

I nodded and said it would be just my seven-year-old son and me.

Lazar looked puzzled. "Only one child?"

"One, and sometimes *he's* too much," I replied, using the same lilt as Lazar's.

"But children. They're a *mitzvah,* and only one you have? Why only one?"

"So, how many do *you* have?"

Lazar smiled, showing his teeth. "Seven, and that's not nearly enough!"

Seven, I thought—unusual for a Lubavitcher family. Why so *few?*

"Why only you and your son come to *Shabbos?* Your wife? She doesn't come?"

Then, on second thought, Lazar whispered, "She gentile?"

"She's Jewish, all right," I said, amused by Lazar's inference. "But she needs to study for her finals in law school."

"A law-YAH! She's gonna be a law-YAH?"

I smiled, more out of the absurdity of hearing in northeastern Iowa the word "law-yah."

"But even *law-yahs* break for *Shabbos.* A Jew not celebrating the Sabbath with *Shabbos* dinna? Tell your wife my wife takes care of all the cooking. Even the dishes. All your wife needs to do is show up. Full-service *Shabbos* dinna at Lazar's house."

"I'd like her to come, but she can't. Law school exams next week. There'll be other times."

Lazar feigned shock. A wife anchored in the secular world, missing, apparently without regret, the paramount religious meal and ceremony of the week; a mother allowing her family to go separate ways on the Sabbath when *mishpocheh* do whatever it takes to stay together; a Jewish wife not heeding the desires of her husband. And this was just the beginning.

Lazar stifled a frown and lit a Marlboro Gold cigarette. As he inhaled, he began twirling an errant strand of hair from his beard.

"So only you and your son coming? What's his name?"

"Michael, but we call him Mikey."

"MI-KEY?" Lazar said with exaggeration, pulling the name out like kosher taffy. "What kinda name is *that* for a Jewish boy?"

I decided to play. "Hey, you got a problem with Mikey, then you got a problem with me. Dat's the little guy's name!"

"MOISHE, now *that's* a nice Jewish name! I don't know about this MI-KEY business. But Moishe, that's a name I like!"

"So, *you* call him Moishe," I said with a shrug of my shoulders. "His mother, his relatives, his friends, we'll all continue to call him Mikey."

"Ah, but his Hebrew name is important," Lazar said, again peering over the top of his glasses.

Jews traditionally name newborns after deceased relatives, but they seldom use the same names, which is viewed as a bad omen. Instead, Jews generally borrow the first letter of the first name of a dead relative. I was named after my maternal grandfather, Samuel, who died a year before I was born. Shlomo or Shmuel were the closest Hebrew equivalents of Samuel. Mikey was named after grandparents from Iris's side and from mine. We borrowed the first letter in the first names of four esteemed people in our families: Mina, Morris, Regina, and Rose. From it all, we arrived at the decidedly non-Jewish, Irish-sounding appellation Michael Ryan. Two months after he was born, Iris's family had a baby-naming ceremony at which the rabbi gave Mikey the name Moishe; the closest the rabbi could come up with for Ryan was Raffel.

"So, just the two of you then, no wife, right? You and"— Lazar paused for a second—"this Mi-key?"

"Are you sure you'll have enough room for us?"

This was the question Lazar had been waiting for. "Room?" Lazar said, raising his voice, suddenly bellowing, sounding like a rabbi coming to the climax of a Yom Kippur sermon. "Of course, we'll have enough room! You have a big house; you never have room for guests. But," Lazar said, his right index finger vertical at cheek level, "you have a small house; you always find room."

Aphorisms, sermons, Jewish maxims, probably a couple of rants, ready quotes from the Rebbe Menachem Mendel Schneerson, Moses Maimonides, Benjamin Netanyahu—this will be a weekend to remember, I thought, as I made arrangements for Mikey and me to meet at Lazar's house at five on Friday afternoon. I was looking forward to the weekend. I remembered Brenda Bernhard's longing to get to know a Hasidic family, her fantasy to be invited inside one of the Lubavitchers' homes. The Jews were forbidden fruit to the Postville locals, and next weekend I was about to go behind the curtain that separated the Jews from the locals—it was a privilege that many Postville locals would have given a bushel basket of sweet-as-sugar corn to experience. And the only reason I got to partake was because my mother was Jewish.

For twenty-four hours, from the moment the sun goes down on Friday to the precise second it sets Saturday evening, the purpose of honoring the Sabbath for observant Jews is to stop and acknowledge that the world belongs to God. Among observant Hasidic Jews, during those holy twenty-four hours, no electricity may be used, stoves must not be lighted, telephones must not be used, cars must not be driven, certain medicines cannot be ingested. Some Hasidim are so ardent that they tear off pieces of toilet paper and stack them in the bathroom before sundown so that they don't violate the rule against ripping paper on the Sabbath. In my entire life, I had been in only two or three Orthodox shuls, and this would be the first time in a Lubavitcher shul. I knew that Lubavitchers believe in two oppositely directed forces that led to *devekuth,* ecstatic "at oneness" with God. One path is an ascent to the Almighty through prayer by repeating words and gestures over and over. The other path is the reward for such devotion: ten distinct *sefirot,* rays or beams from the Almighty, that literally descend into the supplicant's soul. Those spiritual forces probably explained the *tummel,* commotion, I had heard coming from the shul that first night in Postville.

Something else, much less spiritual, lingered in my mind about the upcoming weekend, and that was food. Quite frankly, the bland and monotonous Iowa chow was driving me nuts. Catfish fries, brats, Butter Burgers and Maid-Rites were novelties that had long worn off. Since moving to Iowa, I had given up trying to find first-cut corned beef or pastrami; hand-carved lox; doughy, fist-sized bagels; crispy, fresh-made potato latkes; fresh fruit blintzes. Oh, you could buy corned beef, pastrami, or lox in supermarkets in Iowa, but it was hermetically encased in plastic, ignominiously placed amid corn dogs, bratwurst, and oval-shaped cans of ham. At Hy-Vee, the only pastrami was turkey pastrami, and the thought of buying packaged *presliced* smoked salmon was out of the question for a kid from Jersey. Lazar's *Shabbos* dinner promised more than spiritual nourishment. It was the tantalizing promise of fresh-baked challah (braided loaves of egg bread), homemade matzo-ball soup, crunchy kugel (noodle pudding), slow-roasted chicken or brisket, sweet wine, and honey cake. Let the meal begin, I thought, patting my stomach.

The Sabbath, in whatever incarnation, stands as the most familiar signpost for Jews throughout the world, and for many, the twenty-four hours carry a host of obligations. When Iris

and I were about to get married, the rabbi who was to perform the wedding, requested that we meet with him twice in
his San Francisco synagogue study. During the first session,
we discussed practical matters of the upcoming nuptials (who
was to bring the glass that I would step on, how the *chuppa*,
"wedding canopy," would be secured), but the second meeting was like a session out of "The Joy of Being Jewish." When
the rabbi got to the point of the responsibility Jews had to
raise their children as Jews, he asked if we intended to start a
family. We both nodded.

"When you start is none of my business," he said, and
then paused as though to prepare us for what was to follow.
"But I like to counsel Jewish couples to have intercourse on
the Sabbath, *every* Friday night," the rabbi said, looking each
of us straight in the eye. "It'll be the end of the week, and one
or both of you will be tired. I know that sometimes the easi-
est response will be 'Catch you in the morning,' but resist
that. It is a *mitzvah* to have sex on the Sabbath."

Iris and I were so tickled by the rabbi's conjugal counsel
that, like giddy teenagers, we instinctively knew that if either
of us looked at the other, we'd start giggling. The rabbi's ex-
hortation seemed totally out of place: advice from someone
we hardly knew who was putting himself in our bedroom. I
half expected the rabbi to go into details about positions too,
a *Mazel Sutra* of sex, but none were forthcoming.

And that was a Reform rabbi. Hasidic Jews *require* sex on
the Sabbath. Lubavitcher rabbis counsel that sex is integral to
a couple's devotion to each other, as well as to the Lord, but
they also stipulate that the man has a specific obligation to do
whatever his wife requires so that she achieves an orgasm.
The founder of Hasidism, Ba'al Shem Tov, who died in 1760,

believed that physical desire increased a man's love for the Torah and God, and that intercourse with one's wife was an instrument for uniting with God. Among Orthodox Jews, intercourse on Friday nights is commonly referred to as "doing the *mitzvah*," and the conjugal union is one more of the scores of required rituals to be performed on the Sabbath.

As a warm-up act, on Friday nights some Hasidim chant the highly charged erotic verses from the Bible's Song of Songs, of which probably the most well-known line is one Iris recited at our wedding: "I am my beloved's, and my beloved is mine." Here are excerpts, not from a steamy Harlequin novel, but from the Song of Songs

> My beloved is white and ruddy, pre-eminent above ten thousands. His head is as the most fine gold, his locks are curled, and black as a raven. His eyes are like doves beside the water-brooks; washing with milk, and fitly set. His cheeks are as a bed of spices. As banks of sweet herbs; his lips are as lilies, dropping with flowing myrrh. His hands are as rods of gold set with beryl; his body is as polished ivory overlaid with sapphires. His legs are as pillars of marble, set upon sockets of fine gold. His mouth is most sweet; yea, he is altogether lovely. This is my beloved, and this is my friend.

I put out of my mind the sounds of a squeaking mattress, as well as any thought of an embroidered hole in the bedsheet. As Mikey and I drove to Postville from Iowa City early Friday morning, I was excited about sharing the upcoming Sabbath. One of the Batman movies had just come out, and Mikey was nestled beside me with his newest acquisition: a Batman pillow, a stitched Kmart special in the shape of Bruce Wayne's alter ego. Mikey was stretched out on the front seat, mostly sleeping, as we drove past carpets of green, the gentle hills of northeastern Iowa, an occasional scarecrow stuck on a pole in family vegetable patches. I half expected to see kids setting up lemonade stands on card tables. There was an early-morning mist hanging above the corn in the fields around us, and even though it was early summer, there was still a snap in the air.

I wanted to get to Postville early. I had promised Mikey that I would take him on a boat tour of Spook Cave, a family-run attraction near McGregor, eight miles west of the Mississippi, twenty miles east of Postville.

We pulled off Highway 18 into the Spook Cave parking lot and paid our admission at a souvenir concession stand that had everything from foot-long rubber snakes to black bats on elastic strings. Led by Dennis, our seventeen-year-old tour guide, Mikey and I gingerly stepped into a dented aluminum fishing boat that wobbled precariously as we scrambled for our seats on slats in the boat's rear. Dennis advised us to crouch down to allow the boat to slip into the small mouth of the cave at the base of a wooded hill. Inside the cave, the temperature was cold, forty-eight degrees. We glided along the cave floor, moving steadily in the four-foot-deep water, passing orange and gray stalagmites and stalactites, which Dennis illuminated with a flashlight. The sounds were a combination of the low drone from the outboard motor that propelled our boat; a ticking, guttural noise I assumed came from nesting bats overhead; and water dripping from the cave's ceiling, plinking on the underground river.

Midway through the tour, Dennis pulled up to a ledge, flipped the cave's electrical lights off, and then asked Mikey and me to gaze upward. High in what Dennis described as the Cathedral Room was a backlighted red, yellow, green, and blue stained-glass etching of Jesus Christ. Dressed in a white robe, with locks flowing, this huge, inside-the-cave visage of Christ was spooky, even for me. Suddenly, Dennis turned into a Holy Roller, talking about Jesus, the immaculately conceived son of God and Mary, the man who would account for our salvation. Mikey and I looked at each other and tried to appear unimpressed, but after the sight of this larger-than-life Savior staring us down from above, the party was pretty much over. Mikey and I kept quiet on the return trip, which may have prompted Dennis to turn in his Bible for the day. He didn't say another word, which made our passage back all the spookier.

Mikey said nothing about the stained-glass apparition as we got back in the car. I think we both chalked up the Christ countenance to the price of living in Iowa. Iris and I knowingly accepted our minority status here, and so did Mikey, mostly because we realized there wasn't anything we could do to change it. Our lives were patterning the lives of other Jews who had emigrated to Iowa for the last one hundred years— except the Hasidim. Jews here had always sought to blend in with their Christian neighbors. The Iowa Jews from the beginning were Reform Jews—who else would move so far from the flock? Eighty percent of the Jewish settlers in Iowa had emigrated from Germany, and most had come from the emerging middle class. Their German heritage allowed them to mix in with other immigrants of the time, also German and most often Lutheran. By and large, their religion was subsumed within the dominant rural farm culture.

As we drove west on Highway 18 toward Postville for our weekend with Lazar and his family, I realized that what I was wearing—an IOWA T-shirt, jeans, and sneakers—would hardly be appropriate. Again, I heard my grandmother, hunched over

the kitchen table in her apartment, saying, *"This* is smart?"
Male Lubavitcher garb, even in July, was unvarying: black
pants, white shirt, and black shoes.

But this was who I was, the assimilated Jew I had always
been. Even if I had the necessary clothing for a transforma-
tion, I wasn't going to stop the car on the side of Highway 18
and pull a costume out of my suitcase. I wasn't about to put
Mikey into long pants and a long-sleeved white shirt as the
hotbox Iowa summer was about to begin in full force. What
was wrong with a little boy wearing shorts and a tank top on a
hot day?

Just before we got to Lazar's house, before we stepped
out of our lives and into our weekend as Lubavitchers, Mikey
and I stopped at the Postville *Herald-Leader* to say hello to
Sharon. In the back shop at the paper that day, pasting up display ads, was a blue-eyed high school student, Kari Berns,
and when Sharon told her where we were going, she couldn't
believe it. "You're really going to spend a whole weekend with
them?" Kari asked. "You really are?"

Like Brenda Bernhard, Kari could barely contain her excitement when it came to the Jews. "That is the *coolest* thing
I could imagine! You're going to be with them the whole
weekend? Will you be eating with them? Going to their
church? You're going to actually sleep in one of their houses?
Really? I'd give anything to do that!"

The Jews went out of their way to spurn the locals, yet
some of them, like Brenda and Kari, refused to get the message. Maybe it was their religion, their natural optimism, their
wide-eyed curiosity, or an upbringing that stressed determi-
nation and persistence. Kari was wild to learn more about the
Hasidim. She yearned to make contact despite the Jews' continual snubbing of her people. She longed to stop one of the

Jewish girls on the sidewalk and ask her a barrage of questions—Why do you always wear dresses? Why can't you ever show your knees and elbows? Have your parents already picked out the man you're going to marry?—but even in Postville, you just couldn't do that kind of thing. Since none of the Hasidic girls went to public school, the chance of Kari ever getting to ask them questions was almost nil. Kari had thought about politely stopping one of the girls on the street, introducing herself, and then asking, but she was afraid she'd embarrass, or worse, insult the girl. Who knew what reaction the girl would have if Kari did anything more than just smile? Were Jews like the Amish? Did they have rules against taking photographs of them? The Jews were something to steal glances at, to whisper about, but to approach them? That was out of the question.

Mikey and I said good-bye to Sharon and Kari, invigorated about our upcoming adventure. As we strode up the front walk to Lazar's brick house on Williams Street, I felt as though we were two guys about to embark on a blind double date. We didn't quite know what to expect, but we knew that we'd have plenty to talk about once it was all over.

I pressed the buzzer.

Moishe   and   Shlomo

A fter three or four minutes, a beautiful, dark-haired woman in her early twenties opened the door. Could this possibly be Bielke, Lazar's wife? The woman said nothing to us and seemed flustered. Once inside, she backpedaled, then scurried away, disappearing into the bowels of the house, leaving Mikey and me alone in the living room.

The woman couldn't have been Bielke. Hasidic law mandates that a married woman never find herself alone with a man who isn't her husband or family member. The woman who answered the door must be a housekeeper. Bielke must be upstairs. She must have opted not to greet Mikey and me outside the presence of Lazar, who hadn't arrived home yet from work.

Mikey and I tried our best to make ourselves at home, but we felt awkward. We didn't know what we could or should do. Despite Lazar's comment that he lived in a modest house, the Kamzoil home was huge, one of the original great Postville homes built in 1890, Stanley Schroeder had told me. I peeked in the kitchen, and noticed that, like many Hasidic homes, it was equipped with two refrigerators, two stoves, two sinks, two separate cupboards.

Somehow I felt we were being watched. I heard a creaking sound, and sure enough, from behind a mahogany breakfront in the dining room, about twenty feet away, I spotted three children, two girls and a boy, lined up, one head atop another. As Mikey and I locked eyes with them, for the briefest of moments, the children gave us deer looks, frozen, frightened and curious at the same time.

The girls were dressed in freshly pressed cotton floral-patterned dresses and black patent leather shoes. Their hair had ribbons. The boy was wearing a long-sleeved white shirt, and under it, a *talliskatan*. His hair was a longish crew cut, but he already was growing sidelocks and covering the crown of his head was a blue velvet yarmulke.

"Hi," I ventured. "Come out here and let us know your names."

Without saying a word, the three pointed in unison upstairs. They came out from the dining room and motioned for Mikey and me to follow. We dutifully trailed the trio up the steps, marching to a front bedroom with twin beds, where I assumed Mikey and I were to sleep. Then, like mute Munchkins, they disappeared, closing the door, only to retreat to the other side, where they took turns looking through the keyhole at us.

As we unpacked to the keyhole stares and giggles coming from the other side of the door, Mikey glanced up at the wall. Between the beds was a large framed color photograph of the Rebbe, the Lubavitcher spiritual leader. He had an enigmatic, almost stern, smile vaguely discernible through a full white beard; his blue eyes seemed to sparkle. In a Lutheran home, this photo of the Rebbe was exactly where a laminated picture of Jesus with flowing locks would hang, and probably where one had hung, considering the long line of Lutherans who likely had lived here.

I asked Mikey if he knew who the bearded man in the picture was.

"He's the king of all the Jews, but I don't know his name."

I had no idea where he knew this from. I started to amend Mikey's admission with "the king of *some* of the Jews," but stopped when I heard a commotion downstairs. The front door had opened, there was a stamping of kids' feet, and then the sound of babies crying. Lazar had arrived.

By the time Mikey and I made our way downstairs, Lazar was seated in a big easy chair, a twin baby in each arm. Either the dark-haired maid or Bielke must have appeared with the year-old twins, handed them off to Lazar, and retreated back into the recesses of the house. The three children who had been spying on us through the keyhole were now jumping up and down on the living-room rug, elated that their father was at last home. Lazar rocked the twins back and forth, singing a Yiddish song. A minute or two in his big arms and they stopped crying.

"Welcome!" Lazar shouted to Mikey and me as we walked tentatively downstairs. "Welcome to our home!"

Lazar made the introductions: five-year-old Hodel, nine-year-old Chava, and seven-year-old Yussel. Lazar's children ranged from the twins to a fifteen-year-old boy away at a Lubavitcher boarding school. It didn't take long for Mikey and Yussel to break the ice. They ran back upstairs to play the card game Uno with Hodel and Chava tagging along.

"So, Lazar," I started, "how was your day at work?"

"And how *should* it be?"

"Busy?"

"Every day is busy. If I weren't busy, then I'd be worried!"

I tried a different tack. "So, tell me. What's a nice Jewish boy doing in a place like Postville?"

Lazar looked up from the twins. "What," he shot back. "A nice Jewish boy *doesn't* belong in Postville? And how do you know that I'm a nice Jewish boy? Jewish, yes, but nice?"

"When you were growing up in Toronto, did you ever imagine yourself in a tiny town in Iowa?"

Lazar knew where I was going but steadfastly resisted my entreaties at each turn.

"There's nothing unusual with our being here. It's where we choose to have our community. It's where we have our business. It's a good place. We like it here. You make too much of it. What's the expression? Mountain out of a molehill? This is a molehill, but it's our molehill."

Mikey and Yussel came down the stairs, and Lazar announced to us the ground rules for the weekend. There would be two, and our compliance with both, Lazar said, must be total and absolute: (1) Mikey and I were to wear yarmulkes at all times, which Lazar referred to by the Hebrew word *kippah*; and (2) Mikey and I were both to be addressed only by our Hebrew names. We were not to use Steve and Mikey any longer. We no longer were a part of the secular world outside.

I had used my Hebrew name exactly twice in my life—when the rabbi who married Iris and me inscribed in the *ketubah* (ceremonial marriage contract); and when I was called to the alter during the bat mitzvah of my niece.

"Call me Shlomo," I told Lazar, reinventing the first line of *Moby Dick*.

"And you," Lazar pointed to Mikey, "you are Moishe. You

understand? Your name is Moishe." Mikey shook his head, a little bewildered, but eager to get started.

The next bit of business was keeping the satin yarmulkes attached to our curly hair. With every step we took, the small flat disks seemed to fly off our heads. Lazar produced a pair of bobby pins, which I gratefully accepted, but Mikey was a different story. Bobby pins were for girls, and he would have nothing to do with them.

"OK," I explained, "but each time your yarmulke falls off, you'll have to pick it up and put it back on your head." Mikey said fine, but I anticipated trouble.

As Yussel and Moishe began tearing through the house, Mikey's yarmulke flew off his head every five minutes, and each time, Lazar shouted in a booming voice, "Moishe, your *kippah!*" Mikey, in turn, would stop whatever he was doing, get down on his hands and knees, scramble for the errant yarmulke, plop it back on his crown of curls, and go back to running with Yussel. "Moishe, your *kippah!*" became a chorus of sorts for the entire weekend.

After about an hour, Bielke came down the stairs. She was a tall striking woman in her late thirties, wearing a floral-patterned caftan. I wasn't sure whether Bielke shaved her hair or whether her hair was concealed under the white turban she was wearing. Just as when I had met Leah Rubashkin, I stifled the urge to reach out and shake Bielke's hand. "The mere touch of a woman's body, where there is neither intent nor even a suggestion of affection, is in itself indecent, because it might lead to unclean desires or thoughts," writes Louis M. Epstein in *Sex Law and Customs in Judaism*. "Indulgence in small talk or repartee with a woman should be avoided as bordering on indecent flirtation." Decidedly distant, Bielke never looked me in the eye; her steely gaze seemed to bore through me.

Among the truly observant, only the husband of a Lubavitcher woman is allowed to see his wife's natural hair and her bare arms and legs. The myriad laws of *tzniut*, female modesty, are as all-encompassing as the rules governing orthodox Muslim women. In traditional Lubavitcher homes, a kerchief, *tichl*, is allowed to cover the woman's head, but once outside the home, women must wear a *sheitel*, a wig. The Rebbe writes:

> When a Jewish woman walks in the street without a *sheitel* there is no (discernible) difference between her and others. However, when she wears a *sheitel* one can tell that here is a Jewish religious woman. It is not necessary to go in the streets loudly proclaiming 'I am religious,' but...what is one embarrassed of? Of one's friend? Should they say that this is a religious Jew—what is the shame of the matter?!...The difference between a *sheitel* and a kerchief is the following: It is easy to take off a kerchief, which is not the case with a *sheitel*....Wearing a *sheitel* is especially appropriate now, when one can obtain a *sheitel* in various shades, which looks even nicer than one's own hair.

As for Bielke's clothing, it was in perfect accord with the Rebbe's dictates on women's attire. The Lubavitchers' weekly organ, *Chabad* magazine, quoted the Rebbe on how an observant woman should dress:

> As regards modesty of women, the general rule is that the longer the garment, the better. Just because some *goy* from France decides what the latest fashion should be, Jewish women do not have to obey....In practice, I do not wish, and it is unnecessary to rule exactly what length clothing should be; the local rabbis should decide. One will require an inch longer, another an inch shorter. Nevertheless, my opinion is clear: the litmus test is that the length when one is standing

should be so that when sitting, the knees are covered. Those of a liberal cut will try to find a way around this—by making garments long enough, but so tight that they emphasize the body's contours, and so arouses the *yetzer hara* [inclination to evil] even more. Obviously, this must also be negated.

While Lazar was busy entertaining the twins, Bielke went from room to room, picking up toys, rearranging dishes and bowls, all the while conversing with Lazar in English, Hebrew, and Yiddish. She scarcely paid any attention to Mikey or me.

Darkness was fast approaching and Lazar told me that we had to get to the shul before sundown. Bielke was not going; instead she would stay at home, caring for the twins, and preparing *Shabbos* dinner. Mikey and I changed to long khaki pants and white short-sleeved shirts. Lazar put back on his waistcoat and Borsalino hat that covered his yarmulke. Just before Lazar and I gathered up the brood of four kids into his Land Cruiser, Bielke lit the wicks to the Sabbath oil, and intoned a blessing. Most Hasidic Jews use oil in the *Shabbos* candelabras they light each Friday evening at sunset. There was a pointed reason not to use Sabbath candles and it went to the core of Hasidism: Oil does not mix with any other liquid. The oil used on the holiest night of the week represents the Jewish people who must remain separate; any mixing with non-Jews is thought to contaminate Hasidic culture and ultimately defile it. Such fraternizing is the beginning of assimilation, a concept anathema to all sects of Hasidism.

We were late, and in the Land Cruiser we barreled over the seven blocks to the shul, racing to arrive before sundown. As we walked toward the entrance to the shul on East Lawler, we were joined by a dozen more men who all seemed to have arrived at exactly the same moment.

Mikey ran after Yussel, his yarmulke sailing off his head again.

"Moishe, your *kippah!*" Lazar bellowed. Mikey picked up the skullcap and set it back on his head as the two boys raced inside.

As Lazar and I stepped into the shul, we literally crossed from the twentieth century to the nineteenth. The shul originally had been one of Postville's oldest homes, a hundred-year-old mail-order home, once owned by Stanley Schroeder's paternal aunt, Maude Gass. It was built for Maude's father-in-law, Jacob Gass, who was pastor at St. Paul Lutheran Church from 1882 to 1894. Today, the Gass family would hardly recognize the once-regal parsonage. Neither could the older Postville residents, who grew up attending teas and piano recitals there. Beat-up cars without mufflers were parked in the shul's driveway—or worse, on the front lawn. The once pristine, scrubbed exterior of the parsonage now had peeling paint and windows that were either broken or cracked.

Inside, the shul was different from synagogues I had visited, which were orderly, decorous, quiet, and clean. Stretched throughout a double-room sanctuary, long brown metal tables and folding chairs were haphazardly placed; bookshelves had books in no order, and in the center of the makeshift sanctuary stood a shaky ark that held the scrolls of the Torah. A room off to the side had a padlock on it. I glanced over toward the kitchen adjacent to the hallway and saw dirty dishes piled high in the kitchen sink, garbage spilled onto the floor, dirt and mud from the men's boots on the oak floorboards. Frankly, I was glad the locals weren't allowed inside. The old parsonage looked like a flophouse.

No matter how messy the shul was, once inside, the temporal secular world ceased to exist. In front of the ark, a rabbi was davening, singing, and then reading from a prayer book in Hebrew. The rabbi was giving it his all, wailing with full, open lungs, but all the while, the shul's three dozen male congregants seemed to be ignoring this holy man's communion with the Almighty. There were shouts across the room, greetings, gazes of surprise directed at the two strangers, short and tall, Lazar had brought with him. The scene reminded me of a session of the state legislature: Something seemingly solemn was going on up front, yet dozens of members of the august body were gabbing, grabbing hands, and slapping backs.

Hodel and Chava had disappeared inside the shul and were nowhere to be seen. In fact, there were no girls or women in the sanctuary at all. By nine in the evening, about four dozen men were seated, scattered around the tables. Some, like Lazar, were wearing Borsalino hats. Other Hasidim, who were not Lubavitchers, wore large round fur-lined hats, *shtreimelech,* and some had on *spodikem* that looked straight out of a Russian shtetl. All of the Lubavitchers had beards, while members of other sects of Hasidim had *payot,* the curly sidelocks that either hung from above each ear and flopped back and forth as the men davened or were wrapped and curled tightly around the ear—all a reference to the command in Leviticus (19:27) when God told Moses: "Ye shall not round the corners of your heads, neither shalt thou mar the corners of thy beard."

We joined the other men as they faced east, looking toward cornfields, toward Jerusalem, as is prescribed. Iowa farmers have a saying that corn should be "knee-high by the Fourth of July," and this year, the corn seemed well on its way, certainly shin-high. The green leaves, clustered along budding stalks, looked as though they were aspiring to get closer to the blue sky, the sun, even the heavens. Like the Lubavitchers, the corn for just a moment seemed to be praying in the evening dusk.

After the prolonged prayer ended, we all sat down— Mikey and I next to Lazar and Yussel at the far end of one of the metal tables. The worship was in full swing. There were approving glances our way, nods and smiles. Several men nudged one another with their elbows, as they gazed at Mikey and me, while the rabbi, standing at the *bimah* (podium), continued singing and davening. Mikey picked up his cues from Yussel, and just as Yussel was sitting next to his father, Mikey sat close to me, almost too close. I could feel the side of his little thigh pressed against mine under the table. With his index finger, Mikey was playing with the hair on my fore- arm, twirling it. Yussel occasionally whispered something to Lazar, cupping his hand over Lazar's ear. He waved to other boys entering the shul and seemed completely delighted to be where he was, sitting with his "Poppi," as Yussel called Lazar, in this male-only devotion to the Lord. I looked toward Mikey, whose face was a combination of wide-eyed fascina- tion and feigned nonchalance. He crossed his arms, elbows resting on the table.

Mikey's right arm sported a temporary tattoo of an orange tiger, a giveaway from a Dannon Yogurt Kids' Kit Iris had bought at the Hy-Vee a couple of days ago. Mikey noticed my stare and hiked up his sleeve, flexing his pint-sized biceps as though to say, "Hey, doesn't this look cool!"

Lazar glanced our way. "What's that?" he whispered to me. "On his arm."

"Tattoo," I said.

Lazar's eyebrows shot up. He placed the long, slender fin- gers of his right hand on Mikey's upper arm and traced the outline of the orange tiger.

"Tat-too? For REAL?"

I nodded.

"PER-man-ENT?"

"Is there any other way?" I asked.

"C'mon," Lazar said, staring in disbelief.

I nodded. Lazar paused.

"No kidding?" he asked.

I nodded as solemnly as I could.

Lazar shook his head and rolled his eyes, as though to say, "*Oy!* These nonobservant Jews will do anything!"

I cracked a smile, and for a split second, I don't think Lazar understood. Then at precisely the same moment, we both laughed. We had to stifle our giggles as the rabbi up front began a twenty-minute-long recitation from the thick black prayer book.

I had been to hundreds of Friday-night services at countless synagogues, Reform and Conservative, on three continents, but this service was foreign to me. As I'd seen from afar the first night in Postville, there was much singing and, at the end of the service, stamping of feet and pounding of hands. I was struck by how spiritually and physically close these men in the shul were. They were one another's family, and as in all families, there seemed to be an exacting pecking order. The different hats, the waistcoats, the beards, where the men sat, how loud and fast the men read aloud Hebrew passages, how low a man could daven, all of it showed degrees of adherence to Hasidic strictures, and all of it was a test of devotion, a window to the highly structured world of Hasidic worship and kinship.

At about eleven, just as the service ended, one of the men, the least Hasidic-looking in the shul, a man with a short cropped beard and round wire-rim glasses, came up to me and introduced himself as Martin Appel. He looked diffident and uncertain, as out of place in the shul as I must have looked.

"So, you're staying with Lazar," he said, putting out his hand to shake mine. "That's good. He will give you a good idea of what life is like here." Martin looked distant, still wary of my motives. Perhaps he thought I would spread word of his Orthodox devotion among his *goyishe* colleagues back at the university. Before Martin and I could go any further, Lazar had corralled Moishe, Yussel, Hodel, and Chava and wanted to leave—"*Shabbos* dinner is ready. We must hurry!"

Because driving on the Sabbath is strictly forbidden, Lazar left his Land Cruiser in the shul's driveway. The driveway was stacked with cars, and there were still more cars parked on Lawler Street in front, most of them looking as though they had come from the bargain corner at a used-car lot. To gardening mavens like Rosalyn Kambeer and Marie Schlee, I could see why the shul was viewed as an abomination, but to the men who prayed there, such temporal issues were trivial matters that only gentiles could possibly concern themselves with.

Walking from the shul, Mikey and I joined two dozen other Jews heading north on Lawler. The Sabbath was upon us, a twenty-four-hour respite during which no work would be performed, just holy devotion to the Almighty. There would be magnificent food awaiting the men at home; their wives would wear ornate dresses; their children would be attentive. The men would solemnly lead their families in rituals more than three thousand years old. As prescribed by the Rebbe, sexual pleasure would follow, which served as much a bond between spouses as a commitment to the Lord.

On this Friday, religion had once again imbued these men with a sense of peace and well-being. Hasidic Jews believe that angels quite literally accompany them from the shul back to their homes on the Sabbath, flying with them just above their heads. Devotion to faith and testosterone-driven camaraderie once again had been salve to the men's grimy, bloody jobs at the slaughterhouse. The men surrounding me seemed to be strutting, their chests pushed forward, chins held high. There was a sense of shared serenity, strength, power, and righteousness.

As we approached Moore's IGA, a group of eight teenagers was milling in the parking lot, leaning against bicycles, talking in the fresh evening air, slurping Icees from paper cups. Just as we walked past them, they stopped talking. However many times they had witnessed the Jews' procession after Friday-evening shul services, the local kids couldn't help but stare at the men wearing the tall hats and long black coats, walking on this lovely Iowa summer night. Their heads swiveled 180 degrees, watching twenty-six Hasidic Jews striding by, buoyantly conversing in Hebrew and Yiddish as though it was a perfectly normal and natural thing to see. The Jews, illuminated by the glow of fluorescent lights from Moore's parking lot, held implicit power in Postville, and with each step they took, they walked with the might of that authority, whether it was religious, economic, or both.

As we arrived at Lazar's house, Lazar glanced at Mikey. "Moishe, your *kippah*! Where is your *kippah*?"

Mikey scrambled on his knees, and found the yarmulke just beyond the front doorstep. I placed it back on the crown of his head and asked again if he wanted to try the bobby pins. No way.

Waiting for us in the dining room, Bielke was transformed. She was wearing shiny gold earrings, her hair had been assuredly coiffed (could this possibly be a *sheitel*?). She wore expertly applied cherry-red lipstick, rouge, mascara, and eyeliner. She moved with precision in a thick silk-embroidered caftan. The dining table was equally stunning: an heirloom tablecloth, shining sterling-silver service, Lenox plates, cut-crystal goblets, oil-filled silver candelabra with orange flames that flickered as the gentle breezes from the opened windows fluttered over the dining-room table.

While the dinner was to be Bielke's show, the ritual preceding it belonged wholly to Lazar. Before we sat down, Lazar chanted three times, "*Shalom aleichem,*" which means "Peace unto you," honoring the guardian angels that had squired us along Lawler Street back to Lazar's house.

There was a series of hymns, including one to praise the evening's *Shabbos* queen, Bielke, who (with the tongue-tied maid, I suspect) had worked to prepare the feast. Bielke never once allowed her eyes to rise above the level of the table, but she was smiling, immensely pleased to be acknowledged in such a public way.

Lazar filled his silver Kiddush cup with so much sweet red wine that the goblet overflowed, spilling onto a plate. He held the base of the silver cup in the palm of his right hand and intoned the Kiddush, the blessing over the wine. Then we all marched single-file to the kitchen to wash our hands. Mikey grabbed for the soap, but Lazar shook his head. The rinsing of hands before meals, like everything else in a Hasidic household, is executed with exacting protocol. It not only ensures a modicum of physical cleanliness, it symbolically removes defilement and impurity, becoming an act of consecration. We each took turns filling a pewter chalice with tap water, then poured the water first over our right hand, then over our left, all the while reciting a benediction in Hebrew: "Blessed art Thou, Lord our God, King of the universe, who sanctified us with his commandments and commanded us concerning the washing of hands." We splashed water over our hands twice more.

Back at the dinner table, Lazar took two loaves of challah out from under a velvet covering and cut them into large chunks. These were passed around the table, and we each dipped our piece in salt as Lazar pronounced in Hebrew: "Blessed art Thou, Lord our God, King of the universe, who brings forth bread from the earth."

We were now ready to eat. Besides Mikey and me, there was Aaron, a Canadian in his mid-forties who lived in one of the rooms in the shul and worked as a *mashgiach,* a kosher inspector, and a taciturn rabbi in his sixties from Israel, also housed upstairs at the shul, who spoke no English and was a *shochet.*

The meal's first course was (what else?) homemade gefilte fish. "I came all the way to Postville, Iowa, to get this?" I kibitzed. Everyone nodded and laughed in agreement. We all looked toward Lazar and waited for his signal to commence. Lazar delicately swabbed a piece with *chrayn,* horseradish, chewed a forkful, and then paused for three or four seconds, all the while scanning our faces around the table.

Silence.

He took another bite from his fork and swallowed. He paused again.

"Of course, it's good!" Lazar boomed.

He suddenly pushed his chair out from the table, grabbed

the ample spare tire flopping over his belt, and exclaimed: "Look at this! It's gotta be good!" to which everyone laughed.

With Lazar's seal of approval of the first course, I took a bite of Bielke's gefilte fish, and it did what primal foods are supposed to do. For a quickly passing moment, I saw myself as a boy Mikey's age, sitting around the dining room table in the cavernous apartment of Grandma Rose, my father's mother, who lived on West Eighty-ninth Street just off Broadway, in New York City, years before she migrated to Miami Beach. As with any *bubbe*, food was central to her life, and a visit by the grandchildren amplified her matriarchal imperative. But even Grandma Rose, as formidable a culinary *baleboosteh* as they come, never attempted to make gefilte fish.

Bielke's gefilte fish, of course, was just the beginning. She followed the gefilte fish with the old standard: chicken soup with noodles and matzo balls, the soup meticulously skimmed. Roasted chicken was the main course, with soggy green beans, and kugel that was crunchy on top and gooey in the middle—just the way it is supposed to be. No wonder Lazar had so much flab to grab.

Bielke brought out serving after serving, all the while furtively lifting her eyes, spying on Mikey and me, making sure we were eating her offerings. She certainly should have been pleased. I mainlined the food and within minutes could feel it in my blood; Mikey, not used to such a potent narcotic, balked, hiding the gefilte fish appetizer under a leaf of lettuce and slice of tomato.

It became clear why Sholom had chosen Lazar's house as the showcase of Postville *haimischer Yiddishkeit*, homey Jewish feeling. Bielke was a Sabbath Queen Extraordinaire; Lazar was a model Lubavitcher, a *mensch* as well as a *tzaddik*, an honorable, righteous man. As the evening's gastronomic event was coming to an end, the table now was reserved for a colloquy that went beyond food. Bielke and Chava cleared the table as the talk turned to the longevity of the Jewish faith.

"I am a racist," Lazar said, seemingly from nowhere. "Why is it that Israel has persisted to exist for so long? Why haven't the Jews been extinguished after scores of attempts throughout history? That we are still here defies logic. There is only one answer. We are better and smarter. That's why!"

The assembled nodded in approval and went on to talk about the election of Benjamin Netanyahu over Shimon Peres, whom the Lubavitchers detested. Everything revolved around Judaism. The Sabbath was not for discussion of secular matters, and invoking Israel and its leadership was at the core of Lubavitch today. The discussion ebbed and flowed, and during the ebbs Lazar led everyone around the table in Hebrew and Yiddish songs. Since Mikey and I didn't know the songs, we tried to hum along. Mikey kept beat with his right foot, which wasn't able to touch the floor, and with his right hand, which he tapped on the tablecloth. The Lubavitchers love singing, loudly and boisterously, although I noticed that Bielke was not joining in. Women at family gatherings often choose not to sing, since this, too, like a handshake, a naked elbow, knee, or uncovered pate, could arouse a man. Discreetly, Bielke soon had disappeared into the kitchen and was preparing dessert, a nondairy variation of ice cream.

After half a dozen songs and two servings of dessert, the time was close to twelve-thirty. Mikey's head was bobbing up and down like one of those football-player dolls whose heads are attached with a spring. Yussel, Hodel, and Chava showed no signs of fading and were leading everyone around the table in songs, but I was afraid that if Mikey didn't get to bed soon, he'd pitch forward into his dessert plate. I carried him groggy and limp to the couch in the living room and laid him down, careful not to upset his *kippah.* As Mikey nestled against a big feather-stuffed pillow, his right hand touched the crown of his yarmulke. Thus reassured, he was ready to visit the sandman.

Back at the dinner table, Lazar was railing against assimilation, a not-so-veiled condemnation of the Jewish life Iris and I led. He and Aaron were trading comments about the poor Reform Jews who celebrated Chanukah and Christmas. They shook their heads in contempt. For the sake of the Israeli rabbi, they translated, and the rabbi nodded knowingly, his mouth wearing a grimace.

The night continued, past one, and then one-thirty. Most conversations started out in English, trailed off into Yiddish or Hebrew, but it really didn't make much difference now. Israeli politics, the Rebbe, 770 Eastern Parkway, *baruch Hashem,* back to the Rebbe. It was a circle that started and ended with the Rebbe, the great leader, the *Moshiach* who was God's emissary. Everything boiled down to a story, an allegory, a riddle, harkening back to the scholar Hillel or the philosopher Moses Maimonides, but always back to the Rebbe. One by one, Yussel, Hodel, and Chava asked permission to leave the table, and before doing so, each had to *bentshen,* recite a Hebrew grace after the meal.

My own eyelids were starting to droop, so I bade my hosts and the other dinner guests good night, and carried a limp Moishe upstairs to our room. I crawled into bed, took out a notebook, and started jotting down notes from the evening, even though the Rebbe's stern visage was staring down on me. I was breaking the rules of the Sabbath, but they weren't my rules, nor were they rules my host had asked that I follow. The late hour, goblets full of wine, and the vast amount of food had a narcotic effect on me. I put my pen down, but as I was falling off to a fitful sleep, I could still hear the men around the dining table, talking and laughing.

CHAPTER 13

Shikker at the Shul

By seven forty-five the next morning, the hubbub in
the Kamzoil house had resumed. Moishe, *kippah*
firmly planted, washed sleep from his eyes and brushed his
teeth. After a battery of morning prayers, Lazar and Yussel
emerged, and soon the boys were playing tag around the
house. Lazar and I tried to get Mikey and Yussel to sit down
to eat breakfast before we walked to the shul. Bielke was
nowhere to be seen, at least by me.

We got out the front door by eight-thirty. On the way to
the shul, we saw five or six Postville locals fifty feet ahead, on
the other side of the street, equipped with picks, sledgeham-
mers, shovels, next to a large pile of dirt and several fifty-
pound bags of sand and concrete mix. It looked as though
they were about to begin laying a new sidewalk as their weekend project. When Lazar saw the neighbors, he looked at me,
raised both eyebrows, and then quickly crossed to their side of
the street. Yussel, Mikey, and I followed, walking fast to catch
up. There was no apparent reason to get closer to the neighborhood work crew. The sidewalk was under construction,
and besides, it was out of our way. There seemed to be only

one reading: Lazar wanted the locals to get an up-close look at him and his entourage.

The locals said hello to Mikey and Yussel, who darted by, too engrossed in their game of tag to reply. When Lazar and I passed the men, they said nothing to us. Small-town Iowans, even strangers, simply do not walk by one another without saying something: "Good morning!" "Nice day!" even a plain "Hello." To say nothing was plain rude.

Before I could help myself, before I even realized what I was doing, I heard the words "Good morning!" leap from my mouth. The men replied in kind and smiled awkwardly. Lazar gave a stoic nod and walked by quickly without saying a word.

I wasn't sure if I had committed a transgression. I couldn't imagine Lazar complaining about my mixing with the *goyim*. But indeed, as we rounded Military Road, Lazar launched into a parable about how macaroni will always be macaroni, no matter how you dress it up. "You can put cheese in it, serve it as—what do you call it?—Hamburger Helper, make a casserole out of it, but it'll always be macaroni. You can only do so much with macaroni. Macaroni is macaroni. Right?"

I paused.

"You follow me? You understand?"

"Yes, I understand," I said, "if macaroni means what I think you want it to mean."

"The *goyim*," Lazar told me, as we crossed the street again, three blocks from the shul, "will always be the *goyim*, no matter how nice they are to you. So what's the point?"

Lazar's comment underscored the Hasidim's contempt for non-Jews, which wasn't limited to the Postville gentiles, but to all Christians. In fact, as I was to learn, the Postville locals were fortunate that the Hasidim were so lenient when it came to marking their territory. When a newly established Luba-vitcher community becomes large enough to encompass a few blocks, its boundaries are often marked by an *eyruv,* a wire, strung above the streets, outlining the religious neighbor-hood. Under religious law, this allows Lubavitchers to carry certain items on their person during the Sabbath.

I didn't think the Postville Lubavitchers would ever try that, and if they did, I think even the most taciturn of the men at Ginger's would put a stop to it. But if truth be told, Lazar's anti-gentile sentiment wasn't limited to just Hasidic Jews. The Hasidim put into practice what many Jews just talked about. Lazar's gentile-bashing reminded me of the Yiddish aphorism *Er shmekt nit un er shtinkt nit* ("He doesn't smell and he doesn't stink"), used derisively to describe non-Jews, who are viewed as inconsequential and unimportant. The maxim wasn't very different from the expression my own parents used about the simpleton who's got a *goyisher kop.*

Jews trusted Jews, perhaps in the same way blacks trusted other blacks, Lutherans trusted Lutherans, vegetarians trusted vegetarians. Hasidim like Lazar have a total disinterest in any-thing or anyone who isn't Jewish. The *goyim* were invisible. Then why did Lazar cross the street to confront the gentiles with his presence? I think, in part, it was because Lazar didn't want to slink by, like a nice Jewish boy causing no trouble. Crossing the street was cheeky, in-your-face, confrontational. No shrinking violet, no Milquetoast, no skittish deer, Lazar stuck his chest out, held his bearded chin up, and was saying to his gentile neighbors, "Look at me in all my Hasidic splendor!"

The Hasidim were waging a cultural holy war in Postville, Jerusalem, New York, Los Angeles, Paris—everywhere. Their world was Jew vs. non-Jew, and the dichotomy existed in every-thing they did. Hasidic children went to separate schools; their parents arduously stayed among themselves. If the city of Postville tried to enforce any ordinance the Jews disagreed with, the immediate cry was anti-Semitism. If a local com-plained about noise from the shul, if anyone disagreed about annexation, he or she was quickly branded an anti-Semite. Ultimately, I discovered, carrying on a conversation with any of the Postville Hasidim was virtually impossible. If you didn't agree, you were at fault, part of the problem. You were paving the way for the ultimate destruction of the Jews, the world's Chosen People. There was no room for compromise, no room for negotiation, no room for anything but total and complete submission.

Just as Lazar, Yussel, Mikey, and I got to the shul, Lazar announced to no one in particular, "You know what? I feel like doing a *mikveh* now." He and Yussel were going to im-merse themselves in the ritual bath for men in the shul's base-ment.

Images of pristine, healing waters trickled through my head. For years, I had read about the spiritual realm of the *mikveh,* and like the *Shabbos* dinner the night before, I had long anticipated partaking in this singularly Jewish ritual.

"Can we come?" I asked before Lazar even extended an invitation.

Lazar paused, not so much, I think, because he was wary of our sharing in the sanctity of a ceremonial bath, but, as he put it, "This *mikveh* needs some work. It can be pretty gross at times." No matter, I said, and the four of us gingerly stepped down the steep wooden stairway to the shul's clut-tered and musty stone-walled basement, illuminated by light-bulbs dangling from black electrical wires.

Like all Lubavitcher customs, the *mikveh* is surrounded by stringent and rigorous rules. Oral tradition, passed from rabbi to rabbi, calls for water not already drawn, that is, the water must not be still or stationary. Rainwater, called "living waters," is usually mixed with tap water, and the confluence of the two waters has to be running without chemicals or artificial disinfectants.[1] The *mikveh* must contain at least forty *sa'ah,* an amount equal to about two hundred gallons. The forty *sa'ah* alludes to pivotal events in the Bible: the Great Flood lasted forty days and nights; Moses was on Mount Sinai for forty days and nights; the spies sent by Moses to explore Canaan took forty days to return; forty days is how long an embryo takes to turn into a living being, according to Jewish law. The pit that holds the water has to be built directly into the ground, so that it cannot be moved or disconnected in any way. The *mikveh* and its exacting specifications are of such importance that Jewish law requires a bathhouse be erected even before a community builds a synagogue.

Mikvehs are gender-specific. Hasidic men generally bathe in a *mikveh* before the Sabbath begins, women the nightfall of the seventh day of menstruation. Most *mikvehs* have showers so that men or women can vigorously clean themselves before entering the holy water. *Mikvehs* and the healing powers of water are central to Orthodox Judaism, connecting today's Jews to Adam and Eve. Water was the one substance that existed before creation itself, predating heaven and earth,

---

[1]Much of the discussion of rules surrounding the *mikveh* is taken from Samuel Heilman's *Defenders of the Faith: Inside Ultra-Orthodox Jewry* (New York: Schocken, 1992), and Aryeh Kaplan, *Waters of Eden: An Exploration of the Concept of Mikveh Renewal and Rebirth* (New York: JPI, 1984).

according to the first page of the Bible. Since all water comes from the river that flowed out of Eden, immersion in the *mikveh* thus reestablishes a Jew's connection with Eden, and places the supplicant in the womb of creation. Unlike Christians who believe baptism washes away original sin, Jews believe the newly born are pure. When a Jew submerges in the waters of the *mikveh,* he or she rids the soul of defilement, *tumah,* and is restored to a purified state. Hasidic Jews view the *mikveh* experience as a constant rebirth.

In *Holy Days: The World of a Hasidic Family,* writer Lis Harris described her three dunkings in a *mikveh* as a spiritual reunion with relatives living and dead. She wrote of seeing her grandmother floating by, "curled up, like me, like a little pink shrimp," and on her third submersion, she saw her sons as fetuses inside her womb, awaiting birth. With such a grand buildup, I was primed to experience my own epiphany in the Postville *mikveh.*

The run-down condition of the shul should have been a clue as to what I was to discover. The *mikveh* before us was a makeshift square tank under a single lit bulb, atop the sloping basement floor. There was no filtration, and the unheated tap water inside the tank was very still. The only thing living about these waters might have been a persistent fungus. A multitude of curly black hairs floated on the surface, which seemed to glisten with a sheen of body oil. I thought of sweaty, beefy men, just off the killfloor, soaking in the *mikveh* because the mildewed shower on the shul's second floor had been stopped up for weeks.

Lazar and Yussel hurriedly stripped off their clothes and lowered themselves into the water, as Lazar recited Hebrew prayers. Yussel happily flopped around in the tank, while Lazar carefully placed his glasses on the adjacent basement floor, and then merrily dunked his head three times along with Yussel, each holding his nose as he went under. Lazar, his beard soaked with water, looked up at me and apologized for the condition of the *mikveh,* but added, "This one is nothing like some I've seen. You should see those!" He shook his head and chuckled. "You coming?"

I had envisioned a world of wizened white-haired men gingerly emerging from the living waters, drying their steaming bodies with thick towels, leaving the *mikveh* spiritually cleansed. I had choreographed my own plunge, conjuring images of my own life, my own rebirth. Perhaps I would be reunited with my father, who had taught me about my faith, about manhood, about how to be a good father and husband, or with Uncle Jack, or with Grandma Rose. All these hopes drowned in the reality of the dank basement of the shul.

Instead, what flashed through my mind were images of thousands of slaughtered chickens, cattle, and sheep, bloodied work aprons, sweaty clothes, and scores of plump and hairy butchers. The spiritual side of the *mikveh,* the holy confluence of waters from Eden, God, and Creation, wasn't enough to overcome my reserve.

"*Nu?*"

Lazar was shouting from the water. "Shlomo. You coming in?"

Mikey suddenly glanced my way. He looked terrified that I might be thinking of joining Lazar and Yussel. In the dim light, Mikey shook his head, opened his mouth, and pantomimed the word "gross."

Lazar looked up expectantly from the middle of the *mikveh.*

"Next time," I said.

When Lazar and Yussel climbed out, they horsed around like boys in a locker room, cracking rolled-up towels at each other's pale rump, then rubbing themselves dry, and putting on clothes again. We climbed upstairs without saying a word. As soon as we emerged in the sanctuary, Lazar looked at Mikey.

"Moishe, your *kippah*! You MUST wear your *kippah* at all times!"

Mikey stopped in his tracks, looked right and left like a fawn with a semi barreling down on him. He made an about-face, ran back down the steps to the *mikveh,* and within fifteen seconds, emerged victorious, holding high the missing yarmulke.

Mikey and Yussel disappeared into the back of the shul with a dozen other boys. Twenty minutes later, Mikey came back and found me sitting next to Lazar. He tapped me on the forearm.

"Dad," he whispered, "if my Jewish middle name is Raffel, does that mean then that Raphael on the *Teenage Mutant Ninja Turtles* is Jewish, too?"

I had no idea what kind of conversation Mikey had gotten himself into. "I guess it does," I said, as the rabbi up front was leading the congregation in a long, rousing prayer. "He's the Jewish turtle stuck in the sewers." Mikey looked satisfied and walked back to his gang of new friends.

Meanwhile, Lazar handed me a large *tallis* and told me to drape it, not over my shoulders, but over my head. I wasn't sure if Lazar was embarrassed by my reticence or if he was enforcing a spiritual dress code. "It's the right thing to do," Lazar said, raising his eyes toward five or six other men davening. Someone had opened the windows to the shul, and there was a pleasant midmorning breeze coming from the east, which seemed to inflate the men's *tallises* and momentarily made them billow like sheets.

"Do it," Lazar told me.

I watched Lazar, whose protocol for the tallis was elaborate. After placing it over his head and shoulders, he continued davening. "My soul, bless the Lord!" Lazar implored in Hebrew from Psalms (104:1–2). "Lord my God, you are greatly exalted; you have garbed yourself with majesty and splendor. You enwrap yourself with light as with a garment; you spread the heavens as a curtain." Lazar began softly singing a benediction.

I put the thick prayer shawl over my head and slowly began swaying back and forth, mimicking the men around me, facing east, toward the green cornfields. With the *tallis* draped over my head, on either side of my ears, following the contours of my face, I suddenly understood that *tallises* act as blinders. You were unable to see what was happening on either side of you so that you could pray without being distracted.

I was surrounded by Jews praying and chanting, beseeching the Almighty for salvation, but I felt like a guy with a raincoat pulled over his head, as much an outsider as when Sholom had wrapped me in tefillin. As I stole glances around me, my initial reaction was to be put off by the dramatics of the other men. However much I respected their commitment to faith, their actions seemed drowned in showmanship—who could wail loudest, bow farthest without falling over, read the longest Hebrew passage fastest and without taking a breath.

For two hours we prayed, davened, sat down, and rose up. Just as I was wondering when it all was going to end, Lazar elbowed me. "The rabbi has called you," he whispered, pointing toward the ark, motioning for me to go to the center of the shul. Suddenly, the two dozen men sitting around me turned my way and began urging me in a medley of languages to step forward. A great honor was being bestowed upon me. The rabbi had invited me to give the required blessing on a portion of this week's Torah reading. Called an *aliyah,* literally "going up," such a practice is usually accorded to a person of high distinction. In my case, I think, it probably meant that the Postville shul got so few visitors that when an out-of-town guest like me showed up, he was automatically given such an honor. Perhaps, also, the invitation was an effort to ignite in me a fire of belief, to deepen my commitment to Judaism.

There are generally seven *aliyot.* The Hebrew word connotes that the honored person actually makes a spiritual ascent, but for me, any ascent was fraught with peril. As I arrived at the *bimah,* I whispered to the rabbi that I didn't read Hebrew.

"Just tell me your Hebrew name and your father's Hebrew name," the rabbi replied as we both went into an extended set of *davening.*

"Shlomo and Jacov."

The rabbi gave me a push in the small of my back, toward the open Torah—parchment scrolls containing the five books of the Hebrew scriptures, wrapped around two wooden handles. A heavyset man with a wiry red beard standing to my left was the Torah reader, and as I stepped closer, I saw that he was the "No problem" rabbi from Sholom's office, who had swiped the Marlboro Gold cigarettes.

The rabbi indicated that I was to touch the edge of my tallis next to the section of the Torah to be read and kiss the fringe of the tallis, which I did. Then I grasped the scroll's wooden handles, called *atzei hayim* (tree of life). Four dozen Hasidic men waited for Shlomo ben Jacov—Shlomo, son of Jacov—to introduce the week's Torah section, Numbers 13–15. I looked up to see if this was Lazar's way of getting back at me for the tattoo prank of last night, but his head was shrouded under a white *tallis.*

When I paused at the Hebrew lettering, the rabbi began whispering a long string of Hebrew into my right ear. I was like a TV newscaster getting fed words through an earpiece from the studio control booth. Hebrew magically began to spring forth from my mouth.

"Bless the Lord who is blessed," I started out.

The assembled men collectively responded in Hebrew. "Blessed is the Lord who is forever blessed."

"Blessed art Thou, Lord our God, King of the universe, who has chosen us from among the nations and has given us his Torah," I intoned, as the rabbi vigorously whispered in my ear. "Blessed art Thou, Lord, who gives the Torah."

On it went, until my first act was over. The "No problem" rabbi, another newcomer, I assumed, spoke next, reading the Hebrew fast and furious, all the while davening. The Torah portion, I found out afterward, contained elements that bound Jews to the Lord and revealed commandments funda-mental to a Jew's existence, such as devoting the Sabbath solely to reverence of the Almighty and wearing vestments with tasseled fringes on all four corners.

When the "No problem" rabbi finished, I rolled the scroll back together. The other rabbi whispered in my left ear this time and I repeated:

"Blessed art Thou, Lord our God, King of the universe, who gave us a Torah of truth, and planted within us eternal life. Blessed art Thou, Lord, who gives the Torah."

Either my Hebrew wasn't all that bad, or no one cared, or no one was listening, or it just didn't make any difference, or my hosts were exceptionally gracious. Dozens of men congrat-ulated me, slapping me on the back. If not a full-fledged mem-ber of the club, I had at least been allowed a weekend pass.

At one in the afternoon, we all broke for refreshments and

entertainment. The *tummel* was about to begin. Lazar broke out a gallon of Smirnoff vodka, plastic cups, several tins of baked Manischewitz-mix cakes, and a large jar of sliced dill pickles. We passed everything around, and then we got heavily into the vodka. Lazar downed a plastic tumblerful of straight vodka to the cheers of everyone. I gulped one shot and then nursed a second, biding my time. The last time I had been to such a lively celebration where vodka was the main course had been at our going-away blowout at the Russian Renaissance in San Francisco. In the shul, Sholom's brother-in-law Yosi trumped Lazar by downing *two* eight-ounce tumblers of vodka. The men cheered, but then Yosi put up his index finger. He reached for a *third* tumbler, which he threw back in one swallow.

The men stamped their feet and clapped their hands in appreciation of Yosi's feat. This was an old-fashioned chugging contest. Toast after toast followed, with more laughter and more backslapping, followed by a slew of Hasidic songs. By now, Lazar had drained all the juice from the pickle jar into a plastic cup, and he was using the juice as a chaser for knocking back more shots of vodka.

The booze was starting to have an effect. The men's songs got louder and rowdier. These revelers pounded the tables with their fists and stomped on the floor with their heavy shoes. It was an uproariously good time, with jokes, putdowns, and rapid-fire kibitzing, all in Yiddish. The "No problem" rabbi got into the act by standing up and singing a tune in Yiddish that got louder and louder with each stanza. I couldn't follow the words, but it was a story that seemed to have endless stanzas, and after each stanza, the rabbi sang, "AYE-YAI-YA-YAI" at the top of his lungs. Soon everyone had joined in, singing either the stanzas or screaming, "AYE-YAI-YA-YAI" over and over again. "Aye," I was to learn, was a vocalization of the mystical name of God.

The guys before me, belting out chorus after chorus of Hasidic songs brought to America from Hungary, Russia, or Poland, reminded me of black gospel singers, ripping out all the stops while singing their way to heaven's gate. It was as good an example of Hasidic *devekuth* as I could imagine. If repetitive prayer and raucous song hadn't yet connected these men to one another and to the Almighty, the ample lubrication from the vodka would accomplish the task. Sweating profusely, praying to the Almighty, shouting not just for supplication but because they were on their way to getting splendidly drunk, these men were a jolt to my own notion that religion had to be moderate and orderly. Rapturous song, powerful drink, and overwhelming body heat was the Holy Communion of these believers.

Everything about the day was intense and bodily: the dirty *mikveh,* drinking, singing, the body odor, the pounding of fists and feet. It was primitive ritual designed to strip you to your bones and unite you with your brethren, your ancestors, and the good Lord above. Maybe this was what Robert Bly was talking about. No women, male bonding, getting in touch with your primal feelings. These men worked together, prayed together, played together, even bathed together. As they belted out the same songs their forefathers sang two centuries ago, the men closed their eyes, swayed back and forth, a combination of the alcohol and the davening, singing so loudly that the exhalation of air alone would have made for a heady experience.

The party eventually wound down, and as the songs and jokes came slower and slower, I went over to the presiding rabbi.

"I appreciated your making me feel so welcome here," I told him.

The rabbi recoiled. "You're a Jew, aren't you? All Jews are welcome in the shul. You *never* have to thank me for that. At least, I hope not!"

Couldn't these guys ever take a compliment?

Completely wasted, Lazar and I corralled Yussel and Mikey, who played tag once again as we walked back to West Williams Street. Along the way, I mentioned to Lazar a conversation I had had with a Lubavitcher rabbi in Minneapolis, Moshe Feller, a few months earlier. I had asked the rabbi to explain how the Postville Hasidim could stay so close to the traditions of Chabad so far from their homeland. Rabbi Feller had told me, "If you're committed to your faith, there is no culture shock. Postville and Crown Heights are one and the same." I had thought the rabbi's comment absurd. How could two places—Postville, Iowa, and Crown Heights, Brooklyn— be any more different? But after getting *shikker* at the shul, I had to reconsider. This men's club didn't disband when the members walked out of the shul. Cultural, religious, and familial ties bound these men together twenty-four hours a day. There was no cultural friction for the Hasidim because they acknowledged nothing but their own insular reality and the *Yiddishkeit* surrounding it. What Hasidic Jews did in the secular world was of trifling importance when compared to their religious devotion. What occupied the minds of those who were righteous was uncompromising devotion to one another and to their religion. For months, I had been unable to understand how Hasidic Jews could possibly fit into life in Postville, or for that matter, any place tainted by the goyim. But it all seemed simple now in my pickled state, as I struggled to walk in a straight line.

"Wherever we go, we don't adapt to the place or the people," Lazar preached, as we rounded the corner of Reynolds Street. "It's always been like that and always will be like that. It's the place and the people who have to adapt to *us*."

Good luck, Leigh Rekow, Stanley Schroeder, and all the guys back at Ginger's, I thought.

Back at the house, Lazar and I went to the backyard, as Yussel started teaching Mikey a kid's song in Yiddish, a rousing Hasidic version of "Head, Shoulders, Knees and Toes." I brought up Leigh Rekow's criticism of the Postville Jews' bargaining.

"Here in Iowa, we agree with the shake of a hand," Rekow had told me. "To bargain would mean that we had done something shady when we arrived at the price in the first place."

Lazar couldn't have disagreed more with that anti-Semite Rekow. To Lazar, bargaining was a thoroughly Jewish endeavor. Negotiating the lowest price wasn't *chutzpah,* it was tradition. "I don't feel like a Jew *unless* I bargain!" Lazar bellowed. "I feel bad when I *don't* make a deal. That's part of being a Jew! A Jew has to know he got something for the absolute lowest price—or he feels rotten." If Lazar hadn't been telling me this, I'd have thought it was one of the regulars at Ginger's. Lazar meant what he said, and his remarks were totally anti-Semitic. If anyone else were saying this, Lazar would have him by the throat.

Out of the corner of my eye, I noticed Mikey leaving the backyard and within minutes returning with his Batman pillow from our car parked out front. After two days of submersion in Yussel's culture, Mikey wanted to show off a prized possession from his own world. But as soon as Lazar spotted Batman, I knew Mikey was in trouble. Lazar, who seldom watched television, rarely read a book, or saw a movie secular in content, was blind to the kid pleasures of the Dynamic Duo. "That doesn't have any batteries that go with it?" Lazar asked peevishly, raising his voice. "It isn't part of an electronic game, is it? We can't have that in the house on the Sabbath."

Mikey handed Batman to Yussel, who carried the satiny pillow across the yard, laying his smooth cheek against Batman's. But as soon as he looked at Lazar, Yussel realized how much Batman must have displeased his father. Lazar had a look of disgust, and in a few seconds dismissed Mikey's cherished pillow with a quick backhanded flick of the hand.

"*Goyisher chozzerai.*"

Yussel dutifully handed Batman back to Mikey, who handed him to me. I felt like I was holding an Easter ham. I laid Batman down in a corner of the back porch, the Caped Crusader relegated to criminal status.

Then Lazar noticed another infraction. "Moishe, your *kippah!*"

Mikey reached up to touch his head and all he felt was hair. His face was a combination of panic and anguish.

"Daddy, I had it on a little while ago. "It just...disappeared."

"Yussel, go into the house, and get Moishe another *kippah*. And don't lose this one," Lazar said sternly to Mikey, doubly angry after the intrusion of Batman.

"Are you sure you don't want to use a bobby pin?" I asked. "Yussel uses one, and it'll make wearing your *kippah* easier." No way. Mikey held steadfast to his tried-and-true system: right hand to the *kippah*, teetering precariously atop his head.

Lazar returned to the topic at hand. He had no apologies for Rekow or anyone else in Postville. Lazar was proud that he and the other Postville Hasidim bargained for everything, from cars to computers. At the slaughterhouse, he haggled with one computer vendor for weeks until he had the salesman right where he wanted him. Just as they were closing a deal, Lazar changed the terms. Lazar insisted the vendor throw in the demonstration model—or he'd call the whole deal off. Lazar wanted the demo model for his own personal use at home.

"And my boss is right there," Lazar said. "Sholom is standing right next to me, as we're going back and forth over the phone, the vendor and me, and you could see this guy sweating, thinking he's going to lose the deal. But meanwhile, Sholom, he's enjoying the whole thing. We're both cracking up.

"So the guy says, 'OK, OK, I'll give you the friggin' computer, but we gotta make the deal thirty-days net instead of forty-five-days net, and I say, 'Sure, sure, no problem,' so we sign off on the deal.

"And you know what? I had no intention of paying him in thirty days, not even forty-five days. *Let him sue us!* We'll pay him—eventually—but on *our* terms, not his." Lazar pressed his lips together and smiled as though he had just swallowed another forkful of Bielke's gefilte fish.

It seemed to Lazar that *hondling*, fierce bargaining, was a sport, more for pleasure than for actually saving money. It was the equivalent of hunting or fishing for the Iowa *goyim*. Instead of recounting the adventure that culminated in the stuffed buck's head or trout mounted on your rec room wall, the Hasidim bragged about how they were able to get rock-bottom prices they went to battle for. The Hasidim not only *hondled* with alacrity, but enjoyed boasting about the terrain, equipment, first sighting, and ultimate kill.

Lazar and I went back and forth throughout the afternoon

and evening, Bielke showing up only to put dinner on the table and smile serenely as she served and cleared our plates. By eleven that night, Mikey and I were in bed again under the watchful eye of the Rebbe, as I wrote out my notes, this time guilt-free since the Sabbath had officially ended at sundown. On Sunday, Lazar had to leave at six in the morning to catch a plane to New York. Cliff Olson was to take him to the airport in La Crosse for the thirty-minute flight to Minneapolis, where he would transfer planes. Mikey and I had planned on leaving at eight-thirty Sunday morning, so I told Lazar that we would let ourselves out of the house on our own. Bielke wouldn't say good-bye, presumably since it would have put her in the compromising position of being in the presence of a man who was neither husband nor relative.

As Mikey and I drove out of Postville that Sunday morning, a soft rain began to fall. The air was fetid, close, and humid. We drove past the shul on our way out of town, and a queue of Jews was at the front entrance, and farther inside, I could see there were more donning tallises, getting ready to pray once again. It was never-ending, all encompassing. There was no room for anything else. I had wanted to like Lazar and his merry band of tippling Hasidim. Iris had joked that she didn't want Mikey and me coming home after our weekend converted by the Hasidim. No chance of that happening. It was time to leave, time to re-establish our own sense of identity, instead of being subsumed into someone else's.

Near Independence, we drove by a front yard filled with just-budding wildflowers—purple coneflowers, bonesets, Turk's-cap lilies, Solomon's seals, and black-eyed Susans. Closer to town, two lanky teenage girls, barefoot in cutoffs and T-shirts, stood under a half-dozen balloons tied to a telephone pole. They held a hand-stenciled sign:

CAR WASH

TODAY ONLY

INDEPENDENCE HIGH

I realized, then, that Mikey and I were no longer Moishe and Shlomo. We were back to our secular Iowa lives of pork tenderloins, catfish fries, and sloppy Maid-Rite sandwiches.

Nestled against his Batman pillow, Mikey looked up at me. "In the shul, one of the boys told me that Santa Claus was made up by some rich *goy* who wanted to make lots of money. Is that true, Daddy?"

I laughed. "Maybe. But that depends on how you look at Christmas and your reason for giving gifts," I said.

Mikey mulled over the answer, and it seemed to satisfy him. We never got further into the issue. By Marion, he was in a deep slumber.

In a way, Lazar's ethnocentric I-told-you-so rule-dominated cosmos made the environment inhabited by the Postville locals seem carefree, giddy, even liberating. Lazar's world was insulated against the secular vulgarities that Iris, Mikey, and I had learned to tolerate. There was no television, no Ninja Turtles, no Nintendo, no discomfort come Christmastime or Easter. Yussel listened to his father better than Mikey listened to me. If Lazar ruled supreme in his household, though, then where did that leave Bielke? I thought their relationship was primitive and unacceptable. Iris would never have allowed herself to be treated in such a subservient manner, but neither would my mother or my grandmother Rose.

CHAPTER 14

Mom - Calling

As soon as Mikey and I got back to Iowa City, I wrote Lazar and Bielke a thank-you note. They had opened their house to us, Bielke had cooked a feast, and Lazar had been honest and forthright with me—warts and all. I closed my note by inviting their family to Iowa City, so that Iris, Mikey, and I could reciprocate. I suspected they would never take me up on the offer, but I half hoped that they would. I wanted to show Lazar how Jews like us lived. I wanted Lazar, Bielke, and their children on our turf, so that they could see another version of the world. I never got a reply, which, I thought, was in keeping with Lubavitchers' behavior—why be bothered when it takes us away from our primary tasks: family, prayer, work.

I knew in my heart that the conflict between the Postville locals and the Hasidic Jews continued to be a metaphor for my own transplanted life in Iowa. I wanted to belong, I just didn't know to which group. Even after months of making the 115-mile trip between Iowa City and Postville, I still found myself smack in the middle of an evolving conundrum. I was a Jew—and by now, all of Postville probably knew it—but I also had become makeshift Iowan. Neither group took my roots to be deeply sunk into either legacy, but that didn't matter to me. I felt an obligation to understand the Jews and the Iowans and the slippery nexus that bound them to each other. My stay with a Hasidic family accomplished, I wanted to go deeper into the Postville locals.

By now the political campaign to annex the land on which the kosher slaughterhouse stood was gaining steam. Leigh Rekow had been successful in his drive to place before the voters of Postville a ballot measure calling for the annexation question. The Postville City Council, led by Leigh, had voted for the referendum, and now all that was left was to get the final approval of the exact wording from the Secretary of State in Des Moines. If everything went as planned, the referendum could be on the local ballot within a year's time. And if it passed, then the showdown that might determine whether the Jews would stay or leave would begin.

As far as I could tell, Leah Rubashkin had planned no gala barbecue to convince the locals to vote against annexation. Either she had forgotten about the idea or Sholom had put the kibosh on it. Anticipating war, Sholom had stepped up his threats: If the city annexed his land, the Rubashkin family would move the slaughterhouse lock, stock, and barrel out of Postville. There would be no negotiating, no compromising. He vowed that all the Jews and the economic clout they had brought with them would follow him out of town. Postville would be reduced to a dying prairie town, so economically bereft that not even a QuikTrip would want to set up shop there.

It was just more bluster, Leigh Rekow counseled worried merchants in town. The Jews can't move; they've got too much invested here. The locals knew the Aesop fable about the boy who cried wolf. Most doubted whether Sholom would ever leave Postville, so the annexation vote was really a local referendum, a straw vote on the Jews and how they went about their lives in Postville. Still, I knew it would take a massive sense of outrage for the Postville locals to harness their resentment and channel it politically.

If my four years in Iowa had shown me anything, it was that Iowans don't like to take stands, and they don't often mobilize behind a cause—unless it had to do with football or public education, which they back ferociously. In my precinct in Iowa City, during the Iowa presidential caucuses, the local Republicans and Democrats civilly discussed the merits of each candidate while they sat in miniature wooden chairs arranged in a semicircle in the second-grade classrooms at Longfellow Elementary School. Politics are rowdy and raucous; people should feel passionate about whom they send to the White House. So, where were the posters, the long-winded speeches, the sense of mission and urgency? Iowans approached politics the same way they drove: in a pleasant, moderate, easygoing manner. But, if my stay with Lazar had shown me anything, it was that the Lubavitchers' collective behavior toward the Postville locals was atrocious. Some of what the locals at Ginger's had said was right, but could Leigh Rekow and the others translate their anger to a majority of the town's voting to kick the Hasidim out?

When I was last in Postville, Sharon Drahn had mentioned the town's annual Agricultural/Industrial Days. Sharon and her student assistant, Kari Berns, had made me promise that I wouldn't miss the two-day upcoming fair. "This is Postville at its best," Sharon promised. The locals pull out all the stops for Ag/Industry Days, and this year's blast coincided with the hundredth anniversary of the Postville Volunteer Fire Department, so it would be a double celebration. Elementary-school kids would vie to win a Mom-Calling Contest and the Little Miss & Mister Postville Pageant. A midway would feature more than a dozen attractions, including a scary ride called the Scrambler, as well as the perennial favorite, the House of Mirrors. On Saturday morning at eleven, an old-fashioned parade would take over downtown Lawler Street.

I didn't want to miss the festivities. Neither did Mikey when I told him about it. So, several weeks after our *Shabbos* weekend, Mikey and I planned to return to Postville, this time with Iris, who by now had finished her law-school finals. The trip was to be a celebration: Iris had just completed her second year of law school; school was out for Mikey and me. The three of us had the same intoxicating feeling every student has when June rolls around. School was over and we had the entire summer free! To do whatever we wanted for the next three months was a luxury I still hadn't gotten accustomed to, but each year it had reaffirmed our decision to trade the world of big-city journalism for life in fly-over country.

This time for accommodations in Postville, we opted for neither the Kamzoil home nor the Pines Motel. We planned on staying at Rosalyn Krambeer's bed-and-breakfast, the Old Shepherd House on Tilden Street, where fifty dollars got you a private room with a Murphy bed, wine and cheese before dinner, and a farmer's breakfast the next morning. I didn't plan on calling or stopping in at either Lazar's house or Agri-processors. Instead, this time I wanted to return to the local Lutheran community, and what better time to do that than during this civic blowout, during which everyone in Postville showed up. Everyone, of course, except the Jews.

Ag/Industry Days went from Friday afternoon at five until Saturday midnight, which pretty much knocked out any chance of participation by the Hasidim even if they wanted to go. The big party was designed quite naturally to fit into the locals' timetable, anyway, which meant that when the soiree ended Saturday night, everyone could nurse a pleasant hangover and still attend church the next morning. That Ag/Industry Days coincided with *Shabbos* wasn't really an issue. No one could imagine the Hasidic Jews in their long coats, *tzitzit,* and hats ever taking a spin on the Scrambler. And Hasidic women in the House of Mirrors?

It had been a little more than two years since I had made my first trip to Postville. On the ride up this time, the corn by late June was so eager to grow that it seemed to crackle as we drove by. We drove with the windows down, and as we sped past pig farms, the stench, though still strong and unmistakable, wasn't foreign to us any longer. For Iris and me, the pungent smell of porkers had become a marker to celebrate our transition from city to country life. In fact, the three of us had devised a family game: The first person in the car to whiff the scent of an approaching cloud of swine-manure stink would yell, "PIG!" At Mikey's insistence, we devised an elaborate system of points, bonuses, and dares. Roadkill did not count, and if you confused the smell of skunk with pigs, you were penalized.

I told Mikey about the Mom-Calling Contest, and he immediately wanted to enter. Somewhere between Strawberry Point and Elkader in Clayton County, he started practicing. Mikey had a sound to be reckoned with. He cleared his throat and started out "Mom" slowly, riding a crescendo, holding his breath as long as he could, ten, fifteen seconds, getting shriller and shriller as his prepubescent voice got higher and higher and then cut out. A couple of cows looked up quizzically as our car rushed by, then went back to chewing their cud contentedly. A flock of cawing red-winged blackbirds perched on a slack telephone wire along Route 13, fluttered simultaneously, alarmed, and took flight.

We arrived in Postville with plenty of time to spare, and after checking into Rosalyn Krambeer's house, we got ourselves over to the Ag/Industry Days Registration Desk. A half hour before the contest was to begin, we registered budding Placido with the officials sitting behind a card table. The contestants were to yell into a microphone set up front and center on a stage in Roberts Park, to be judged by a panel of civic leaders, one of whom was a disc jockey at an FM station in Decorah. Mikey was slotted fifth out of twelve contestants.

The first four entrants were tentative, shy, unsure of themselves, hardly able to croak even an audible "Mom" into the microphone. One boy approached the microphone, and then ran crying back to his mother, who was waiting in the wings.

Mikey, the dark horse from downstate, walked confidently to center stage, baseball cap turned backward. He nodded to the audience. As he took in a deep breath, there was a moment of silence. Then he let loose a scream from the pit of his little diaphragm: "MOOOOOOOOOOOOOOOOOOOOOOO OOOOOOOOOOOOOOOOOOOOOOOOOOOOOOOOOOOO OOOOOOOOOOOOOOOOOOOOOOOOOOOOOOOOOOOO OOOOOOOOOOOOOOOOOOOOOOOOOOOOOOOOOOM!" The loudspeakers attached to the telephone poles in Roberts Park rattled as Mikey's voice seemed to go on forever—ten, fifteen, a full twenty seconds. When he finished, Mikey took several steps back, bowed, and then fell spent into a folding chair on the stage.

Seven contestants later, the judges huddled. The head judge raised Mikey's right hand like a heavyweight champ's and presented him with a prize, a gift certificate from Pizza

Time Pizzeria on Greene Street. Sharon, who also served as the *Herald-Leader* photographer, snapped Mikey's picture with the runners-up. As we walked through the crowd, many of the locals I had interviewed during my trips to Postville stuck out their hands to greet the seven-year-old with the ear-splitting voice. Not just a few asked Mikey for a personal screaming, and after glancing up at Iris and me with a "Do-I-*have*-to?" look, the king of mom-calling demurred, which was for the benefit of everyone involved.

The contestants for the Mom-Calling Contest had been polite, timid, controlled. I got the impression that few of these country kids ever raised their voices. They reminded me of young versions of some of my students at the university— calm, nice, unhurried, unassuming, totally civilized. "Clean as you go" is a popular Iowa expression, and it means more than scrubbing the kitchen countertop after each meal. It means staying out of trouble, certainly not asking for trouble, keeping your mouth shut. For the mom-calling kids up on the stage, shouting at the top of their lungs was calling attention to themselves—something that made rural people uncomfort-able, as when Yosi Gourarie strapped the oversized menorah to his car and drove through Postville at Christmas time with loudspeakers blaring Hebrew melodies. Too bad none of the Hasidic kids had entered the mom-calling contest. If they were anything like their fathers who performed weekly at the shul, the loudspeakers wouldn't have just shaken, they'd have exploded.

Mikey's victory was just the beginning of Ag/Industrial Days. Along the midway, you could toss rings on the necks of Coke bottles or shoot water guns at mechanical racehorses that inched forward with each squirt. The prizes ranged from miniature key chains to large stuffed animals. For the adventurous, there was the Scrambler, which spun twenty-eight screaming kids and several reckless adults for what seemed like an eternity but was only three minutes. When the Scrambler stopped and the riders got off, most were so dizzy that they staggered like drunks. For more sedate fairgoers, you could walk around in the House of Mirrors, swearing and laughing that no way were you going to bump your nose again into yet another mirror. Admission to the fair cost six dollars, which included a shredded pork sandwich, corn on the cob, chips, cheese curds, an ice-cream cup, and a half pint of milk. In the tented Biergarten, three steins of draft sold for five dollars. By nine that evening, the Whitesidewalls had set up in the band shell, and by ten there were more than fifty couples dancing under the stars.

Back at Rosalyn Krambeer's house, after a couple of glasses of wine with Rosalyn and her Wayne Newton–look-alike dancing partner, Oren, we went upstairs. Mikey crawled into the Murphy bed, and Iris and I slept in a large mahogany bed in an adjacent room. Rosalyn had fitted the beds with white percale sheets that smelled of starch and a fresh ironing. Atop the sheets lay a fluffy comforter and a square-patterned handmade quilt.

The next morning we were awakened by the aroma of fresh-brewed coffee that wafted up the stairs and into our room. As promised, Rosalyn had prepared a country breakfast: farm eggs, strips of thick bacon, slices of grilled ham, fresh strawberries, waffles and pancakes off the griddle, and just-squeezed orange juice. Rosalyn's offerings were an Iowa version of Bielke's *Shabbos* feast: nurturing food, lovingly prepared and served, but without the prayers, lectures, or guilt.

We filled ourselves with this country sustenance, but we didn't tarry. We wanted to get a good spot along the parade route downtown. I pulled on a T-shirt and shorts and went to get Mikey's clothes from the car.

Just as I turned the key to the car trunk, I glanced over to the alley next to Rosalyn's house and saw a doleful, stooped, solitary figure plodding by. The man looked like he was carrying the weight of the world on his shoulders. For a second or two, I didn't quite know what I was seeing. Hot day, a guy dressed all in black? He looked like the grim reaper. But that was me wearing a *goyisher kop,* not a *kippah.* I looked closer and saw a familiar Borsalino, black beard, and waistcoat.

"Lazar!" I shouted.

He barely lifted his head.

"Hey, Lazar!"

Lazar turned my way, muttering to himself, softly but audibly so I could hear. "Who's this *goy,* someone in shorts, shouting at *me*?"

"Lazar, it's me, Shlomo, son of Jacov! Moishe's father. Remember?"

Lazar continued to walk, then looked up, smiled, and stopped.

"What are YOU doing here?" He paused. "What are you doing THERE?" Lazar shouted, pointing to Rosalyn Krambeer's house.

"I came back to talk to more people."

"Why would you want to talk to anyone else? You already talked to me."

"Because someone else might have something else to say."

"I doubt it. I told you all you need to know. Why waste your time?"

"I need other viewpoints."

"From the *goyim?*"

"From people who might have a different viewpoint."

"*Viewpoint?* What does *that* mean? *Viewpoint?* Sounds like a *goyishe* word. I don't know about this *viewpoint* business. You already heard the truth. Why do you want to confuse yourself? You don't trust *me*, a fellow Jew?"

"I do my job; you do yours."

"But what is this *job* of yours, Shlomo? You start snooping around, asking everyone questions, you're liable to confuse things. You understand what I mean? Your *job,* as you call it, is plain and simple: to be a Jew."

"If I need help with that, I'll come to you."

"Good. I'm glad to hear that."

The comment, for a moment, silenced both of us. We had reached a temporary standoff until Lazar said, "Always remember this, Shlomo: You are one of the Chosen People. This is a free country, and don't you forget it. Ever! Now, you come to shul with me. It's late. Then you come to the house for lunch."

"We can't go to shul."

"*We?* Who's *we*? Moishe here, too?"

"Moishe came with me. So did my wife."

"The wife? She here this time? She finished with the law exams?"

I nodded.

"Excellent! Then you and Moishe come to shul now, and your wife joins us at the house in the afternoon. It's all settled."

"We can't come to the shul. We're going to the parade downtown."

"The PARADE? That's more important than shul? A Jew

can't come to shul? This I cannot understand. Shul loses out to a parade with the *goyim,* with animals, cows, *pigs?* Whaddaya *meshugge?* You're a Jew, Shlomo. You come to shul."

"Can't. I promised Mikey we'd go to the parade."

"Moishe'll understand. I'll explain it to him. He should be in shul on a Saturday morning. Not at some cockamamie parade with all that *chozzerai.* And you, too, Shlomo, son of Jacov."

"Nope," I said, smiling now. "*You're* going to the shul; we're going to the parade."

Lazar looked up toward the heavens. He put his hands out, palms up, as though feeling for raindrops. "You do what you want to do, I suppose."

"Thank you."

"You're welcome!"

"What time should we come by the house?"

"Time? What do I know from time? It's the Sabbath."

"About two o'clock?"

"We'll see you whenever."

"You want to ask Bielke first?"

"Bielke? Why should I ask *her?* My wife is the boss of our family. I just write her script. That reminds me of a thought I had today as I was looking at myself in the mirror. I said, 'My wife is a very stupid person. The more she listens to me, the stupider she gets.'"

"We'll see you at about two."

"Whenever. But wait, Shlomo. Listen to this: A guy gets interviewed by a top Israeli general to be an Israeli spy. As a test, the general asks, 'If you had a chance to kill an Arab or a cat, which one would you kill first?'

"'Why the cat?'

"'You're hired!' the general says."

Shul could wait. Lazar was on a roll.

"Listen to this one: The president of a company interviews three job candidates to be his accountant.

"'What's two plus two?' the boss asks the first guy.

"The guy says, 'Four.'

"'Get outtahere!' the boss says.

"'What's two plus two?' the boss asks the next guy.

"'Twenty-two.'

"'Get outtahere! You're *meshugge*.'

"'What's two plus two?' the boss asks the third guy.

"'Vell,' the guy says, 'that all depends on vhat you vant it to be.'

"'You're hired!'"

Just as Lazar was reaching the punch line, Iris and Mikey had made their way to the alley. "Moishe," Lazar admonished. "It's the Sabbath, and you still don't have your *kippah* on!" For a kid who sixteen hours earlier had screamed louder than anyone, Mikey suddenly was speechless. He looked at his sneakers.

Lazar came over to us, bent down, and with the index and middle fingers of his right hand, grabbed hold of the taut, rosy skin of Mikey's cheek and pulled it—the same gesture my grandfather used to do with me. Mikey grimaced.

Lazar stood up from Mikey and shifted uncomfortably when I introduced him to Iris. Like all observant Hasidic men, Lazar was proscribed from addressing a woman who was not his wife. He looked at Iris, not directly but instead focusing somewhere between her nose and neck. For Iris's amusement, I wanted him to kibitz, but instead, Lazar nodded to her solemnly, almost shyly.

Iris was in a state of shock. Though she grew up in the Lubavitcher stronghold of south Miami Beach, she had never talked to a Hasidic Jew in her life. She was wary of Lubavitchers, with their proselytizing and their roving Mitzvah Tanks. What most troubled her was how Hasidic men treated their women: the professional matchmakers, the mandatory *sheitels*, the long dresses with long sleeves, the obligation to give your husband twelve or fifteen children, the rumored hole in the bedsheet. Iris didn't know quite what to make of Lazar. Which seemed fine by Lazar, who kept shifting his weight uncomfortably from one wing tip to the other.

We agreed to meet at his house for lunch, sometime in the early afternoon. "Don't worry about the time. When you get there, you get there," Lazar said with a shrug of his shoulders.

We said good-bye and went off to the parade. The two big events were a bed-racing competition and a cinnamon roll bake-off. The locals hauled out their lawn chairs, set them up along the parade route, and in the strong June sun, some women opened parasols. At noon, farmers rolled up and down Lawler Street in their twelve-gear tractors. Four-H kids ("thinking head, feeling heart, skilled hands, strong health") strutted with ribbon-festooned heifers, goats, hogs, and sheep. The high school marching band played "YMCA" by the Village People, and from atop a float, the Republican Party band blasted a rousing rendition of "Louie, Louie." County politicians handed out pencils, miniature American flags, and refrigerator magnets. They shook as many hands as they could and even kissed a few babies. (I could only imagine what a Hasid would do if a *goyisher* politician tried that on one of their babies.) Sitting with her court high atop a float, the newly crowned Dairy Princess, wearing a pink gown and white gloves that came up to her elbows, waved to everyone as though she were Miss America.

After the parade, we changed our clothes for Bielke's upcoming lunch. Iris was in a quandary. She didn't have a kerchief and certainly wasn't about to cut her hair, which stretched down to the middle of her back. The Kamzoil family would have to get used to what a modern woman looked like.

CHAPTER 15

Matchmaking

Just as I was about to press the buzzer to Lazar's house, I jerked back my hand. To press the buzzer on the Sabbath would be an unpardonable sin, akin to driving or doing business. I knocked on the screen door, and within seconds, this time, Bielke appeared. She nodded at me coolly, but smiled welcomingly at Iris and Mikey. Without being told, Mikey and I picked up *kippot* from a table near the door and put them on our heads, once again transforming ourselves into Moishe and Shlomo. Yussel and Mikey exchanged high fives and ran to the backyard to play. But the girls, Hodel and Chava, wearing puff-sleeved dresses with white collars and white tights, stood paralyzed, holding each other's hands. They couldn't take their eyes off Iris.

"Those are very pretty dresses," Iris offered, getting down on her knees. "How old are you two?" The girls didn't answer. They peered at Iris for several more seconds, and then ran away, giggling hysterically.

With a wave of her hand, Bielke ushered us into her dining room, and we took seats around the table. "Yussel, Hodel, Chava!" Bielke called out. "Come."

In an instant, they ran back into the dining room, but chose to sit as far away from Iris as possible. Lazar made a point of having Mikey sit next to him. Bielke brought out the meal of the day, *cholent,* a traditional stew prepared on Friday that cooks by simmering overnight. We ate the beef and vegetable dish and drank red wine as Lazar again took center stage.

Lazar was paying special attention to Mikey. What better opportunity was there than this to spark a Hasidic interest in a seven-year-old—a boy—despite how his parents had raised him? Mikey sat transfixed by Lazar's lengthy rendition of Moses being cast off in a basket as a baby. Mikey was grilled on stories from the Torah and played the dutiful student, which seemed to please Lazar immensely.

When the conversation switched to the shul, Iris mentioned a recent bar mitzvah we had attended at an Orthodox synagogue in Los Angeles, where the men and women were not allowed to sit together. The shul had been by divided sheets stitched together, *mechitzah,* which afforded the women a side view of the bar mitzvah boy. The boy's own mother, sisters, aunts, and grandmothers were shunted to one side of the synagogue, barely able to see their little boy become a man. Iris thought such discrimination was terrible.

"But that's how it should be," volunteered Bielke, speaking slowly, at first not quite sure of herself. "Whenever women are introduced into a situation, it invites an element of sexual attraction. It would interfere with the men praying." Lazar nodded approvingly. Hasidic rules governing *kol isha,* women's voices, prohibit men, other than a husband, from hearing a woman singing and, at times, even speaking.

Such prohibitions made Catholicism sound like a guilt-free ride in a convertible with the top down. The Hasidim could treat their women like inferiors, bargain ruthlessly, renege on financial agreements, snub their neighbors, do whatever they rationalized as acceptable—all in the name of religion. Looking at Bielke across the table, I was perturbed that Jews—my people—could be so mired in a closed system of such misogynistic customs. Bielke was extolling a practice that oppressed her all the more, like a prisoner thankfully defending the guards, the warden, and the prison.

"How does introducing a woman to a situation necessarily invite sexual attraction?" I asked Bielke. "Doesn't that depend on the particular woman and man?"

There was a pause. Bielke seemed taken aback. So did Lazar. Iris didn't know where I was going. Mikey's eyes got big. Hodel, Chava, and Yussel looked over to their father.

"What you're really saying," I continued, "is that a man doesn't have enough willpower or concentration to pray if women are present, that he's powerless to control his urges. Do you really believe that? These aren't biblical times. This is 1996, for goodness' sakes!"

Bielke smiled uncomfortably, not wanting to go further into any of this. I was a renegade Jew in the eyes of Lazar and Bielke, too far out to be reeled in. Iris looked alarmed and from across the table shot me a pointed look that said, "Watch what you say."

The children peered my way, then back at Lazar. There was silence. We would get nowhere with this topic, and everyone knew it. Lazar was allowed his harangues, as were Sholom and the other Lubavitcher men. But when an outsider spoke up, the world skidded to a stop.

We were at a standstill, until Bielke abruptly changed the subject. "What do you do with your days while Moishe is at school?" she asked Iris.

When Iris said she was a law student, Bielke's response was immediate. "Lazar would make a wonderful attorney," she said, smiling beatifically at her husband, redirecting the conversation back to Lazar, ending any more talk with me or the she-devil who forayed outside the home.

Bielke's remark led Lazar to go on a jag about a notorious crime in 1978 in Crown Heights when an elderly Hasidic man who after leaving the Shul one Friday night, was stabbed by youths from the surrounding neighborhood. Lazar said the Hasidic man crawled back to synagogue, pushed open the doors, and yelled "*Shvartzer!*" (a derogatory term for a black person, from the German *schwarz* for "black"). Ultimately, the man died from injuries sustained in the mugging. "You ever want to get the attention of a hallful of Jews, don't yell 'Fire!' or 'Help.' '*Shvartzer!*' will do it just fine."

Lazar laughed and Bielke smiled, as Iris and I glanced at each other. Lazar went on to recount the story of Hasidic Jews who, in retaliation, surrounded neighborhood blacks in Brooklyn and pelted them with stones. Like many Hasidim, Lazar made no point in concealing his dislike of "the niggers," as he called them. They were not only the *goyim,* they were black—two of the worst characteristics that anyone could possess.

Lazar's reference to *shvartzers* bought back a memory from long ago. During the summers I spent in Miami Beach as a boy, my grandparents automatically referred to blacks as *shvartzers,* as did millions of American Jews at the time, and as some American Jews still do. When I got a whopper of a tan once, my grandmother laughingly said, "Stevie, you're so black you look like a little *shvartzer!*" Another time, Grandma Rose told me that "the *shvartzeh*" was coming.

"Who's *that*?" I asked.

"You know, the cleaning lady," she replied.

It wasn't until I got home at the end of the summer that my parents set me straight. "That's a very bad word," my mother told me. "And if I ever hear you saying that again, I'll wash your mouth out with soap."

My parents may have harbored prejudice, but they certainly never talked about it, not even, I think, between themselves. To use slurs directed at other ethnics was plain wrong. They had heard slurs like *kike* their whole lives. They knew about restricted country clubs and hotels, quota systems at universities and companies, neighborhood covenants that prohibited Jews from buying homes. They weren't about to continue the tradition. Back at the dinner table in Postville, I suddenly felt like my mother. I didn't want *my* son to learn and ever use a word like *shvartzer.*

But why should Lazar be governed by my rules? Hasidic Jews *were* a separate culture. They lived apart and wanted to remain apart—such separatism was fundamental to their existence and to their beliefs. Lazar and Sholom had repeatedly made that clear to me. Their behavior followed the rules of their community—governed by its social mores, helped along by whatever they wanted to cite from the Torah, Talmud, and the Rebbe to justify their actions. *Shvartzer* to the Hasidim was as benign a word as *goy*. Used as code, it amounted to innocuous shoptalk, like a waiter telling a short-order cook, "BLT to travel, hold the mayo."

At the *Shabbos* table, the conversation moved from *shvartzers* to other stereotypes. Bielke said she had a difficult time telling Iowa women apart. "When they get old, they all have the same haircut—short and a curly permanent. They really all look alike. It's the strangest thing." If Bielke had a hard time telling *them* apart, how could the locals tell the Jews apart? I thought of saying that, but I just listened and smiled.

Lazar poured more red wine into our crystal goblets. After several Hebrew benedictions, Lazar returned to the discussion he and I had had in his backyard—rules of commerce. "I get bills and throw them away," he said merrily. "The more bills I get, the faster I throw them away. If they want to get paid that badly, they'll send me another notice, and then another. When *I'm* ready to pay them, I pay them!" Lazar's monologue confirmed everything the locals had said about the Postville Hasidim.

Eager to change the subject, I asked Lazar how he and Bielke met. Maybe this would steer us clear of controversy. Lazar leaned back and smiled. Bielke sat primly in her chair, a Mona Lisa smile on her face. *"This* was a story," Lazar said, looking smug. "I was in my early twenties, living in New York, when my uncle called my father and said he had an excellent girl for me. He gave me her name, and I said, 'Let me do my homework, and I'll get back to you.' So I called her neighbors, friends, relatives, investigated who the parents were, where they came from, till I came to the conclusion that this was the type of person I was looking for. So I called my father and said 'yes.'

"So he called my uncle, and my uncle calls the girl's father, and they worked out a time for us to meet. So I fly up to Montreal from New York, never seen this girl before, but it all somehow seemed right to me. We were going to meet in front of my cousin's house in Montreal. I got dressed up in my best suit and a tie. I knew this was going to be an important day in my life, and I wanted to remember it.

"So, at the time we were to meet, Bielke and her father arrived, and he introduced us. Then the father left. He didn't take an extra second. He just took a hike. I remember she wore a cream-colored winter coat, a maxi-length coat. It was a knockout, custom-made coat. Under it, she wore a blue dress with red trim and boots. They were classy boots. I was impressed she didn't come laden with jewelry. She wasn't flashy, but she was elegant. A real knockout."

Bielke smiled, but said nothing.

"We went to the Queen Elizabeth Hotel and sat down in the lobby and we talked. We talked for about eight hours. It was amazing. My first reaction was that she was sure of herself. We got straight to the point of whether we had the same focus in life, the same goals, what aspirations we had, what we could live without, what things were most important, what kind of home we wanted to set up. I guess you could say we talked about marriage.

"I drove her back at four A.M. But I didn't ask her then if she wanted to go out with me again. I didn't want to put her on the spot. I did, though, call her uncle, and he asked, '*Nu?*'

"I said I was interested in pursuing it. So my uncle called her father, and it was decided that there was mutual interest. We arranged to meet for a second night, at my cousin's house this time, who was out of town. This time, her mother brought her, but her mother didn't take a hike very fast. I had prepared a *nosherie* at the table. The mother left ten minutes later, and then I hear someone opening up the front door, and it was my cousin, who had come back unexpectedly. He said, 'What the hell is happening here?' But I guess he figured out fast since he made a U-turn and took off.

"The third night, we took a drive downtown to the Bonaventure Hotel in Montreal, at the top, which has a revolving restaurant, and ordered cocktails, but no food. She drank soda, and I had a rum and Coke. That night we sat for about six hours. We talked about our lives some more. I learned about her job—she was a teacher at a girls' day school—and then I asked her if she wanted to meet another night, and she said yes."

Bielke continued her Mona Lisa smile, sitting upright like a coquettish girl.

"On the fourth night, we went back to the Queen Elizabeth Hotel, and by the end of the night, I asked her a stupid question, 'What if I were to ask you whether you'd like to marry me?'

"And she answered, 'If I were to hear that question from you, the answer probably would be yes.' So, I took a deep breath, and I asked her, and she answered yes.

"We immediately went back then to my cousin's house, and we both wrote separate letters to the Rebbe, asking whether he agreed with us, and for his blessing. Bielke signed hers and sealed it in an envelope. I took her letter with me, but before I left Montreal, I knew I was in trouble"—Lazar, at this point, raised his eyebrows in a Groucho Marx imitation—"because she asked me to call her as soon as I arrived in New York, just to make sure I got there safely."

"Was there something wrong with that?" Bielke asked, in mock protest, from across the dining-room table.

"That's when I knew you had your hooks in me for good!"

"Oh, Lazar," Bielke said teasingly. "You're going to give them the wrong impression."

Lazar shushed Bielke and went on with his story. "So, I gave the letters to the Rebbe's secretary the next morning. He had never met my people, but he had supernatural abilities, even if he didn't know the person. He's like a prophet, like he knows more about the person than the person knows about himself. That same day, I got a call from the Rebbe's secretary, saying that the Rebbe had already responded to the letters, and that he approved of the marriage.

"Then we congratulated ourselves via long distance."

It wasn't much of a fairy tale, more like a business contract, with the intervention of parents, uncles, cousins, and a Supreme Being who put his stamp of approval on the marriage, even though he had never met the betrothed. But for reasons known to Lazar and Bielke, the marriage seemed to work. There was a division of labor, a sense of commitment that each shared for the other, and seven children to keep them busy.

The breezes coming through the open windows now had died down, and the air suddenly seemed still and oppressive in the house. Mikey, Yussel, Chava, and Hodel were getting fidgety. Iris kicked me under the table. We needed to go; we wanted to get back to Iowa City that evening.

The moment seemed like a natural place to break. Lazar said he wanted to get back to the shul before sundown, and Bielke had already gotten up, clearing the table with Iris's help. At the door, Iris smiled and nodded to Lazar. Again, he seemed nervous and avoided looking at her. I shook Lazar's hand. Bielke, in the breezy manner to which I had grown accustomed, said, "Good *Shabbos.*" Mikey and Yussel exchanged one last high five. Before we left Lazar's house, Mikey and I removed our *kippot* and left them on the table next to the door.

Once again, leaving the big brick house on West Williams Street brought a sense of relief. We were free from the stifling rules, prescribed rituals, mandatory list of dos and don'ts. We could get back to our own lives, lives that *we* controlled, or at least, tried to control. But I also felt sorrow, perhaps a sense of yearning. I wasn't sure if my reaction was about the opportunities Lazar, Bielke, and their children never would experience or whether it was regret that my family would never be so single-mindedly devoted to a cause we could so earnestly believe in. However foreign their lives were to me, Lazer and his family had found their life's purpose.

If Iris and I had gone to the devil, it was done already, but my lingering doubt was about Mikey—that by choosing to raise him, as the Hasidim would have put it, in *goyisher* Iowa, we had isolated him from the urban stimulation of art, culture, and lively conversation, that somehow we had done him wrong. Not to mention isolating him from the wonderful world of Jews, all kinds of Jews, who talked fast, who were able to juggle angst, anxiety, success, failure, and guilt, with aplomb.

Walking back to Rosalyn Krambeer's house, Mikey suddenly stopped in his tracks. He was exhausted. The rapid-fire give-and-take, Lazar's soliloquy about his courtship with Bielke, had been too much for Mikey. Iris picked him up, and within five steps, he was asleep in her arms, legs wrapped around her hips. We laid him on our bed back at the Old Shepherd House, as Iris started packing. As had been the case the last time I was in Postville, there was too much to digest from the day, and I didn't mean just the food. The wine had left me hazy, so I took a walk, back to Lawler Street.

Despite their many differences, there were similarities between the Jews and the Postville locals. The Jews paraded with regal, unbearable gall in look-at-me clothing; they maintained slavish devotion to faith. But they also loved their children and seemed to love one another. They looked after each other in their community. The men seemed to be good providers; the women, devoted mothers and homemakers. Was the story of Bielke and Lazar's arranged marriage all that different really from how the locals went about marrying their young? Wasn't the idea in both cultures to consolidate families and property? Glancing through the society pages of the *Herald-Leader,* I could see that it was an unusual bride and groom who weren't from the three-county area of northeastern Iowa. In most local marriages, the families of the bride and groom had known each other for years and had sanctioned their children's union. The Jews were just more up-front about it, usually hiring professionals to make the match. Wasn't that the same as what some busy, successful people in cities even do?

I must have still been tipsy from all the wine. Walking alone on the streets of Postville, I started singing softly from *Fiddler on the Roof.*

> Matchmaker, Matchmaker,
> Make me a match,
> Find me a find,
> Catch me a catch.
> Night after night in the dark I'm alone,
> So find me a match
> Of my own.

For the Postville locals, matchmaking as well as marriage, too, had its roots in religion. The Lutheran church sought to encourage boys and girls of the same faith to marry one another. When girls and boys start dating in rural high schools and then marrying, their unions were religiously, socially, and familially sanctioned, just as the marriages of the Hasidic Jews were. That's why there were so many Schlees, Schlitters, Schmeltzers, Schmitts, Schroeders, Schultes, Schultzes, and

Schuttes in this northeast corner of Iowa. Just about everyone was related to everyone else. The community was as inbred as that of the Hasidim. There, of course, was an underlying difference between how the Hasidim and the local Lutherans went about perpetuating their respective faiths: With the Lutherans, while certain relationships were endorsed by eager parents, if their children married outside the fold, it might anger their families, but the offending couple seldom would be ostracized or shunned as the Hasidim were apt to do. The stakes in marriage, as they were in everything else, were higher for the Hasidic Jews.

I was sobering up as the sun started to set. Daylight was quickly turning into dusk, the time of day I've loved most ever since I was a little boy. The corn, as golden as could be, did strange things to the day's last rays of light. As the sun dipped to the horizon, its rays grew longer and longer, covering acres and acres of fields.

Suddenly, my reverie was broken. Someone was tugging at my arm. It was Moishe Tamarin, the blue-eyed *shochet* from the slaughterhouse's killroom, who had invited me to join him in the bloody pit. "We must hurry," Moishe said in his thick Russian accent, tightening his grip on my arm and pulling me while he ran. "We need to get to shul. We have no time."

"No. I can't go to shul tonight. My family is here. I'm going back to my home."

"*This* is your home. We go to shul together." Moishe squeezed my arm harder. "Let's go. We must hurry if we intend to get to shul on time."

I turned to look at him, and his eyes caught mine, just as they had in the slaughterhouse. There was something about the slightly crossed, watery blue eyes that was mesmerizing. They locked on to my eyes and wouldn't let go.

"No!" I said, breaking his hypnotic stare. "I'm not going to the shul. *Leave me alone!*"

Moishe looked puzzled. Then he smiled knowingly, in almost an angelic way, and released my arm. "I must go then," he said.

My eyes followed Moishe, his long waistcoat flapping, his shoulders moving back and forth, right to left. He took quick, small steps, his Borsalino bobbing. He raced past Greene, Tilden, then Military Road, until in the distance, he disappeared.

CHAPTER 16

The Crime

Two years after my first trip to Postville, the locals were still in limbo: Make a separate peace with the Jews or vote yes in the annexation referendum, which the state had finally approved and set for the first week in August. If the referendum passed and the Hasidim left town, then no one could say that the locals had pushed the Jews out. If the referendum passed and the Jews stayed, then Sholom's bluster would have been just what the locals had figured it was all along: a scare tactic to intimidate them. And if the referendum failed, then the Jews were more popular than the guys at Ginger's had ever imagined, and they deserved to stay in Postville and do whatever they wanted.

Perhaps in another state with another set of locals, the story might have played out differently. Other townspeople might have tried to scare the Hasidim into leaving. There might have been truly ugly incidents of anti-Semitism. But the Postville locals were too decent or docile to resort to anything like that. Couldn't the Hasidim understand that the locals weren't hungry wolves about to eat them, as Rabbi

Feller had made all gentiles out to be? Most all of them were honest, plain, decent folks. Maybe they were wary of the Jews, but some of the Jews' actions merited wariness.

The problem, as I saw it, was that although the locals might have been right about the atrocious behavior of some of the Postville Jews, not a few of the locals began using this behavior to generalize about all Jews. At least that's what Cliff and Ida Mae Olson, Toey Kelly, Ralph Gustafson, and William Erickson had told me. Some of the locals were beginning to weave stories about Jews everywhere, based on what they saw happening under their noses with just the Hasidim. Stanley Schroeder, however a noble historian he was, couldn't be everywhere, patrolling what the locals were saying about Jews. And, look what happened to Reverend Chuck Miller—that is, should you choose to believe Ralph Gustafson. When Reverend Miller started preaching tolerance to his congregation about the Jews, many parishioners complained and Miller left his pulpit. Some of the locals did what seemed natural—they extrapolated, they generalized. All Jews were greedy, all Jews bargained, all Jews reneged on their agreements. Not counting a couple of *Seinfeld* episodes on TV, to most of the locals, their experience with Jews had been pretty much limited to the Hasidim who had come to Postville. There might have been a single exception, and that was Doc Wolf, the Jewish physician, whom I was to learn about.

Since my first trip, I had traveled to Postville more than three dozen times, each time going deeper into the relationship between the Hasidim and the locals, all the while trying to figure out where I fit in. It wasn't until my eighth or tenth trip that I came to believe that there was something awry about the Postville Hasidim, and the more time I spent in Postville, the more I became convinced of a subtext that no one wanted to talk about. It was something palpable, something I could sense. To the casual visitor, Postville was a veritable *shtetl* on the prairie, a remarkable outpost of ultra-orthodox Jews. The Hasidic mission in Postville went something like this: The Jews were hardworking, deeply religious men and women who had come to Postville to fulfill a kind of biblical destiny. These Hasidic pioneers had fanned out to the territories to provide fellow Jews with a sacred spiritual commodity. In the process of performing the holy task of *kashered* meat and poultry, the Hasidim had fashioned a community of families with the three basic obligations of religious life: *mikveh*, shul, yeshiva. The choice of Postville was a rerun of Moses leading his flock, following God's holy command-ment. Aaron Rubashkin was a modern-day Moses; his sons, Sholom and Heshy, were Gershom and Eliezer; Lazar Kam-zoil was his most trusted ally, Joshua.

But the more time I spent in Postville, the more I began to suspect that I was getting a filtered, sanitized version of the truth. I wasn't surprised; that's what happens whenever an outsider seeks access to a family, whether the outsider is a fu-ture son-in-law or a stranger asking questions. Whenever I questioned the Hasidim's prescribed version, the answers al-ways wove back to the same standbys: the evils of annexation and assimilation, the wonders of Israel and the Chosen People, the supreme Rebbe. It seemed as though Sholom had made sure that the only Jews I came in contact with were up-standing members of the local community, people like Lazar Kamzoil or Moishe Tamarin. When I tried to meet other Jews at either the slaughterhouse or the shul, it was a replay of my phone conversation with Martin Appel two years earlier. The

Hasidim were guarded, seemingly scared to talk to me. I sensed that Sholom or Lazar had warned them about me.

The Hasidim didn't need me poking into their business, and there were good reasons to be protective. Agriprocessors was a privately held corporation, owned solely by the Rubashkin family, and as such had no public stockholders, no one to whom they had to be accountable. Agriprocessors was an immensely profitable, dirty business that kept rolling along, raking in more and more money from observant Jews around the world. Healthy, hearty steers and chickens were in ample supply in northeast Iowa, and the slaughterhouse, while antiquated and small compared with mega-operations like IBP or Empire, had far surpassed the Rubashkins' wildest expectations.

If there was a problem at Agriprocessors, it wasn't in procuring animals, it was in attracting and maintaining a pool of reliable labor. The slaughterhouse had a voracious appetite for a never-ending supply of workers. The burly, unemployed guys who drank too much at Club 51 or around the corner at the Horseshoe Lounge would do fine for hauling and deboning sides of the richly marbled beef, as long as they could hold down a job and stay sober at the same time. Most were unskilled laborers who welcomed the money, and some even enjoyed the hard, physical work. The other group of unskilled laborers at the plant were Russian and Ukrainian immigrants like Leonid and Pasha who happily gravitated to Postville for menial jobs that started out at six dollars an hour.

But the locals and gentile foreigners could do only so much at a kosher slaughterhouse. A sixth of all employees at Agriprocessors had to be Jews, skilled in the arcane rules and practices of *shechita,* the rules of kasrut. *Shochtem* were regarded as holy men in the Hasidic community, but the mitz-vah of transforming the hearty Midwestern steers into hot dogs, briskets, and flanken went only so far. Slitting the throats of steers or soaking tens of thousands of dead chickens in salt vats wasn't work that appealed to many Hasidim. What kind of city-bred Hasid would want to chuck everything to move to Iowa to work in a grimy, bloody slaughterhouse?

Gelt—money—was the answer. To feed the never-ending need for more and more Hasidic workers, the Rubashkins had to find and transport scores of Jewish slaughterers into *goy-isher* Iowa. Sholom paid their plane fares from Brooklyn to La Crosse, Rochester, or Minneapolis, and then sent Cliff Olson in his big Olds 88 to meet them at the airport and chauffeur them down to Postville. A *shochet* at Agripro-cessors could make as much as fifty, sixty thousand dollars a year—with hardly any expenses. And that didn't include the bonuses—incentive pay for overtime before the Jewish holi-days, plane tickets back to Brooklyn, a room atop the shul, an apartment or a house owned by the Rubashkins, cut-rate prices on anything the slaughterhouse processed. On payday each week, the Hasidim stashed their money away in Jim Lage's Citizens Bank or sent it in postal orders back home. Some Hasidic slaughterers would come for a year, others for six months or for a summer. Some, like Lazar, brought their families and lived in big houses and would stay for years. All isolated themselves from the *goyisher* killfloor workers. They spoke in Hebrew or Yiddish. They had a separate break room that the gentiles were prohibited from entering.

But *gelt* was only part of the reason for taking the de-manding jobs. Many workers were in flux, confused over their next stage in life. Some were questioning their spiritual commitment to the rigors of Hasidism. Others were escaping painful divorces; some were vagabonds unwilling to settle down. Many came to the wilderness of Iowa to find themselves; others came to the remote Midwestern plains to hide. To these men, Postville wasn't a Garden of Eden, as Lazar had once described it. Instead, Postville was more like Siberia, a place where Hasidim came and went, working monotonous, mind-numbing jobs around the clock.

Almost all had spent their entire lives in either Crown Heights or another Hasidic enclave, constricted by family, religion, and obligation. A stint in Iowa brought with it an intoxicating dose of freedom, a break in the rigid order of Hasidism. In Postville, these Hasidim had absolutely no responsibility, other than to show up for their rote jobs at the meatpacking plant. No Aunt Sadie, the *shadchen,* matchmaker, trying to fix them up with nice girls from good families, no rabbis drilling into their ears complicated passages from the Mishnah or Gemara. The amount of freedom was more than most of them would likely ever have again in their lifetimes. To these Hasidic men, Postville was the last breath before a lifelong commitment to a wife and a city apartment full of children born one after another.

One man who came to Postville was a Jewish Vietnam War veteran, who everyone in Agriprocessors simply called the "knife freak" because of his habit of viciously slashing and stabbing the beef carcasses. Another was a fanatic who became maniacally obsessive in his unyielding demand that the salt in the salting vat penetrate to each and every crevice of meat carcass, as strictly required by rules of *kashrut* processing. Another drawn to Postville was a blustery, charismatic rabbi who, uncharacteristically for a Jew and a rabbi, was an expert marksman.

The Hasidim were faceless lookalikes to the locals, bearded men in black who came and went, but the names of two were burned into every mind in Postville—Jew and gentile alike. Phillip Stillman was a tough, street-smart con man with a ready smile, who without provocation would fly into a rage. Pinchas Lew was a lean, ascetic rabbinical student who looked the role of a Hasidic intellectual: bookish, crooked wire-rim glasses, pale skin, a sparse beard. These men were drawn to each other, each seeking refuge in the other. Both were restless, looking for action in a place with none.

In September 1991, Stillman and Lew went on what passed in small-town Iowa as a crime spree. In northeast Iowa, where missing a taillight on your pickup was as bad as crime gets, Stillman and Lew's offenses were the equivalent of "wilding." With Lew driving the getaway car, Stillman robbed a popcorn vendor at gunpoint and, forty-five minutes later, shot at point-blank range a forty-nine-year-old convenience-store clerk, who, to this day still carries the .38-caliber slug in her spine.

Several locals told me that I needed to learn about Stillman and Lew, but no one would talk about their crime. Stanley Schroeder, who seemed to know everything about Postville, confessed he knew hardly anything about the pair. Sharon Drahn shrugged her shoulders, as did Cliff and Ida Mae Olson. Leigh Rekow said Stillman and Lew had gotten into a heap of trouble, but he didn't know anything more than what he had read in the newspapers. Other locals seemed reticent to say anything about the pair.

When I asked the Postville Jews about Stillman and Lew, they flatly refused to discuss them. Lazar quickly shook his head. "I don't know anything about those guys, but why would you want to go into *that*, anyway?" he asked, looking suspiciously over his glasses. When I asked Sholom about the pair, his eye narrowed into slits. "Bunch of rotten apples," Sholom said, with a quick, dismissive flick of his right hand as though shooing away a fly.

In the late afternoon of Friday, September 27, 1991, Pinchas Lew, dressed in jeans, a T-shirt, black Reeboks, and a red string necklace, stuck a blue New York Yankees baseball cap over his yarmulke, just as the Sabbath was about to begin. Phillip Stillman wore a long-sleeved white cotton shirt, jeans, a green Army fatigue jacket, and black Nikes. To observers, the two were going out to celebrate: Lew had just turned twenty-two years old.

Stillman and Lew met at the shul on Lawler Street and got into one of the clunkers parked in the driveway—a rusted 1986 black Oldsmobile without a front grille. With Lew driving, the two men stopped at Casey's on Tilden Street to buy two forty-ounce bottles of Old Style beer. Stillman and Lew then headed northwest on Highway 52 to Ossian (population: 810). Somewhere along the way, Lew stopped the car. Either he or Stillman got out, unscrewed the Oldsmobile's Iowa license plates from their frames, and placed the plates on the floor in the backseat.

In downtown Ossian, Lew pulled up to Brockman's Grocery, and Stillman went in. He opened the cooler, got out a six-pack of Budweiser, and placed it on the checkout counter. Cashier Vicky Svendsen glanced suspiciously at Stillman. She knew just about everyone who ever came into the store. Stillman looked like he probably was twenty-one, but he was so short, no more than five foot five inches tall. Better card him. Instead of a driver's license, Stillman produced from the front pocket of his Army jacket a green passport from a foreign country. When Stillman tried to put the passport back in his jacket pocket, Vicky noticed he kept fumbling, missing the pocket.

With the six-pack, Stillman returned to the car, parked in front of Mane Street Styles, the beauty parlor in Ossian.

On East Main Street, Stillman got out and approached a sixty-six-year-old retired high school teacher by the name of Albert Tinderholt, who was working at Uncle Frank's Popcorn Stand in front of the Laundromat in town. Lew stayed in the Oldsmobile, gunning the engine.

"Give me all your money," Stillman said to a startled Tinderholt.

Tinderholt couldn't believe his ears. "I looked at him, you know surprised and startled, and I thought, 'Gosh, is this a holdup? Here in Ossian?'"

When Tinderholt hesitated, Stillman moved closer. "I got a gun. Give me all your fucking money!" Stillman pulled a .357-caliber Colt revolver ever so slightly out from his right pants pocket, so that Tinderholt could see the gun's brown wooden butt.

"Dig out that change and put it in my hand," Stillman said in a low no-nonsense voice. As Tinderholt scooped up the silver, he got so nervous he started dropping coins. "Pick it up, and put it in my hand and hurry up!" Stillman ordered. "Now take out your fucking billfold and give it to me."

All during the stickup, Tinderholt was struck by how calm Stillman seemed. "After he robbed me, he walked back to the car, got in, and the car drove away at just a kind of normal rate of speed, like they were in no hurry. I was a little surprised at that; I figured they would tear out of there." The entire robbery took no more than two minutes.

Tinderholt ran into the middle of Main Street to see if

he could spot the license plate but saw there was none. He raced over to Becker's Hardware store and told Ron Becker about the robbery. Becker called the Ossian Police Department and when no one answered, he dialed the sheriff's office in Decorah.

Meanwhile, Stillman and Lew drove farther north, this time on a bumpy county road that took them to Decorah, where Stillman walked into the Petro-n-Provisions convenience store on Montgomery Street, next to Mom's Diner. It was 6:00 P.M. With Lew in the car, Stillman went to the cooler with all the deli sandwiches in it and took one out. The clerk, Marion Bakken, thought that Stillman was "kinda checking out the store, walking around. I didn't know what he was up to." After a couple of minutes, Stillman brought a sandwich to the counter and asked how much it was.

"Two dollars and ten cents," Bakken said matter-of-factly.

Stillman checked his pockets and slapped two dollar bills on the Formica countertop. Bakken said he still owed her ten cents. Stillman put the sandwich down on the counter next to the two dollars and went back to the car.

When he returned, he was wearing the jacket, which seemed strange to Bakken. The late-September evening was balmy. Fall had officially begun just five days earlier, and the temperature was in the mid-seventies.

Stillman stood directly in front of Bakken at the counter and leaned toward her. "I want all of your money in the cash register," he told Bakken her quietly.

At first, Bakken thought this runty kid with greasy black hair was playing a prank on her. She cocked her head and placed both palms on the counter. "Are you kidding?" she asked with a half smile, as though Stillman was about to say with a big grin, "Gotcha!"

But Stillman reached into his jacket pocket and pulled out the .357. He pointed the gun directly at Bakken, holding it at waist level with his elbow tucked in near his side. "This is no joke. This is for real. Give me all your fucking money!"

Bakken had never heard such language before. What took her breath away, though, was the gun. To Bakken, it looked like a cannon.

As Bakken turned to open the register with her left hand, she managed to press the button to a newly installed silent-alarm system under the counter. At that instant, Stillman's index finger slid to the gun's trigger and squeezed it. The weapon discharged a bullet that first grazed the countertop, then ripped into Bakken's torso, traveling through her liver and her right kidney. The bullet never exited Bakken's body, and lodged in the third lumbar vertebra of her spine.

"I felt like someone hit me in the side with a baseball bat," Bakken said later. "I couldn't get my breath and my right leg went numb. I locked my legs so I wouldn't fall down, and I leaned on the counter. I thought if I went down, I'd never get up."

Stillman quickly walked out the front door, still holding the gun at waist level. Marlys Cook, who had been waiting in the parking lot for her husband, heard the gunshot and saw Stillman leave the P-n-P.

"What have you DONE?" she screamed at Stillman.

Stillman got in the Olds, and with Lew at the wheel, the two drove away, again at a speed of less than twenty-five miles per hour. One of the customers at the P-n-P, Tor Roppe, ran out to see if he could spot the license-plate number. Marlys Cook dialed 911 from inside the P-n-P, as Tor Roppe grabbed a towel from behind the counter and put pressure on Bakken's ribcage. By now, the purple Jordache sweatshirt Bakken was wearing was soaked. She was standing in a pool of her own blood.

By seven that night, practically all of Decorah had heard about the robbery and shooting. "You don't hear a siren very often in Decorah and armed robberies are so rare in Winneshiek County that we sometimes go twenty years without one," said Karl Knudson, the county attorney whose job it was to put Stillman and Lew behind prison bars.

Immediately, the Decorah police mobilized. Dave Naeseth, a Decorah police officer on duty, spotted Stillman and Lew in the Oldsmobile and called in their location. Off-duty police chief Al Etteldorf got into a squad car with Knudson to join in the pursuit, as did police captains Robert Ward and Warren Leeps.

It was a slow-speed chase that lasted no more than ten minutes. Two miles past Trout Run, outside the city limits, Naeseth turned on the flashing red light atop his squad car and forced the Oldsmobile onto the gravel shoulder. Surrounded by four police officers with their guns drawn, Stillman reached out his car window and feebly turned over a can of Budweiser, emptying it. That was pretty funny, the officers thought. Driving in a car with an open container was the least of Stillman and Lew's worries.

Meanwhile, Marion Bakken had been transferred via helicopter from the local hospital to a larger medical center in Rochester, Minnesota, ninety miles north. Physicians in the trauma unit decided against removing the .38-caliber slug for fear that it would further damage her spinal cord. The doctors told Bakken to expect excruciating lower-back pain and chronic headaches, but she would be able to walk.

At the Decorah police station, Stillman's hands were

swabbed for gunpowder residue; the test came out positive, indicating he had recently fired a gun. Stillman waived his Miranda rights and confessed to the crime, saying Lew had encouraged him to commit the two robberies. He said the gun used in the shooting belonged to Lew. For his part, Lew refused to say anything. When asked to acknowledge that the officers had read him his Miranda rights, Lew refused to sign the affidavit, citing the Hasidic prohibition against writing on the Sabbath. Police thought that was a good one: This man had been involved in two robberies and an attempted murder, but he couldn't pick up a pen or a pencil because his religion prohibited it.

The case against Stillman was straightforward. There were at least four witnesses to the P-n-P robbery. Once charged, Stillman was held in the Winneshiek County Jail in lieu of $200,000 bond. Four months after the crime, Stillman pleaded guilty to attempted murder and first-degree robbery. He received the maximum penalty: fifty years in prison.

The case against Lew was more complicated. Lew spent thirty-two days in the county jail before he was released on cash bond. Two checks, each for $100,000, were made out on a bank account from Ezrat Israel, Inc., a not-for-profit corporation located in an apartment house a few doors down from the Lubavitchers' world headquarters in Crown Heights, Brooklyn. An affidavit filed with the court said that the money had "been collected from various friends, relatives and members of the Defendant's religious order."

Observant Jews are compelled to post bail that will allow a fellow Jew "imprisoned unjustly" to be released. Called in Hebrew *pidyon shevuyim,* the "ransom of captives" is a particular obligation of the Hasidic community. The dictum is so strong that a person who delays "the fulfillment of this duty and causes an undue prolongation of his fellow Jew's imprisonment is regarded as if he has spilled his blood," according to the Halakah, the code of Jewish law. Such a sacred obligation should have made for the speedy release of both Stillman and Lew. But *pidyon shevuyim* benefited only Lew.

That Lew was able to post $200,000—not merely a percentage of the bail—dumbfounded the judge who set the amount of the bond. "I never dreamed he would put up the bond," said Judge Joseph C. Keefe. "I never conceived anybody would come up with that kind of money." Lew's family hired Lawrence F. Scalise, Iowa's former attorney general and one of the state's most high-profile criminal-defense lawyers.

While awaiting trial, Lew was allowed to have kosher food prepared by the Postville Lubavitchers and served to him at the Winneshiek County jail.

For the Jewish holiday of Simchat Torah, Lew was allowed to pray in the jail for three days with his uncle, Rabbi Posner, one of the men who would raise Lew's bail.

Judge Bauch said he was struck by the solidarity that Lew's family and the community of Lubavitchers publicly displayed in the courtroom. There were so many high-powered attorneys and Hasidic *machers* in the courtroom during one of Lew's hearings that three cellular phones rang at the same time, a rarity in Decorah, Iowa, in 1992. While Lew was free on bail, awaiting sentencing, Judge Bauch allowed him to travel to Israel and England to visit his family. While on bail, Lew was introduced to his future wife, his *bashert* (destined marriage partner), and the two married while Lew was out on bond.

Lew eventually opted to accept a plea agreement of conspiracy to commit a forcible felony, which carried a maximum penalty of ten years in prison and a $10,000 fine. Michael Juergens, the county probation officer assigned to the case, recommended to Judge Bauch that Lew be sentenced to the maximum term, and Bauch formally sentenced him to spend ten years in prison.

But on March 30, 1993, in a judgment that stunned the prosecution, Judge Bauch made a complete turnaround and placed Lew on probation. All told, Lew had spent just eighty-one days in jail for a crime he was sentenced ten years to serve. Judge Bauch placed Lew on five years' probation and mandated that six months be spent at the Lubavitchers' Rabbinical College of America, in a "rehabilitation program" in Morristown, New Jersey. Lew's confinement was to be monitored by the Lubavitchers' Miami Beach–based Aleph Institute. That was to be followed by six months of "house arrest" at Lew's father-in-law's home in Brooklyn.

County prosecutor Karl Knudson couldn't believe his ears when he heard the judge's ruling. "I was outraged that the judge intervened and reconsidered the sentence," Knudson told me. "If you look at the court record, we had pretty strong evidence against Lew. There were reasons they were together. There is no way that Lew was just giving Stillman a ride that night, as was his alibi."

Jim Burns, Stillman's court-appointed attorney, also had a hard time accepting Bauch's ruling. "Lew sure got a deal. I remember thinking, 'Whoa! You've just given this guy a pass.'"

Marion Bakken seemed to be the most upset. "The whole court proceeding was like a giant slap in the face. At least Stillman apologized to me, but I never got anything from Lew, not a word."

When I asked Judge Bauch why he reversed his own sentence, Bauch said he was swayed by Lew's previous record of good citizenship. "I expected Pinchas to do very well when he got away from these elements [Stillman's influence]. My decision to put him on probation wouldn't have occurred if he had a prior record. There were a host of balancing factors." The judge said he was "impressed by many of the Jews who came. The courtroom had a significant number of rabbis. They were very intellectual individuals."

If the crime had stunned the locals, the double standard of punishment for Stillman and Lew took their breath away. "People around here say those boys must have had an awful lot of pull to get away with damn near killing Marion Bakken, and then one of them getting paroled," said Ralph Gustafson, one of the few locals who would talk about Stillman and Lew. "If one of our boys did that, not only would the judge throw the book at him, we would, too. Seems like when a Jew does something as bad as this, then it's a whole different story." Gustafson shuddered to think what the Postville Hasidim would have done if a local boy had shot a Jewish woman.

To the locals, the Hasidim had a lot of explaining to do. The locals had welcomed the Jews to Postville—and now it seemed they were paying the price. Letting the grass on your front lawn grow ankle-high was one thing, nearly killing a forty-nine-year-old grandmother was another. For a religion that professed so many rules, Stillman and Lew's crime, at the least, had to require some kind of public acknowledgment from the Hasidic community.

Ultimately, though, how the Jews responded didn't really surprise anyone. None of the Hasidim denounced the shooting of Marion Bakken. No one apologized to her. They didn't

raise money for her. No one from the Jewish community donated anything to her as a token of their sorrow or shame.
None bothered to visit her or her family. They didn't even
offer her free meat from the slaughterhouse. The Hasidim
treated Marion Bakken the way they treated all the *goyim*.
They ignored her.

CHAPTER 17

No-Goodniks

With its towering sentry turrets and limestone arch-
ways, the Iowa Men's Reformatory in Anamosa resembled a medieval castle. Well-tended flower beds lined the
double-football-field length of the prison, and an expanse of
manicured lawns surrounded the penitentiary built in the
grand old style of nineteenth-century houses of detention. On
a sweltering August day, I sat inside a glass-walled interview
room, gathering together my notes, waiting to meet Phillip
Stillman. A guard slouched outside on a vinyl seat.

Wearing denim pants and a maroon T-shirt, Stillman
walked in and stuck out his hand, a big easy smile on his face.
He had a mass of black hair, combed straight back, and was
stocky, bulked up from weight lifting. Stillman said he had
spoken by phone to Pinchas Lew in Brooklyn the night before. Both were curious why I was interested in a solved five-
year-old crime. Stillman, after all, had confessed to forcing
Lew to drive him to Ossian, then to Decorah. Stillman had
recanted his original statement and had accepted the version
that Lew had watched helplessly as Stillman committed the

robberies and shot Marion Bakken. The misadventure had been Stillman's idea from beginning to end.

Phillip Stillman was not the Hasid I had envisioned. Born in Bogotá to a destitute woman who left him and his brother on the front steps of an orphanage, Phillip was known in Colombia as a *gamín,* a child who roamed the streets, begging for food and money. In 1974, Miriam and Nathan Stillman flew to Bogotá, appeared at the orphanage's door and had the director line up all children under age six. Miriam and Nathan picked out a half-dozen boys and girls and took them to an English-speaking physician. The Stillmans chose four children: Phillip, over his biological brother, and three other children younger than Phillip.

The Stillmans brought their ready-made family back home to Howard Beach in Queens. Nathan Stillman was in the dry-cleaning supply business—selling chemicals, hangers, rolls of plastic; Miriam, a housewife, had grown up in Tripoli and had emigrated to the United States when she was twenty. Both were observant Jews, but not Hasidim. They immediately arranged a *bris* (circumcision) and submersion in a *mikveh* so that Phillip and his brothers could be pronounced Jews. When he was nine, Phillip was sent to Lubavitcher schools. During the summers, he attended a Lubavitcher camp, Gan Israel in the Catskill Mountains, where he first met Sholom Rubashkin, a camp counselor there. At age twelve, Phillip enrolled in a Lubavitcher secondary school in Crown Heights, down the block from the Lubavitcher world headquarters. Phillip moved into a dormitory at the Lubavitcher yeshiva, but because of a raft of disciplinary problems, he was asked to leave. For a while, he lived with at least one of the Rubashkin brothers on President Street in Crown

Heights. Phillip celebrated his bar mitzvah, as is customary, in his thirteenth year. As a teenager, he grew *payot* and wore the usual Hasidic vestments—yarmulke and *tzitzit*.

But Stillman's life as a Hasid was anything but pious. In his early teens, he began drinking heavily "with the *goyim*," he told me during the prison interview. "I used to take off my yarmulke and *tzitzit*, throw them behind a bush at the Jewish school, and then leave every day. I'd go to shul on Friday night to check out the chicks, but they were upstairs. It wasn't easy." He started hanging out with two Crown Heights hoodlums from Lubavitch families—Yosef "Yossi" Gorodetsky and Nahum Leibowitz. The three were inseparable, an unrepentant trio of Hasidic *no-goodniks*.

Gorodetsky came from a long line of *machers*, deeply revered within the Lubavitch community. He had *yiches*, pedigree. Gorodetsky, like Stillman, had been adopted at an early age from a gentile family. Gorodetsky got into so much trouble during his teenage years that his adoptive parents shipped him to Israel to straighten out. Back in Brooklyn, from March 1988 to August 1990, Gorodetsky was arrested at least nine times for an assortment of crimes: criminal mischief, petty larceny, grand larceny, theft, joyriding, possession of stolen property, forgery, resisting arrest, possession of a controlled substance, possession of marijuana, harassment, criminal possession of a weapon.

The third spoke in Stillman's wheel of Lubavitcher wise guys was Leibowitz. When I contacted Leibowitz in the fall of 1996, it had been six years since he had last seen Stillman, and for the last year, Leibowitz had been working as an apprentice diamond cutter on Manhattan's Forty-seventh Street. Leibowitz waxed rhapsodic about the trio's salad days in Brooklyn. He asked that I not use his real name.

"We owned Crown Heights," Leibowitz told me. "Nobody messed with us. Not the niggers, the Puerto Ricans, the Italians—nobody messed with us. As soon as I met Phil, we clicked. Crown Heights was ours. If we wanted to rob the drug dealers, we robbed the drug dealers. The Jews, the blacks, no one fucked with us. We always were packing. You looked at us the wrong way, and you'd have a 9-mm in your face. We had everything we ever wanted. We were a gang of three, Yossi, Phil, and me. We were the mobsters in the neighborhood. We did whatever we wanted to do.

"We always had drugs with us. We had them up the ass. Yossi loved drugs. He had to get high. We used to smoke all day long. I caught Phil two or three times with a needle in his house, but Phil's problem wasn't drugs. It was alcohol. He packed vodka like water. We'd sit in his basement in Crown Heights. He never had a lock on his door, but no one ever fucked with the place. We used to shoot up his wall just for fun. Yossi was so nuts that one time we were playing with guns at his place, and Yossi was saying a .22 wouldn't do shit, and Phil and I said it would, and before we knew it, Yossi shot himself in the ass. We were nuts.

"We used to sleep all day and stay out all night. The only reason we'd get up in the daytime was to rob a couple of houses. We used to go to a house and we'd whack people over the head with a brick or hammer, brass knuckles, bare hands—you've got two hands and two feet, you used them.

"One night this Jewish guy pulls over and waves to me to come over to his car. I figure he needs directions, so I go over. But he thought I was a faggot. He asked me to suck him off. I picked up a brick and pulled him out of the car and pounded his fucking face in. Another time, Phil and me were coming home from the Village. We were at a traffic light, and maybe we were over the white line at the crosswalk or something, and it was late, and there was a guy walking in front of the car, and he knocked the hood with his hand, then cursed at me. So Phil takes a metal bat he had in the backseat and he beans the guy with the bat so hard I remember seeing parts of the guy's head come apart.

"We were three Jew boys and we wanted to get off. Once we were on the nigger side of Crown Heights. There were eight niggers, and we were two. So Yossi shouted, 'Nigger!' and they said, 'Who *you* calling nigger?' and they came at us. Yossi opened his coat, and he had a 9-mm and they backed off. That kind of shit was a daily fucking occurrence.

"We'd be hanging out on the corner, and the *frums*, Orthodox Jews, from Flatbush would come, and if someone came by and gave us a look, we'd beat the shit out of them. If anyone ever made fun of the Rebbe, I'd be like, 'Yo, don't talk that shit when I'm around,' or they'd catch a beating. Flatbush Jews would sometimes laugh at the Lubavitcher Jews and we'd brawl with them. If you disrespected someone from our turf, you passed your boundaries, you'd pay. We had a reputation to keep.

"One kid smashed a bottle on Phil's head, and he took two stitches for it. So we saw the kid one day, and he ran into his uncle's restaurant. Phil and I went in there and talked to the uncle and said the kid had to catch his beating. We could have done the kid in the deli and ruined the whole place, or do him outside, so the uncle gave up his nephew, and we took care of him."

During the late 1980s, Nathan Stillman tried to get his son away from Leibowitz and Gorodetsky. He sent Stillman on an odyssey of Lubavitch schools and rehabilitation programs. Stillman enrolled in yeshivas in Boston, Pittsburgh, and Los Angeles. He also spent time at two substance-abuse centers in Wichita and Tampa, and was hospitalized at two psychiatric facilities in the New York metropolitan area. On November 9, 1989, Stillman was arrested and charged with raping a twenty-two-year-old woman who had once worked with him at a bakery. The woman told police that Stillman had invited her to his basement apartment, then pinned her down on his bed and raped her. Although police entered into evidence the woman's bloodied underpants, Stillman denied that any physical contact ever took place and plea-bargained the charge to one count of sexual misconduct, a misdemeanor.

I traced down a neighbor in Crown Heights who knew both Stillman and Gorodetsky. He said Stillman and his friends were punks out of control. "Yossi could con his way past the dead. He and Stillman always had these shady guys coming over to his place. Gorodetsky's own father told him that someday he was going to get killed." Suddenly, the conversation switched gears. "Are you familiar with the expression, 'Vonce a *goy*, alvays a *goy*'? the neighbor asked me. "Vell, that vas the story of Gorodetsky and Stillman. They vere trouble from the very beginning. *Goys*, vhat can you do?'"

The gang of Stillman, Leibowitz, and Gorodetsky crashed in the early months of 1991. Leibowitz was sent to a rehab program, so he was out of the picture. Stillman said that Gorodetsky had gotten involved in a drug deal gone sour. In March, at least one person entered Gorodetsky's basement apartment and shot and killed the twenty-five-year-old execution-style through a pillow. Police said Gorodetsky had been dead for three or four days when his brother, Yankel, found the body in bed.

Gorodetsky's killer or killers were never caught, but his murder was a watershed in Stillman's life. Shortly after the slaying, Stillman added a third tattoo to his body, this one, etched into his shoulder, read "In Memory of Joe" (Yosef is Joseph in English). That same week, Stillman called Sholom Rubashkin, who invited him to Postville with a job offer, plane fare, and a place to live. "I was freaked. I wanted to get out of New York," Stillman told me. "If I stayed there, it was just a matter of time before I would be dead."

Stillman arrived in Postville in the summer of 1991, still on three years' probation from the sex-crime conviction. Stillman quickly found the bottom feeders of rural Iowa, insinuating himself into a ragtag group of losers who frequented biker parties, drank copious amounts of alcohol, and smoked marijuana daily. He was arrested twice for drunk driving. Within his first month, some of the Postville Hasidim thought Stillman was more trouble than any Jew could possibly be worth. One rabbi accused him of stealing coins from the shul's *pushkes*, charity boxes. Another rabbi was aghast when Stillman sneaked a *shiksa* into his room upstairs at the shul. "At first when I met the *shiksas*, I would talk to them, and they couldn't believe that I was Jewish," Stillman told me. "They asked me where my hat was. I'd have girls call me at the shul, or we'd go to the motel. I got along with everyone I met. They called me 'Phil the Jew.' Crank, acid, coke, pot—there's all that crap up there. I never really got addicted to drugs. My thing was alcohol. I was drunk pretty much every day. I drank vodka, tequila, Old Style beer. I used to eat at the Pirates Den, the Horseshoe, and at first, it would freak people out. But then, I think, they grew to appreciate me. The Jews said I couldn't do this, but I told them to go to hell."

Alarmed by his behavior and fearful that he might do something to undermine Agriprocessors, the Hasidic *machers* came up with a plan to rehabilitate Stillman. As was Sholom's style, he approached Stillman with an ultimatum: Get married—or leave Postville. A nice Jewish girl—that's what Stillman needed, that would settle him down. So Sholom convinced Stillman to ask a Lubavitcher girl from Brooklyn to fly out to Minneapolis, where she was chauffeured to Postville. But within a week, the two got into an argument over marijuana and the girl flew back home.

In early September, Stillman got other companionship in the form of a recruit to Agriprocessors. Pinchas Lew, whom everyone called Pinny, had worked at the slaughterhouse for sixteen months, two years earlier, and had returned to Postville just before Rosh Hashanah 1991 to pick up some quick cash. Lew moved into a room atop the shul, where at least four other Hasidic men also lived.

Stillman and Lew became fast friends. Lew acted as a listening post for Stillman's *mishegoss*, his wild, crazy ideas. They were indeed different. Lew, the fifth in a family of fifteen brothers and sisters, was born in England, the son of a *macher* in the Lubavitcher movement. His father was second in command of Chabad in London, a key post in worldwide Lubavitch. By the fall of 1988, Lew wanted a break from Torah and Talmud meditation. Minneapolis–St. Paul has a surprisingly large Lubavitcher community of more than five hundred, directed by Rabbi Moshe Feller, Lew's paternal uncle. One of Lew's brothers was teaching in a Twin Cities yeshiva and told Lew of a Lubavitcher who owned a kosher restaurant in St. Paul. Lew flew to Minneapolis and started making pizza pies, borscht, and knishes at the restaurant. One

Friday night, while in Rochester to help make up a *Shabbos* minyan at the federal prison there, Lew met Heshy Rubashkin, Sholom's younger brother. In 1989, the Rubashkins, ever on the lookout for Jewish workers, offered to double Lew's salary if he'd come to Postville. Lew gave two weeks' notice and started at the slaughterhouse the week after Passover.

Lew's first job was affixing tags on cut-up meat. Then he became a "salter," standing eight hours a day in the ice-cold packing plant, wearing layer upon layer of winter clothing. Lew learned the art of deveining and ultimately became a *mashgiach.* He worked alongside the Jewish Vietnam veteran everyone called the "knife freak," and eventually worked himself up to the killroom, where he learned how to slice the necks of wriggling cattle, for which he earned $120 per day.

In Postville, Lew tentatively began to discover for the first time the world outside of Chabad. He saw up close the enemy—the *goyim.* The stories the Lubavitcher elders had told him about the *goyim* were true. He made friends on the killfloor with several locals, and what he saw and heard amazed him. Some were so drunk they could barely stand. Sex was openly discussed as workers sliced and deboned carcasses. Some of the *shkotzim,* young gentile men, at the slaughterhouse even offered to take Lew to the Club 51 or the Horseshoe to mingle with the locals after work, perhaps even meet a *shiksa,* but Lew demurred. Mostly what struck Lew was how boring, bleak, and meaningless the *goyim*'s lives were.

In October 1990, Lew left Postville for Israel, where he studied at a yeshiva and thought of enlisting in the Israeli army, but eleven months later, he returned to Postville. The slaughterhouse was especially busy prior to the Jewish High Holidays, and the Rubashkins needed *mashgiachs.*

The day of the crimes, Stillman left work early and met Lew at the shul in the late afternoon. The pair then got into the rusty Oldsmobile parked in the driveway and drove away. Their first stop was at Casey's in Postville, where Lew bought the two forty-ounce bottles of Old Style beer. An hour later, Stillman was in the P-n-P, pointing a gun at Marion Bakken.

By seven that evening, Stillman and Lew had been arrested and transported to the Winneshiek County Jail in downtown Decorah. Each was placed in a separate cell, and by law, each was allowed a phone call. But whom could they call? Orthodox Jewish law prohibits the use of phones during the Sabbath. Nonetheless, Lew called Rabbi Aaron Grush at the Postville shul, according to logs of phone calls made from the Winneshiek County Jail.

By the next morning, the Decorah Police Department had traced the Oldsmobile to Agriprocessors and called the slaughterhouse. Agriprocessors operated a skeleton shift during the Sabbath; no processing ever took place, so there were just gentile workers doing secretarial and maintenance work. A secretary took the call and told the maintenance supervisor, Ken Klepper, about it. Klepper drove over to the shul. Everyone was gone except Rabbi Grush, who was incensed that a "Jewish person would be held captive," recalled Klepper. Rabbi Grush mentioned to Klepper the Jewish commandment, *pidyon she-vuyim*, the practice that compelled Jews to release fellow Jews from prison. "He went ballistic," Klepper said of Rabbi Grush. "Grush thought it was horrible. He wanted to see what he could do." Even though it was the Sabbath, Klepper drove Rabbi Grush to the Decorah jail to visit Lew.

Like everyone else in the tight circle of Hasidim, Rabbi Grush knew how revered Lew's family was. Klepper, one of the highest-ranking gentiles at the plant, said his impression was that Rabbi Grush "wanted to move up at Agriprocessors. Grush knew that Lew had a lot of money and clout" and coming to the rescue of Lew, an imprisoned Hasid, "was a way to get a foot up the ladder." Rabbi Grush was the first of the Hasidic community to get to the jail to talk to Stillman and Lew. Speaking in hushed tones in Hebrew, Rabbi Grush first spoke with Lew. While waiting to talk to the rabbi, Stillman saw Klepper and told him that "he would get Lew out of this." According to Klepper's affidavit to police the next day, Stillman said, "Lew could make something out of his life and that his [Stillman's] life was wasted anyway. Then he [Stillman] asked me to remove two guns from Lew's room at the shul."

As Klepper was leaving, he ran into County Attorney Karl Knudson in the jail parking lot, and the two talked. "What came out was that Stillman told Klepper that Lew had two guns in his room, and Stillman wanted to get word back to Lew's friends so that they could remove the guns from his room," Knudson said. That led Knudson to file an affidavit for a search warrant. Police first searched Stillman's room at the Pines Motel, where they didn't come up with much—several letters in Hebrew and jotted-down notes of airline schedules from Minneapolis to New York City. That there was no evidence of guns, gun paraphernalia, or ammunition in Stillman's room, though, confirmed Knudson's suspicion that Stillman may have gotten the gun from Lew, and this provided probable cause for Knudson to obtain a second search warrant to search Lew's room at the shul. Police searched Lew's room the next day. While officers found no guns, they discovered something just as incriminating: inside a zipped-up suitcase, they found a box, and inside the box was a gun-cleaning kit. Anyone trying to get rid of guns in Lew's room would not have thought to look in a suitcase to find a gun-cleaning kit. The gun-cleaning kit posed a simple question: Why would Lew own a gun-cleaning kit if he didn't own or use guns? Lew had told police he had never used a gun in his life.

In the first week of October, police interviewed Gary Goldman, another young Hasid who lived upstairs at the shul. Goldman told the officers that Lew had declared to him that every Jew should own a gun and keep one in his dresser drawer for protection. Goldman also recalled that Lew had boasted that he could get a gun in twenty-four hours.

Goldman was in awe of Lew, in part, because of Lew's Lubavitcher lineage. "Pinny has *emunah shelema* [complete faith]," Goldman told me. "He is *tahor* [pure], from the purest stock there is. He was born on the mountaintop." Goldman said Lew found an ally in Rabbi Grush, whose politics matched Lew's. Both boasted that Jews ought to arm themselves, Goldman said.

Goldman recalled that the day after the robbery, Rabbi Grush had told him that he had cleaned Lew's room at the shul of evidence that could have implicated Lew in the shooting. "I never saw the gun or bullets, but I remember Grush telling me he did it. We were all so involved with the religion that when Grush went into Pinny's room, we didn't think it was illegal. He [Grush] didn't want Pinny to get in trouble. No one cared about Stillman. We knew that Stillman was a bad character: he was a goy; he was *tamay* [impure]."

After the crime, Rabbi Grush moved out of the shul, went back to Chicago, and became a *sofer*, a Hebrew inscriber. When I tried to contact him, he had disappeared into the labyrinthine world of Chabad.

For their investigation, police officers talked to Dick Blocker, the owner of Northern Iowa Sports Shop, a store in nearby Waukon that sold a wide assortment of firearms. Blocker told police that two Jewish men from Postville had bought ammunition at his store numerous times, which would fit 9-mm, .357-caliber, and .38-caliber firearms, the guns found in Stillman and Lew's car after the robberies and shooting. When shown photographs, Blocker identified Lew as one of the men and said Lew had bought ammunition one week before Marion Bakken was shot. Blocker said Lew had bought ammunition in his store as often as ten times but had never purchased a gun from him.

Knudson didn't need much more to conclude that Stillman was taking the fall for Lew, but Knudson got it. While in jail, Stillman had told a fellow inmate that two Lubavitch rabbis from Minneapolis had made a deal to supply Stillman with money for every month he spent incarcerated. A week before the meeting with the rabbis, Stillman wrote to the Brooklyn girl who had visited him, "There is no way I'm going to testify against Lew about what really happened. There are only two people who really know what happened and that's Pinny and myself and that's the way it's going to stay.... I thank God that I have everything I basically need. I have people who will send me money from the outside and take care of me."

At least five rabbis eventually paid visits to Stillman, including Moshe Feller. "When they talked with Stillman, they talked in their own native tongue, so we couldn't understand what they were saying," said Knudson. On January 13, 1992, two rabbis, Moshe Feller and Gershon Grossbaum, visited Stillman at the Winneshiek County Jail. A sheriff's deputy was present during the conversations between Stillman and the rabbis. Jailer Patricia Bullerman couldn't help but notice what was happening. It was clear as day, even if she didn't understand every word of their conversation, which alternated between English and either Hebrew or Yiddish. "They were striking a deal or an agreement among themselves," said Bullerman. "By the part of the conversation that I could hear, and also when they went to leave, they asked Phil to remember to keep his promise, and he said he would as long as they kept their promise to him."

After the rabbis left, Stillman appeared elated. "He was quite excited and glad," Bullerman recalled. "He said things went like he wanted them to. He said, 'I'm going to get a couple sets of clothes, tennis shoes,' and he did mention money and also that he was going to get to choose a motorcycle of his choice when he got out of prison."

To Knudson, the whole episode sounded like a pathetic penny-ante contract to keep Stillman quiet or to induce him to lie on the stand if he was ever called to testify against Lew. When I had talked to Nahum Leibowitz, he said he thought Stillman was crazy for doing time in exchange for what might be waiting for him at the other end of a fifty-year prison term. "When Phil said he was going to take the fall, I was totally against it. I tried to explain to him that he was living in Disney World. So what? They didn't sign anything. When he gets out, he's an ex-con. No one is going to believe him. He knocks on Lew's door and says, 'Pay up,' they're going to call the cops, and if he's packing, he'll go away for a parole violation. He doesn't want to face reality."

As I sat across from Stillman in the prison interview room, he had the same wide smile as when I had first arrived. He knew that I had spent months looking into his life and Lew's. He knew that I had talked to Leibowitz.

"Are you taking the fall for Pinny?" I asked him quietly. "Why?"

Stillman pulled back his head sharply in mock recoil. Then he smiled again. "Most guys get out of prison with nothing," he said, almost apologetically. "But when I get out, I'm going to have a car, a good place to live. That's what I'm going to get. That's something a lot of people know. When Rabbi Grossbaum and Rabbi Feller came to the prison and told me to break off with the past, they said there would be people who would take care of me for the rest of my life. I want clothing, food, a job.

"I'm not telling the whole truth so that someone who didn't do things as bad as I did could get married and start a life. I also don't tell on other people. Why should two people be in here, when only one had to? I pulled the trigger; I know that. They were Pinny's guns, it was Pinny's idea, but I'm the one who did it. We did this crime together. When we got to jail, [Pinny] kept on saying, 'I can't go to prison. I can't go to prison.' So I said to him, 'I'm going to take all the blame.'"

Stillman said what Knudson had believed: "Pinny called Rabbi Grush and spoke in Yiddish from the jail, and told him his combination [(of the lock on his door) and to] get all the fucking guns out."

Guns were a part of Lew's life, Stillman said. "Pinny would come over to my place at the Pines, and a couple of times we went to a field behind the rabbis' house [the shul] and shot at the corn. One day, I was up in his room at the shul, and he pulls out these cases with guns in them. 'Hey, you ever do an armed robbery?' he asked.

I looked up suddenly. The prison guard had gotten up from his vinyl seat and was tapping the glass wall to the interview room. My time with Stillman was up. As the guard led Stillman out of the room, Stillman looked over his shoulder at me.

"Shalom," he mouthed.

The missing link to this bungled crime and seeming cover-up was Pinchas Lew. I wanted to find Lew to get at this sliver of a Chabad netherworld. I also wanted to resolve a sense that I couldn't shake: that the crime and its aftermath were a perverted outgrowth of how the Hasidim did business in Postville. The attitude shared by many Postville Hasidim toward the locals nourished a destructive environment of contempt and scorn providing a setting for Stillman and Lew. While the Hasids would not encourage unprovoked violence against gentiles, their everyday us-against-them mentality helped set the stage for two cocky followers to fantasy into reality.

For more than a year, the Hasidic Jews' imperious attitude toward the Postville locals had stuck in my craw. As a Jew, I was embarrassed by their take-it-or-leave-it mentality. I cringed when I heard Sholom or Lazar regaling me with more stories about *hondling, goyisher kops,* and *shvartzers.* Stillman and Lew had provided me a rationale for my own distancing from the Jews I once hoped I could embrace. The Hasidim's wholesale bashing of the Postville locals was one thing. Stillman and Lew were quite another. The pair had become straw men to justify my sliding over to the side of the Postville locals.

Using the Internet, I located Lew quickly. I e-mailed him and got an immediate response. When I mentioned that I was planning a trip to New York City, he agreed to a meeting. But he messaged that he would talk to me on one condition:

that we not discuss the robberies and shooting of Marion Bakken.

There was good reason for Lew to avoid discussion of the crimes—he owed Marion Bakken $1.6 million in damages. After less than an hour of deliberation, a Winneshiek County jury had returned a verdict against Lew, saying he performed the crimes "willfully and with malice." Despite the judgment, Bakken never recovered any money from Lew.

It had been a year since I was last in New York. I checked into a midtown hotel and dialed Lew's number. He answered the phone in a distinctive British accent. "Sunday would be good. Come over at three," he said.

New York was more than a world apart from Postville: high-pitched steel-grinding squeals of subway cars; steam rising from manhole covers; cold, vacant stares from subway riders; people pushing and shoving at rush hour to get onto packed trains; rockers with spiked purple hair and rings through their noses, lips, and eyebrows; a Felliniesque parade of faces—pursed lips, squinted eyes constantly watching, hands clutching purses, shopping bags, or briefcases.

As the No. 3 train rattled through the dark tunnels from Manhattan to Brooklyn, I closed my eyes and flashed to the lush fields of northeastern Iowa. There was so much light in Iowa. Sunlight, bluish in the early morning, ivory yellow in mid-afternoon, golden by dusk. In my vision, the Iowa moon was always full, always a pure, bottomless white, hanging high over endless rows of green cornstalks that were growing, crackling. A faraway pickup crunched on a gravel road. The crackling and the crunching sounds were the only noises in a quiet and serene landscape. The crowded, dirty subway car ground to a halt at the Kingston Avenue station in the heart of

Lubavitcher Crown Heights. I walked up the littered stairs, out into the brisk November air, toward 770 Eastern Parkway.

As I looked around, hundreds of black-hatted Lubavitcher men were scurrying to get to 770. They were coming out of houses, storefronts, apartments, side streets lining Eastern Parkway, black hats everywhere converging at the shul, two blocks behind me now. Their look and their gait reminded me of Lazar that Saturday morning in Postville as we had passed his neighbors on the sidewalk. Several Hasidim stared sharply at me, a hatless Jew without *tzitzit* or beard. The November air brought with it a sudden chill, as I pulled the collar of my coat closer to my neck. I walked faster.

Five blocks from the shul, I found the brick building that was Pinchas Lew's duplex. When I pressed the building's buzzer, the intercom attached by a rainbow of frayed wires responded with a static "Yes?" in the same royal accent I had heard when I had spoken by phone to Lew. I announced myself and pushed open the heavy iron gate. Before me was a steeply pitched staircase. At the top, peering down at me, was Pinchas Lew.

Lew certainly resembled a Talmudic scholar—tiny brown-framed wire-rim glasses, sallow complexion, a patchy beard the color of chestnuts. We shook hands, warily eyeing each other. Lew rocked a sleeping baby in his arms, and as he moved to the children's room to diaper a second child, he began telling me his story—from England, to Canada, to Brooklyn, to Minnesota, to Postville, to Israel, back to Postville, and finally to Brooklyn, a free man. As Lew laid down the two children to nap, we sat at a dining-room table that had cold kosher pizza slices left over from lunch.

I asked him if he regretted his friendship with Stillman.

All Lew would allow was this: "It was my fault that I got involved with Stillman. For that, I have myself to blame."

As though I had missed something, Lew suddenly whipped
out the black leather phylacteries, and within seconds, he was
wrapping the long straps around my left arm, flipping them
seven times around my biceps and forearm, looping the rest
of the strap around my middle finger, while centering the
square boxes on my upper arm and forehead. There was no
time to protest. Lew spoke fast and nodded that I follow his
lead. I intoned the same prayers that I had recited on the second floor of the Postville slaughterhouse. As with Sholom,
there had been no opportunity to demur.

I was praying with a man who may have cooked up two
robberies, supplied the weapon that discharged the slug still
in Marion Bakken's spine, and consistently lied to officials
about his involvement. While Lew was invoking the Lord's
name in his prayers, he didn't look toward the heavens. His
eyes locked steadily with mine. Was Lew trying to intimidate
me, using the Lord to ensure that his plea would be made all
the fiercer? Was Lew trying to establish a bond with me, a
pact, obligating a fellow Jew to "do the right thing"?

Lew carefully folded up the tefillin and placed them back
in the velvet pouch. There was little more to talk about. There
seemed to be an implicit understanding that we both shared
about his role in the crime and its aftermath. When the infant
in the adjacent bedroom awoke from a nap, Lew told me that
I should leave. "I must attend to the child," he said, his British
cadence and accent in force. Lew and I nodded at each other
and shook hands.

I made my way to Crown Street and Kingston Avenue, a
couple of blocks from Eastern Parkway, where I stopped at an
outdoor market owned by a rotund Lubavitcher who watched

me suspiciously as I looked over the displays of fruit. I picked out three large apples and brought them to him to be weighed. The man eyed me warily. I certainly looked like a Jew, but why such *goyisher* clothes, and where was my beard? The man put the apples on a swinging scale. Two-twenty-five, he said. Experience had taught me to haggle, to make sure the man hadn't put his thumb on the scale. I felt eyes following me. The man snatched my money, grimacing, then held the plastic bag of apples out to me at arm's length, looking at me the same way the two spinsters in Winga's, the restaurant in Washington, Iowa, had glared at me. Again, I was a foreigner.

CHAPTER 18

Sticks in Spokes

The Postville locals had told me that Aaron Rubashkin, Sholom's father, was the mastermind of the Hasidic operation in Postville and that the slaughterhouse had
been his brainchild. Aaron called the shots from his little
butcher shop somewhere in the recesses of Brooklyn. It had
been Aaron's idea to buy the abattoir, paying just $150,000 for
it, and it had been Aaron who reconfigured the old Hygrade
plant, drawing up plans for the killfloor and the killroom.
From Iowa, I had called the butcher shop in the Borough
Park section six times, and each time a busy clerk had told me
that Aaron was out and that she had no idea when he would
return. When I asked if I could leave a message, she said no
and hung up. The only way to get to him was to appear at his
butcher shop, the way Leonid and his two Ukrainian friends
had done. The State City Development Board in Des Moines
had finally set the first Tuesday in August as the date for
the long-awaited annexation referendum. Before the vote, I
wanted to track down Aaron. By midafternoon the next day, I
found myself back on a subway to Brooklyn. Short of a car, the

fastest way to Borough Park from Crown Heights was a privately operated bus, which I queued up to board on a corner not far from Pinchas Lew's apartment. The bus driver barely looked sixteen, had *payot,* and wore a yarmulke and *tzitzit.* The left side of the old school bus was for women; the right side, for men. Husbands and wives, brothers and sisters, traveling together split apart to opposite sides as soon as they boarded.

I took a seat in the back. As soon as I sat down, I looked up and saw a frail man hobbling toward me, tentatively sliding his right hand along the railing above his head, and with his left hand, holding on to the top of each seat, guiding himself down the aisle. The little man, with requisite Borsalino, black coat, and white beard, must have been in his nineties. He shuffled, nodding to passengers on both sides of the bus, invoking the same Hebrew blessing to each person as he made his way to the back. "Ai!" he said as he plopped down next to me, exhausted by the trip. Rabbi Springer, I learned, was an eminent teacher at 770, born in Poland at the turn of the century, exiled to the gulag, emigrated to Israel in 1945, who arrived in Crown Heights in 1952.

I asked whether the rabbi knew about the Rubashkins and the slaughterhouse in Postville. "Of course! All very good, very important people that ensure we eat strictly kosher," he said, nodding again, enthusiastically. "*Glatt* kosher. Very good."

"Have you been to Postville?"

"Too old to travel, but I know all about the slaughterhouse. Very important, very important work for us." The driver suddenly stopped short at a traffic light, and everyone on the bus lurched forward. An elderly woman with shopping bags on her lap shouted, "Oy!" then shook her head in disgust at the driver. "And you," the rabbi asked, "what is your name?"

"Shlomo," I answered.

"Ah, Shlomo! Named after King Shlomo, the son of King David. An important figure in our past. This is good, very good." The rabbi paused, lowering his voice, moving closer to me. "But Shlomo, why no *kippah*?"

Yet another righteous stranger had descended into my life. "Shlomo, you must wear a *kippah* always," the rabbi scolded, eyeing my uncovered head. He leaned toward me, his nose now just several inches from mine. Raising his bony index finger, he beckoned me even closer, bringing his mouth to my ear. I could feel his breath on the flaps of my ear. "*Kippot* are important," the rabbi whispered, "but tefillin is essential."

Rabbi Springer then launched into a long recitation on tefillin wearing. "You *must* wrap tefillin twice a day, Shlomo. It will save your life. Do not doubt me. Tefillin is in praise to our Creator. It will allow you to stay alive. Literally. You must believe me. Your life depends on it."

The bus driver took a sharp turn onto Flatbush Avenue, sending the rabbi careening toward the aisle. I grabbed him by his black coat, pulled him back to the seat, and without missing a beat, he continued. "By giving our Creator praise in this way, it keeps you from acting against his commandments, from engaging in activities that are negative." I had the image that phylacteries were akin to rosary beads. When your mind was being led astray, the tactile sensation of the slick, smooth leather straps moving through your fingers and hands, cinched around your left arm and forehead, pulled you back to holy order.

When I told Rabbi Springer that I had laid tefillin the day before, an immense calm seemed to settle over him. "This is good, but you must do it every day. Promise me, Shlomo. Promise me on this bus. Every day. Please."

I looked toward the rabbi, barely lowering my chin. "Shlomo," the rabbi suddenly asked. "You have children?" But before I could answer, he asked, "How many?"

"My wife and I have one son, Michael—Moishe."

"One son! But why only one when children are such a *mitzvah*?"

It was a replay of my conversation with Lazar Kamzoil. "We're happy," I said, and to that, even Rabbi Springer could voice no fault and nodded back at me.

As we arrived in Borough Park, I helped the rabbi down the aisle and the steep bus steps, and bade him farewell. A half block away, I turned back and saw that he had not moved. Rabbi Springer stood his ground, stooped at the shoulders, watching me as I moved down Thirteenth Avenue. I waved, and he stoically nodded back at me.

With the exception of an Asian-American Brooklyn Union Gas meter reader, I was the only man on the street without fedora and beard. I felt a sudden kinship to Dwight Bacon, the Postville Farmers Cooperative Society manager who had taken his family sightseeing in Brooklyn. Borough Park was so dominated by ultra-Orthodox that residents closed off the streets at sundown Friday with road barriers so that cars couldn't enter or exit on the Sabbath. Hat and wig stores lined the street along with Judaica stores that stocked everything from handmade *tzitzit* to Kosherland, a variant on the children's board game, Candyland.

I found Rubashkin & Sons Inc., the butcher shop, and asked the Hasidic man behind the meat counter if Aaron was there.

"You got appointment?"

I shook my head.

"He know you?"

I shook my head again.

"Then why he want to talk to you? He's a busy man."

"I'm from Iowa."

Iowa was the magic word. The man threw a quick glance to his right, outside the door. "At corner. Maybe talking. Maybe there. Maybe not."

I felt like I was playing Kosherland, throwing dice to hop from square to square. But at the corner, I found Aaron Rubashkin in an old gray cardigan sweater, blue-striped shirt, Borsalino, white beard, and blue eyes. He was talking to a man in Yiddish, and just like his son, Aaron was making a point by vigorously slapping the back of his right hand into the palm of his left.

We walked back to the butcher shop, upstairs where Aaron sat behind a cluttered desk, across from a closed-circuit television that showed four screens of the tiny shop below. Aaron Rubashkin had fled Russia in 1945, lived in Paris for seven years before emigrating to the United States, and had run the butcher shop since. In the early 1980s, a turf war of sorts had erupted, and Lubavitchers placed a ban on all meat that had been *kashured* according to Satmar *shechita*. Righteous Lubavitchers were not allowed to eat Satmar beef, a dictate that prompted Aaron to expand into slaughtering and buy the packinghouse in Postville.

Given a host of different circumstances, Aaron reminded me of Leigh Rekow. Both were about the same age and both had the same watery-blue eyes and crinkly skin. Both had achieved success by hard physical labor. Their accents, of course, were different, but each spoke softly, with the same hesitation, the same lingering at the end of each sentence, as though he wanted to tell you more.

When I asked Aaron about choosing Postville as the site for his slaughterhouse, his eyes widened. "When I first got there, the city was an open place, but on every block there were five homes for sale, closed storefronts. The streets were clean, there was lots of green, and the people, the people were nice—that was my first impression. I felt they wanted us. I felt they needed us. One of my sons, Heshy, went to the Rebbe and asked him whether we should invest in the packinghouse in Postville, and the Rebbe told him 'Yes, that would be good,' so we followed his wishes.

"What upsets me is that some people in Postville think that we came in and took something that wasn't ours. My sons are native-born Americans, just like the people of Postville. We have every right to make a life there—like the Postville people have. This annexation, what this Rekow is trying to make, we don't need people putting sticks in the spokes of our wheels. I wouldn't say they are anti-Semitic, that's what happened in Europe. But Jews are different. We are. No one can deny that. It's not that we're prejudiced, but we are different. The people in Postville don't have any idea what a Jew is. They look at us strange. They aren't evil, it's just that they've never seen people like us before. They are uncertain. We've done only good for them—but sometimes that's not enough." Aaron paused, raising his snowy eyebrows as though to say, "No matter what we do, the *goyim* always find fault with us." He suddenly got up and grabbed my arm. "I want you to eat with us at the restaurant. My family will be there. You be our guest. Let's go."

We walked several blocks to a kosher delicatessen, where

Aaron's wife of forty-eight years, Rivka, was busy serving meals to a roomful of diners. She looked like an elderly Russian peasant woman, plaid scarf covering her head. Aaron plopped a yarmulke on my head, and as we sat, he said a blessing over rye-bread slices in a plastic bowl in the center of the table. The oldest of Aaron's nine children, Joseph, and his family arrived. The dinner was a send-off: Aaron's fifteen-year-old grandson was leaving tomorrow for Paris to study in a Lubavitcher yeshiva.

To diagram the discussion would be impossible. It was rapid-fire machine-gun delivery. Jokes, put-downs, comebacks. No one was able to finish a fragment of a sentence before someone else interrupted. Joseph's wife, an elegant Hasidic woman with a coiffed *sheitel* on her head and a rock on her finger the size of a small walnut, took a look at the necktie I was wearing—red with silver stripes—and said, "So where are the stars on the tie? Oh, I guess you don't need any—you're the star, right? Eat! Join us, let's eat!" No wonder the Postville locals were left in the dust.

Suddenly, matzo-ball soup, breaded chicken fillet, flanken, mushy green beans, and Dr. Brown's Cel-Ray Tonic appeared before me. There was a blur of hands, voices, smells, and more food. Joseph said the only reason that Agriprocessors had succeeded was because of Divine Providence, pure and simple. "We didn't know anything about live cattle. All we knew was dead meat." Wiping the corner of his mouth with a napkin, Aaron said, "We're really just a bunch of *shleppers.* We did what any Jew would do. We worked hard. So?" Aaron's wife, Rivka, placed servings of apple strudel in front of Aaron and me. "You've got to taste this," Aaron boasted. "My wife makes it fresh every day. It's out of this world."

After the strudel, Aaron insisted on walking me to my
subway stop. The sun had long gone down. Aaron folded his
right arm in mine, inside my elbow's crook, two men walking
arm in arm. It was an intimate gesture, something I could
imagine Stanley Schroeder doing. Aaron motioned me toward
a doorway. "Here," he said. "Stand here. We talk."

We stood in the doorway of a walk-up apartment building, side by side on a dirty tile floor, next to a cast-iron gate,
in front of six tarnished brass mail slots. "Sholom tells me
about this Rekow, about all the problems he makes for us in
Postville. Sholom tells me things," Aaron said, again raising
his eyebrows. "But we shall see what happens with this annexation vote. We put money, our own blood and sweat into
that plant. We built that ourselves. We shall see what happens." Aaron wasn't angry, but he spoke with conviction. He
knew he was right. We continued to talk in the doorway,
shielding ourselves from the wind, and it struck me that
Aaron was the vintage city dweller, perhaps the quintessential
New Yorker, who knew how to survive handily anywhere. It
was time to go, and when we shook hands, Aaron reached
over to touch my cheek, under my right ear, almost to brush
it, just for a split second. It was another familiar gesture that
transported me back to my childhood, something Poppa
Charles used to do to me, and at that moment, I thought
Aaron Rubashkin and Stanley Schroeder or Leigh Rekow very
well could have become friends.

I descended into the subway and boarded an empty train
from Coney Island. Religion to Aaron wasn't all-encompassing,
as it was for Sholom or Lazar or any of the other Postville Hasidim I had met. There had been no *baruch Hashems,* no
pulling out tefillin, none of the never-ending preaching I had

come to expect from the Postville Hasidim. Many of the children of foreign-born Hasidim like Aaron were righteously religious, much more so than their parents, and there was logic why. The hardworking parents, émigrés from Eastern Europe, ensuring their children not go for want of anything in golden America, sent their sons to the best yeshivas in the world. In Paris, New York, Montreal, Jerusalem, these boys came back well versed in the Lubavitcher schema of the world, taught by ardent, righteous rabbis like Rabbi Springer. Most became ordained rabbis themselves, even though they went into Lubavitcher-run businesses. I got the impression that to Aaron, Hasidic protocol was important, but not fundamental, as it was to Sholom. Aaron wore a plain blue-striped shirt under a sweater; whenever I saw Sholom he always had on white shirts and *tzitzit* underneath. Post–World War II Hasidic education had raised the religious imperative of now middle-aged Hasidim like Sholom and Lazar. To these men, commerce wasn't just a business, but a holy, zealous mission that had a divine right to flourish.

I climbed into a taxi in midtown the next morning, and headed out of the gray, noisy, smoke-belching city. As soon as I stepped into the main terminal at LaGuardia Airport for the flight back to Iowa, I saw scores of African American men positioned every fifty feet, each with a tiny earpiece, each wearing a nearly identical suit and bow tie. As I walked toward my gate, they formed a veritable wall. Minutes before boarding, Nation of Islam leader Reverend Louis Farrakhan emerged in the center of a fast-moving phalanx of twenty hefty bodyguards. My plane was going to Chicago—where Farrakhan's headquarters are—then I was to transfer to a smaller plane that would take me to Cedar Rapids.

Farrakhan and his men had taken over the first-class section of the plane, as well as a dozen seats in coach. As a journalist, I had covered Farrakhan several times, but the event
that stood out was when he spoke to a raucous rally at the Los
Angeles Forum in 1985. At that point in his career, Farrakhan
was causing jitters among whites and especially among Jews.
He had praised Hitler in a speech, referred to Judaism as a
"gutter religion," and called New York City the "capital of
the Jews." That evening more than a decade ago, Farrakhan's
voice was booming as I found a seat in the crowded Forum. I
quickly sensed that this was a variation of an old-fashioned
revival, and Farrakhan was the preacher, his rolling, fast cadence greeted after each sentence with thunderous shouts
from the assembled of "Amen" and "Oh, yes!"

"I know that right here in your midst is a white JEW-ISH
reporter who works for the white, establishment *Los Angeles Times*," Farrakhan shouted to his flock. He seemed to
spit when he uttered "Jewish," splitting it into two slurred
syllables.

"Oh, yes!" came the reverberating response. "Oh, yes!"

"And, my friends, do you know what this white JEW-ISH
reporter's job is? Do you know? Do you know why he is
here?" Farrakhan was sweating profusely, dabbing his face
with a large white handkerchief, bellowing to the crowd, who
by this time were all standing. Many were stamping their feet,
clapping, singing, chanting. It made for a deafening jumble of
rolling, rumbling noise that filled the Forum to its rafters.
Some in the crowd were swaying, their eyes closed, as though
in a trance.

My initial thought was that one of the security guards
must have given my name to Farrakhan. But on further reflection, I thought not. Farrakhan's business that night was to

stir up his followers, to fill them with a sense of righteous in-
dignation, a sense of power. Why not weave Jews and the establishment newspaper into a single tapestry? The Jews were
to blame for everything, and the newspaper they ran was part
of an evil empire.

"Oh, this reporter's not here to let you all know what *I*
think," Farrakhan roared to the adoring crowd. "You already
know that, don't you? You already know what *I* think. Isn't
that right, my friends?"

"Oh, yes! Oh, yes!"

"This white JEW-ISH man's job is to scare the white
people of America. Yes, it is! This white JEW-ISH man's job is
to distort, to mangle, to change the meaning of what I say
to you tonight. You see, my friends, this white JEW-ISH reporter's job is very simple. Oh, yes it is! His job is to make me
sound like I'm a crazy black racist. That's what his job is! Oh,
yes, it is!"

The crowd roared in approval. I noticed some in the audience staring at me as I scribbled in my notebook, preparing
to phone in my story by deadline; but Farrakhan's followers
inside the Forum that night seemed too enraptured with their
leader and his message to be sidetracked by my presence.

What I saw that night reminded me of what I was to see
over a decade later in the Postville shul and around Lazar's
dinner table. I came to realize that much of Farrakhan's rhetoric at the time ironically echoed the Lubavitcher agenda.
Both peoples had endured centuries of inhuman domination,
and now both sects demanded total devotion. Their time had
come. Followers of Farrakhan and the Rebbe showed unwavering, single-minded devotion to their respective causes.
Some disciples of Farrakhan and the Rebbe advocated a world

based on racial or religious prejudice, a world divided. Anyone who was neither black nor Jewish could not be trusted. Blacks and Jews needed to be reeducated to learn why they were the Chosen People. Blacks or Jews who didn't follow these teachings had to be proselytized, brought into the fold. Black- or Hasidic-run businesses were advocated. Any association with non-blacks or non-Jews was discouraged. Even though the Rebbe had been dead for two years, Lubavitchers talked about him as though he were still alive, and in an observant Lubavitcher's mind, the Rebbe's spirit was indeed alive. The degree to which an ardent Nation-of-Islam follower adored Farrakhan matched the ferocity with which an observant Lubavitcher idolized the Rebbe.

Since that Saturday evening in 1985, Farrakhan's drive to be accepted by more Americans has largely succeeded partly because he has tempered his message, but also because many Americans have grown to accept the theory and practice behind his ideas. That night in the Forum, Farrakhan spoke of black separatism, a thriving black culture, black businesses, blacks educating blacks—his message paralleled the separatism that Hasidism preaches about Jewish communities, ethos, commerce, and education. Farrakhan's once radical message has become mainstream, as has the Rebbe's. It's what Americans have come to expect from any self-respecting ethnic bloc. If you replaced the words "African American" with "Jewish," Farrakhan's and the Rebbe's messages were identical. The way Farrakhan had spoken about the Jews was little different from the way the Hasidim spoke about the *"goyim,"* or how Lazar had referred to the "niggers" or the *"shvartzers."*

The Postville annexation vote, scheduled for the first Tuesday in August, was the showdown in Postville, but it wasn't set on an isolated cultural battlefield in Iowa. The larger issues surrounding the referendum spilled over to the rest of America. What happened in Postville signaled how willing Americans were to accept newcomers who believed they had a mandate from the Almighty to show up in your backyard and pronounce that the rules you had lived by were now null and void.

Our plane taxied into O'Hare, and the covey of bow-tied African Americans exited first, whisking the Reverend Farrakhan to an even larger phalanx of security guards inside the terminal. I found the gate to connect to Cedar Rapids, and as we flew above flat-roofed warehouses, the industrial grid of Chicago, then the cookie-cutter suburbs, and finally the expanse of stubbly fields, I realized for the first time that I was glad to return to Iowa, to get away from the confines of suffocating order, whether it was Hasidic or Muslim, urban or suburban. When I had first come to Iowa for the job interview, I had flown over much of the same landscape. Then the view had been of snow and ice, plateaus of snowdrifts, flurries furiously whipping through the air. Today, that chill had dissipated. There was a pleasant sense of randomness, of freedom, to the rolling, expansive fields below as the last of the late-afternoon sun was about to set.

CHAPTER 19

Doc Wolf

Initially, I had gone to Postville to learn from the Hasidim, to share with them a sense of identity and belonging. Instead, what the Postville Hasidim ultimately offered me was a glimpse at the dark side of my own faith, a look at Jewish extremists whose behavior not only made the Postville locals wince, but made me wince, too. I didn't want to partake in Hasidism's vision that called on Jews to unite against the *goyim* and assimilation. The world, even in Iowa, was too bountiful to base my likes and dislikes solely on religion, and it was that fundamental difference that continued to gall me about the Postville Hasidim. The word *Hasid* comes from the Hebrew, and literally means "the pious one," but the Postville Hasidim I had encountered were anything but pious. You couldn't become casual friends with them; it was all or nothing. They required total submission to their schema of right and wrong, Jew vs. Christian—or you were the enemy.

Sometime after the *Shabbos* weekend with Lazar and his family, my relationship with the Hasidim began to erode. Once they realized that I wasn't going to sign up and become a *baal teshuvah,* returnee to the faith, I noticed a distinct chill. The tension got worse after Iris, Mikey, and I ate lunch with Lazar, Bielke, and their children. By the time the Hasidim discovered that I was prying into Stillman and Lew, I had all but become a nonperson. Whenever I returned to Postville, I was greeted with nary a nod when I passed the Hasidim on the streets. I had become worse than the *goyim.* I was a Jew digging up dirt on other Jews.

That I had alienated myself from the Hasidim, though, did not dissuade me from returning to Postville. In many ways, it strengthened my resolve. On Friday afternoons, when my classes were over, I'd drive along the blacktop of Route 13, turning off at Elkader, taking the same washboard county roads I had driven that first day to Postville two years earlier. I had grown to enjoy the locals and value their opinions. I had come to appreciate Sharon Drahn's self-deprecating laugh, Leigh Rekow's love of farming the fertile Iowa earth, Stanley Schroeder's lectures on local history in his cluttered living room. The locals still looked at me as the city slicker I was, but after dozens of trips to Postville, I think they had begun to see in me an ally. They all now knew I was the same faith as the Hasidim, but that didn't matter. Even though I could get in my car and drive home to Iowa City, I shared their sense of outrage directed at the Hasidim. I, too, had somehow become a stakeholder in the clash of cultures in Postville.

After four years in Iowa, Iris, Mikey, and I were still trying to become Iowans. We still enjoyed the perquisites that came with living in a place as foreign to our senses as Iowa was. Our friends, Joe and Rita Williams, invited us to karaoke night at a local club, where we sang "Somewhere over the Rainbow." They asked us to their cabin at Clear Lake, where we took Mikey for his first ride on a Jet Ski. Back in Iowa City, we went to dozens of potluck dinners, as well as to two sock hops held at a high school gymnasium in Cosgrove, a tiny town of farmers twelve miles west of town. Dick and Nina Norman, who lived in the country, invited us to dine on lamb chops butchered from their flock of sheep. Our across-the-street neighbors, Earl and Marilyn Rose, invited us in for afternoon tea and cookies. Iris and a law-school friend organized a spring garage sale at Longfellow Elementary School and took in nearly five hundred dollars for the PTA. I was a judge for the homecoming pageant at the university and interviewed scores of wannabe kings and queens. If the temperature was above thirty degrees, Iris and I drank Leinenkugels and ate brats at Hawkeye tailgating parties around the corner from Kinnick Stadium. We wanted to partake fully, and we did everything to be ushered to front-row seats.

But Iris and I continued to find ourselves strangers caught in the middle. Mikey, now seven, picked up on our uncertainties, and he, too, shared a sense of confusion. His dad didn't hunt, his mom never Christmas caroled—not that all Iowans do those things, but we had a hard time cozying up to a community where activities like these were viewed as virtuous and noble.

By the spring of 1997, Iris had finished her second year of law school, Mikey had graduated from first grade, and I had been granted tenure at the university. Tenure was a virtual guarantee of a job at the University of Iowa for the rest of my life—a thought that was at once comforting and terrifying. The notion of staying in Iowa forever, which we never had taken seriously during our first years here, had become real.

I'm not sure I was looking for a path to follow or just

someone who could lead me in the right direction, but I wanted to learn about the Jewish physician who Ida Mae and Cliff Olson and Marie Schlee had told me about. Henry Wolf had moved from Chicago to Iowa in the 1930s; he and his wife had raised their family of three children in Elgin, a town twelve miles south of Postville. Henry died in April 1996, just as I had begun to think about writing this book. I wasn't searching for a model in Henry Wolf, just someone who could help steer us through our odyssey as émigrés from the big city to Jews living in Iowa. Henry Wolf and his wife, Rose, had come to Iowa long before Iris, Mikey, and I had. They had made a life here. Perhaps Doc Wolf could serve as a guide-post for me and as a lens through which I could see the Postville Hasidim and myself.

As I knew all too well, Lubavitchers are known throughout the world for their consummate desire to bring nonobservant Jews back to the fold. "Are you Jewish?" young Lubavitcher men yell to passersby on urban street corners. If the question is an-swered affirmatively, the would-be recruit is ushered inside a nearby Mitzvah Tank for phase two of the recruitment drive— books and photographs of the Rebbe, an invitation to *Shabbos* dinner, a visit to a Lubavitcher shul, the laying of tefillin. The Postville Lubavitchers had their opportunity for such a *mitzvah* during the last week of March 1996, when eighty-nine-year-old Henry Wolf made a deathbed request that a rabbi from the kosher slaughterhouse pay him a visit at the Good Samaritan Center on Hardin Drive in Postville. In the early 1970s, Henry had been diagnosed with prostate cancer, and by now the slow-moving cancer had metastasized to his bones. Death could come in a matter of days, certainly no more than a week or two.

Henry's friend and confidant, Judy Deweber, the Methodist pastor in Elgin, had sung the Twenty-third Psalm twice to him at his bedside. When Henry called the rabbi, he knew he was about to die and he was preparing for it.

Henry Wolf was well aware of the gravity of his own medical condition. For sixty-three years, he had practiced medicine in Elgin (population: 637). To almost anyone within a fifty-mile radius, Henry Wolf was known simply as Doc Wolf. Over his six decades as a country doctor serving Elgin and Postville, the kindly, compact physician with the trademark mustache and thick black-framed glasses had stitched up thousands of wounds, removed hundreds of appendixes and tonsils, and brought more than twenty-five hundred babies into the world. He held the record for delivering more babies in northeastern Iowa than anyone else—a record that no other doctor will likely break. More than several people told me the same thing: Doc Wolf could cure you with his bedside manner. Just seeing him made you feel better.

To many, Henry Wolf was a Renaissance man in a part of America where being a man with brawny shoulders, a quick head, and an honest way was usually good enough. For six decades, no one in either Allamakee or Fayette County commanded anything near the respect that Doc Wolf had. He was on the school board, started the local Boy Scout troop and the Little League. Doc revered baseball, the Chicago Cubs in particular. During the first week in April every year, he would take his two sons, Butch and Howie, out of school, and the three of them would drive all the way to Chicago to see the Cubs on opening day—but not before stopping off at a delicatessen on Roosevelt Road for Dr. Brown's sodas, a sack of corned beef sandwiches, and an enormous kosher dill pickle sliced in three. Until he was forty, Doc played second base for the Elgin Cardinals, a ragtag summer team that competed Sunday evenings against teams from Wadena, Strawberry Point, and Clermont. Weighing 150 pounds and standing five feet seven inches, Doc was a solid .300 hitter known for his ability to punch singles and doubles into short centerfield. He and his teammates wore red caps and gray flannel uniforms, each with a number. Before every game, the team held a citywide picnic in the Schori cow pasture, which had been transformed during the 1930s into a baseball diamond with wooden bleachers so that wives, girlfriends, mothers, fathers, grand-parents, children, aunts, and uncles could cheer on the Cardinals. It was *Field of Dreams* fifty years early.

Baseball wasn't Doc's only pastime. He played bridge three times a week, wouldn't put down a newspaper until he finished the crossword puzzle, and would travel at a moment's notice if he could snag a ticket to any opera within three hundred miles. He was a master gardener and consummate reader. He went few places without a well-worn leather-bound edition of *The Collected Works of William Shake-speare,* and whether he was waiting for a patient or a train, Doc devoured the book the way Fundamentalists devour the New Testament. Doc knew every Shakespearean play and character, as well as the moral lessons their actions prompted.

To some, Henry Wolf was also known for something else: his religion. All the old-timers in Elgin knew that Doc Wolf was Jewish. He wasn't a practicing Jew and hadn't set foot in a synagogue—save for his daughter's wedding in 1959 and his grandson's bar mitzvah in 1981—for more than sixty years. But Henry Wolf was proud of his heritage and never hid his religion from anyone. In the Elgin house he and Rose bought in 1958, Doc affixed to the doorjamb under the breezeway a *mezuzah,* a tiny rolled-up parchment with passages from Deuteronomy inside an oblong box. The *mezuzah,* with Hebrew lettering on its cover, was notice to anyone who entered the Wolf house that Doc and Rose were Jews.

Rural towns, though, are worlds unto themselves—keepers of secrets, guardians of tact—and for a host of reasons, Doc Wolf's religion never made headlines up the road in Postville. Some Postville locals knew that Doc was Jewish, but many, especially those under fifty, did not. Few probably would have cared. Doc was an institution in these parts, a physician who made housecalls in the middle of the night even when he was in his late seventies. "I don't think people gave a damn what religion he was," Doc's older son, Butch, told me. "His entire life was as intermingled with the Christian community as it possibly could be. The fact that he was Jewish really never came up."

It really wasn't until the Hasidim moved to Postville that any of the locals would have had reason even to consider Doc's religion. Almost everyone in town was Lutheran, and if you weren't Lutheran, then you probably were Catholic. And if you weren't Lutheran or Catholic, then you were either Methodist, Presbyterian, or Baptist. Most of the locals probably believed that it was nobody's business which church you belonged to, if you went at all. But the Postville Hasidim had changed all that. The stakes were higher now. Religion had been yanked from the Sunday pulpit onto Main Street. The righteousness of the Hasidim had been tossed so often in the locals' faces that these days religion somehow seemed to be the only thing that mattered. You were either for the Jews or against them. You embraced and respected what the Jews had done for Postville—or you detested their arrogant ways. You were either pro-annexation because you thought the Jews needed a lesson in humility or because you thought they were bluffing—or you were against annexation because, like it or not, the Jews had brought prosperity to Postville and the last thing you wanted to do was tempt them into leaving.

So, when a queue of black-coated Hasidic rabbis started forming at Doc Wolf's room at the Good Samaritan Center, word spread faster than an Iowa tornado in spring. Could Doc Wolf be one of *them*? If someone of Henry Wolf's revered stature was seeking counsel from the Hasidim, then how bad could the Postville Jews really be after all? If Doc was asking the Hasidim for guidance, then maybe, just maybe, these men in their long coats and broad-brimmed hats were holy.

For the Postville locals who hadn't known that Doc Wolf was a Jew, the daily parade of Hasidim to his room at Good Samaritan Center (which was run by the Evangelical Lutheran Church) came as a shocker, and not just a few locals were outraged when they found out. At least that's how Cliff Olson saw it. "They were thinking, 'He was Jewish, and he delivered my children!'—or worse, 'He delivered me!'" Finding out that Doc Wolf and the Hasidim were the same religion, I imagined, was for some of the locals like knowing someone all your life, someone with whom you had shared life's most intimate moments, and suddenly, after all those years, you discovered a truth about that person that gave you goosebumps and made the hair on the back of your neck stand on end.

During the last ten days of Henry Wolf's life, as he was slipping in and out of consciousness, the cancer overtaking his now-frail body, Doc had asked Barbara Stockstill, his companion of nineteen years, to summon a rabbi to his hospice room. Doc, though, wasn't seeking salvation, nor was he ask-

ing for penitence. He had made that very clear to Barbara
and to Judy Deweber, the pastor. All Doc Wolf wanted in the
waning days of his life was one last taste of the Jewish food
he had grown up with in Chicago. It was a simple request
from a dying man: Bring me matzo-ball soup. Never one to
embrace organized religion, Doc had told Barbara that if one
of the rabbis could visit with him for fifteen or twenty minutes, that would be fine, but the food was the thing. That's
what mattered.

Barbara contacted Jim Lage's wife, Arlene, the resource-
development coordinator at Good Samaritan, who, in turn,
called Sholom Rubashkin and his wife, Leah. Soon, three rabbis arrived at Doc's room, as did Leah and two Hasidic children. Leah came bearing quart jars of shimmering matzo-ball
soup. As though the liquid were some kind of life-saving ano-
dyne, the nurses spirited the jars to the kitchen and quickly
heated them. With the Hasidim crowding around his bed and
looking on, Barbara spoon-fed the elixir to Henry. The Jewish
penicillin did nothing to relieve Doc's terminal condition, but
it did seem to comfort his spirit. Doc nodded and managed a
smile.

Henry Wolf got much more than matzo-ball soup from
the Postville Hasidim that afternoon and during the remain-
ing days of his life. He had asked for an appetizer. Instead, he
got a seven-course sit-down meal that never seemed to end.
What had started with a simple request for Jewish food
turned into a nonstop procession of Hasidic Jews to the bedside of a man they had never met. The Hasidim had seemingly moved in, taking over the last stage of Doc Wolf's life.
They had mounted a full-court press to save Doc Wolf's soul.

The next day, the Hasidim brought to Doc's bedside three

or four more children, who took to calling Henry "grandpa." Over the coming days, the Hasidim visited Doc around the clock, bringing not just more food, but now prayer books. If Doc was having a particularly bad time, and the Hasidim hadn't shown up yet, all Arlene Lage had to do was call the rabbis and someone would be at his bedside within minutes. The Hasidim took to bypassing the front entrance of Good Samaritan, directly entering Doc's room through a sliding glass door, day or night.

On the Sabbath before Doc died, two teenage Hasidic boys appeared at his bedside. They silently wheeled Doc out of his hospice room and into a light-filled solarium. Dressed in black trousers, white shirts, yarmulkes, and *tzitzit*, the young Hasidic men laid out their articles of faith atop the nurses' station—Bible, *tallises,* and tefillin. The charge nurse at Good Samaritan, Dolores Topel, took Doc's hands in hers and asked whether he was aware of what was happening. Doc squeezed Dolores's hand and nodded.

Dolores was fascinated and asked Doc whether he minded if she stayed to observe. Doc looked up and shook his head. The young Hasidic men seemed pleased that Dolores wanted to remain. They draped a prayer shawl over Doc's shoulders, elaborately wrapped the long black leather straps of tefillin around his left arm, wrist, hand, and index finger, then around his forehead. They began intoning a series of solemn benedictions, rising and falling, in rapid succession. From his wheelchair, Doc rhythmically bent his head, neck, and shoulders in a sort of davening motion, all the while chanting softly.

"They would ask him things first in their language and Doc would answer them in the same language," Dolores recalled, likening the ceremony to a last Communion. Dolores wasn't sure what the language was. It could have been Hebrew or Yiddish, but it certainly wasn't anything she had ever heard before. "In my mind," Dolores said, Doc was "reaching out to do everything he could do in his last hours. He was lucid and aware of what was going on." When the two Hasidic teenagers finished, they packed up their religious paraphernalia, shook Doc's hand, bowed their heads, and then silently exited the building through the sliding glass door in Doc's room.

All told, more than a dozen Hasidic men, women, and children called on Doc Wolf during the last week of his life. Until he was too weak in his final days, Doc would reach into his pajama pocket as soon as the Hasidim would arrive, pull out a yarmulke, and place it on the crown of his head. "I was born a Jew, and I guess I'll die a Jew," he told Barbara. On the Thursday before he died, Henry seemed at peace with his failing condition. "I am ready," he told Judy Deweber.

On April 5, when two of Doc Wolf's children, Marcia and Howie, arrived from Denver to see their father for the last time, they found him surrounded by Hasidic men and children. There were so many people in his room that Marcia and Howie felt they were intruding. It was the Friday afternoon, the day before the Jewish holiday of Passover, and the Hasidic men were all wearing *tallises*. A young Lubavitcher boy was holding Doc's hand, singing to him. Doc's eyes were closed, and he was breathing peacefully. As Marcia bent down to kiss her father's forehead, he reached for her hand, brought it to his lips, and kissed it.

To Marcia and Howie, there was something terribly wrong with the scene before them. Everything about it, from the yarmulke on their father's head to the prayer shawls that

covered his visitors' shoulders, was completely out of character. All his life, Doc Wolf had been a completely assimilated
Jew. His children couldn't recall his ever uttering a single
word in Hebrew. What were these strangers doing there, and
what exactly was their business with their father?

At one-thirty the next day, Doc's oldest child, Butch, arrived. Doc greeted Butch with a faint smile and a weak handshake. He nodded to the rest of his family gathered around his
bed. But within an hour, Doc's condition was rapidly deterio-
rating, and at three in the afternoon of April 6, 1996, Henry
Wolf died.

Butch, Marcia, and Howie left their father's room for several minutes. Crying and hugging, they assigned one another
tasks: calls about a memorial service had to be made to Pastor Deweber, to the local funeral parlor, to far-flung relatives,
and to scores of Henry's friends and former patients.

Judy Deweber arrived at Good Samaritan as soon as she
heard about the death. She let herself into Doc's room
through the sliding glass door and was surprised to find a Hasidic rabbi next to Doc's body, "making Hebrew prayers for
the dead," the rabbi told her. Seconds later, Butch returned to
his father's bedside.

Butch had known the Methodist minister for several years
and he greeted her warmly as she offered him her condo-
lences, but Butch wasn't genial with the rabbi. He was flab-
bergasted. Butch didn't know who the rabbi was or how he
had happened to arrive at his father's bedside just moments
after his death. Most of all, Butch wanted to know who had
invited him. The rabbi looked up. "This is the time for your
father to receive proper prayers and blessings," he sternly told
Butch, as he went back to davening and chanting over the
dead body.

Butch angrily shook his head. "I don't know what you're doing here or who you are, but you have three choices," said Butch, an equine veterinarian who could calm an ornery horse with his smile. "You can leave the way you came in, you can leave by the door, or you can go headfirst. Take your choice. But you *will* leave this room now."

"We are all one, and we should stay together," the rabbi responded solemnly. "We need to stay together at this moment as Jews."

"No," Butch said, getting angrier. "You have alienated yourself. You people have made fools of yourself. My family doesn't want any part of you. Leave this room, now!"

But the rabbi refused to budge. Judy Deweber looked at the rabbi, who stared at Butch, who glared back at the rabbi, all the while Doc Wolf's still-warm body lay under the hospice's starched white cotton sheets. No one would yield any ground. Judy found herself in the middle of a stalemate between two very different Jewish men who each believed he had an absolute mandate to commune with the dead.

Finally, after what seemed like an eternity, the rabbi ceded his post, turning his back and quickly exiting. Judy Deweber led Marcia, Howie, Barbara, and the rest of the family back into Doc's room. They formed a circle around the bed and, as they clasped hands, the pastor led the family in a prayer to God, offering thanks for Doc's life, his wisdom, the years of memories he had left.

Doc Wolf's funeral, as he had requested, was held at St. Paul's United Methodist Church in Elgin. More than 150 people attended the service and lunch reception held afterward at the American Legion Hall, just west of downtown. There was no recitation of the Kaddish, the traditional mourner's prayer for Jews; in fact, the entire service was nondenominational. Sisters Marilana Sutter and Sara Strong sang a rendition of "The Lord Is My Shepherd," and closed the service with Rose and Henry's favorite song, Hoagy Carmichael's "Stardust." None of the Hasidim was in attendance at either the funeral or the reception.

Doc chose not to be buried in the family plot at the Jewish cemetery in Chicago next to his wife, Rose, his parents, or aunts and uncles. As Doc had instructed his children, his body was donated to the University of Iowa College of Medicine. He had been adamant about that decision. "My father wanted to give back to medicine some of what medicine had given him," Butch said. Howie, also a physician, said that his father had repeatedly told him that he didn't believe in an afterlife. "He thought organized religion was hogwash. His feeling was that when people die, they throw them in a hole and that's about it," Butch recalled.

Doc's companion, Barbara Stockstill, said Doc never could have imagined that his single culinary request would have turned into a vigil to shepherd his soul. "It was like asking for a glass of milk and getting a barnful of cows," Barbara told me.

Butch had his own take. "I know when a Catholic is dying, a priest is sent for. That doesn't mean the entire clergy, diocese, and the cardinal court plus the pope be in attendance. That's what happened with Dad. The way in which the Hasidic Jews acted was an outrage. Their attempt to use my father to promote themselves was reprehensible."

That's, at least, what Butch thought the Hasidim were doing. Not only had they taken advantage of a confused, dying man, but they also hoped that word would circulate among the Postville locals that Doc and the Hasidim were on the same side. Maybe once the locals saw that, their attitude toward the Hasidim and annexation would soften.

When Doc Wolf first came to Iowa in 1932, some of the locals thought he had horns. Howie recalled getting into a fight at school because a classmate had called him a "damned Jew." When I interviewed Henry's younger sister, Anne Mich, who at eighty-six still pulled no punches, she said that when Henry and Rose left the comforts of Chicago for the Iowa cornfields, "Jewish people kept to themselves. If Henry wanted the job, he had to keep his religion to himself. Jewish people had a reputation. If they [the rural Iowans] knew he was Jewish, they might not have accepted him. People didn't give us a chance. But if my brother knew people didn't like him *because* he was Jewish, he would have kicked them in the ass."

For more than sixty years, like a January snowfall that covers and shapes everything in its wake, Henry Wolf had subsumed his Jewish faith into the dominant Christian culture of rural Iowa. Henry and Rose could count on one hand the number of Jewish families in a fifty-mile radius. There were the Levines, in the scrap-metal business in Oelwein, and psychiatrist Max Selo and his family in Independence, but that was about it. Out of necessity and purpose, Henry and his family became assimilated Jews; religion became generic: It meant to tell the truth, to treat everyone fairly even though you might not like them, to forgive transgressions, to let compassion be your guide. In Iowa, blending in with their neighbors was the only way to survive. The Wolfs had a Christmas tree and their children went on Easter-egg hunts. During summers, Marcia and her best friend, Pat Anderson, attended a Methodist camp in Clear Lake, not far from where Buddy

Holly, Richie Valens, and the Big Bopper would perform for the last time a decade later.

Henry and Rose insisted that their children be raised with some formal religious training, and the Methodist church in Elgin was the least offensive choice. In the 1930s and 1940s, there were two places of worship: the Methodist church and the Baptist church, both in town. St. Paul's United Methodist was the more moderate, the church that most of the businessmen and their families belonged to. It was certainly different from First Baptist on Main, which had the reputation as a home for Bible thumpers and required its members be baptized and make public their commitment to be saved by Jesus Christ. During Methodist Sunday school, when the children sang "Onward Christian Soldiers," Marcia used to lip-synch the words. Whenever she was called on to utter the word "Jesus," Marcia said under her breath, "Moses." Butch told me, "The three of us went every week to Sunday school. We sang the Bible songs, read the Bible stories, and threw a nickel in the hat. We didn't think twice about doing it." At home, the Wolfs never celebrated Chanukah or Passover, although some years, Rose would order from Leo Falb, who owned the meat market on Center Street, a box of matzos, unleavened bread, with which she made matzo brei, a dish of matzos scrambled with eggs and often sweetened with sugar, cinnamon, or syrup. "The most important lesson, religious or otherwise, I learned from my mother was that, although we were Jewish, there was good and bad in all religions and races, and not to judge anyone based on religions and races," said Howie.

In high school, Marcia dated a boy who was Lutheran, but Rose ultimately discouraged the relationship, preferring that Marcia "find a nice Jewish boy." As a student at the University of Wisconsin, Butch said, "I would look at the Jewish girls and when I said I wanted to live in a rural town, they looked back at me in kind of a strange way. I didn't want to train them, and they didn't want to be trained. My mother had been through that already." At least once while Howie was in high school, he visited his paternal grandfather, Peter Wolf, in Chicago, who asked him if he had a girlfriend and if she was Jewish. When Howie answered, "Yes, I do, and no, she isn't," his grandfather admonished him to choose only Jewish girls. "They're better for you," he told Howie. But to Doc, his children said, it really didn't make any difference.

Like a Holy Communion wafer, Doc's religion ultimately materialized in what he put in his body, as his last earthly request to the Hasidim revealed. For more than six decades, isolated in rural Iowa with no synagogues and few fellow Jews, Doc had no choice but to connect to his faith through food. On trips to Chicago, Doc would haul back home crates full of Sinai and Hebrew National meat and fish—pastrami, brisket, whitefish, nova, lox, fresh bagels, and rye bread with caraway seeds. The larder of Jewish food was a way for Doc to connect with his past, but also a way to introduce his heritage to his children—and anyone else in Elgin or Postville brave enough to try out an onion bagel with lox and cream cheese on it. Don Fauser, who owned the D-X service station in town, has Doc Wolf to thank not just for bringing his eight children and six grandchildren into the world, but for introducing him to Chicago, corned beef sandwiches on rye, kosher dills, and a Cubs game—all on the same day. Whenever Henry's relatives came to town, they would follow Doc's unwavering mandate: Come bearing sacks of Jewish food. In between the care-package trips and his own visits to Chicago, Henry had Leo Falb put in a standing order with the Vienna Sausage Company for kosher hot dogs, corned beef, and skirt steak. He cherished the delicacies because they weren't available in Iowa, they recalled his childhood, they tasted so damned good, and because they were the closest material thing that reminded him he was Jewish.

For the sixty-five years Doc lived in Iowa, assimilation had been essential to his survival and contentment. From the moment Henry and Rose moved to Iowa, they wanted to belong. Like Iris and me, they sought to become a part of their new environment. Like us, they moved, in part, to learn new customs and shed old ones. They were in it for the adventure, and any worthwhile adventure included not just new sights, sounds, and smells, but new people. For Doc and Rose, as for Iris and me, savoring people different from us became essential to realizing our dream.

The afternoon after Doc died, his daughter, Marcia, found in her father's basement a stack of letters and a diary that Rose had kept, still neatly held together by a frayed pink rubber band. Unknown to Marcia, Rose Wolf had begun in 1947 to write a family history that she entitled "And Life Goes On." In the single-spaced typed memoir, Rose recalled Henry and her momentous move from Chicago to Iowa sixteen years earlier.

"It wouldn't be easy to leave our loved ones and lifelong friends," Rose started out. "I pictured us as real pioneers and while I thought, I suddenly decided we ought to give it a try. There were the usual farewell parties and our parents made us feel like we were leaving them for another world."

Rose quickly learned the ropes of small-town Iowa society. "I knew for the good of my husband's practice, I'd have to be a joiner, so I accepted all offers. I met seventy-two ladies at my first meeting of the Ladies' Aid Society. How could I ever remember all their names? I didn't. When they planned a Food Sale, I wondered what that was and asked what I could do to help. 'Oh, bring anything that will sell,' one of the women offered. I ordered special rolls made at the local bakery. I wondered why these didn't sell as quickly as the others—then it dawned on me—they wanted *home-baked* articles for their sales. I took my own rolls back, amid embarrassment. Now I bake my own rolls for food sales, but I know they [Ladies' Aid Society] couldn't have sold the first ones I ever tried.

"We even went in for gardening, and it was fun. It was thrilling to see the seeds we planted grow into big, healthy plants. There's nothing tastier than a bowl of fresh garden greens. I learned to make jams and jellies and canned jars of vegetables to store away for the winter. I had read about things like this but never dreamed I too would be doing the same thing. I'd have something tangible to show our city friends when they visited us.

"We managed three trips a year to the City. We took in some ball games, a few good shows and ate food we couldn't get at home. It always seemed good to get back to our own home. The country was really in our blood by this time. Our friends wondered how we could stay away so long from the city and how we ever managed to make the adjustment so well. When we explained the lives we led, we felt certain they were a bit envious. None of my husband's former school chums had time to spend with their families. We were growing up together as a family and that was worth a lot."

In January 1965, after Butch, Howie, and Marcia Wolf had left Elgin and made their homes elsewhere, Rose developed a gallbladder inflammation. While recovering, she fell and nearly broke her ankle. Doc arranged for Rose to be driven to a physician in Decorah for physical therapy, and at a spot the locals call Horseshoe Bend, on State Highway 51, near Frankville, the car in which Rose was riding skidded. Rose grabbed the car-door handle to steady herself, but as she pushed down, the door swung open. In a freak accident, Rose fell out of the car headfirst, breaking her neck. She was taken to Postville Hospital, where she died of cardiac arrest later that day. Rose was fifty-six.

Henry was just shy of sixty. He threw himself into his work, but also began singing in a local barbershop quartet. He closed down his office on Wednesday afternoons and took to playing bridge with three friends in his parlor till past midnight. In the spring and summer, a daily ritual of his was to pull weeds in his front yard. As neighbors strolled by, Doc would look up from his spot on the lawn and wave.

Doc surprised his friends when he changed his allegiance from the Chicago Cubs to the Atlanta Braves. The only thing good about television, Doc allowed, was that he could watch baseball on it, and since the Braves were among the first teams to be televised nationally, Doc ultimately became a diehard Braves fan. Doc's once-rabid devotion to the Cubs and later to the Braves ultimately turned out to be bluster, though. Baseball had always been poetry to him. Doc didn't care who won; it was the ballet of motion that counted. He appreciated a southpaw pitcher dueling against a right-handed home-run king, a shortstop going deep behind second to throw the runner out at first, an outfielder on the warning track plucking a ball from midair the second before it reached the stands. Baseball was an art form, and when executed right, it was one of life's sweetest pleasures.

Five years after Rose's death, Doc started dating Barbara Stockstill, a retired nurse, who eventually moved to Elgin. In the spring of 1995, at age eighty-seven, as the cancer had come back with a fury, Doc Wolf quit practicing medicine. He was to die eleven months later.

One night, two months after Doc died, Howie Wolf was at his Boulder, Colorado, home when his phone rang at nine-thirty. The caller identified himself as a Hasidic rabbi from Seattle. "As you know," the rabbi said, "your father's soul has departed his body, and this is the time when it is ascending to heaven."

Howie had no idea who the rabbi was or how he had gotten his telephone number. Butch or Marcia hadn't given it to him; neither had Barbara or anyone else at Good Samaritan. The only way, Howie figured, must have been off his father's patient chart. Howie wanted to know exactly why the rabbi was calling. Did he want money, and how did the rabbi know that this was the precise time when his father was about to enter heaven?

In the quick of the moment, Howie asked neither of those questions. But just as Howie was about to hang up, the rabbi asked him whether he was active in the Jewish community of Boulder. "Would you be interested in attending some of our services at the shul?" the rabbi asked. "Would you like to meet any Hasidic Jews who live nearby?" The rabbi said he could arrange for Howie to attend a Friday-night service or eat *Shabbos* dinner with a nearby Lubavitcher family. But like his father, Howie had no wish to make his religion a public matter, and the conversation ended quickly. It was a curious call, Howie thought when he hung up. A stranger calling out of the blue, preying on Howie's emotions over his father's death, trying to save Howie's soul. Whatever the motivation for the call, it reminded Howie of the Yiddish word for nerve—*chutzpah*.

My life in Iowa was different from the life Doc Wolf led. The sixty-five years that separated his migration to Iowa from mine made for a wholly distinct set of experiences. Iowa City was not rural Iowa. I had a choice where to settle; during the Depression, Doc opted to go where he could find work as a physician. We weren't the only Jews who lived in this university community. But there were undeniable similarities. Iris and I were constantly on the lookout for Jewish food in Iowa. When anyone from a city came to visit, we gave specific instructions: "Bring corned beef. First cut." Visiting my mother-in-law in Florida brought with it a culinary bonanza. It was as though we were banking the food in our bodies and souls, training for the long, parched stretch when we would return to Iowa. When we spent holidays in Miami, as soon as we walked into Iris's mother's house, we'd be greeted with a blast of chicken-soup vapors. After the soup, there would be chopped chicken liver, kasha with bow ties, chicken in a pot with vegetables. The beverage was Dr. Brown's Black Cherry or seltzer from blue-tinted bottles that squirted when you pressed the chrome lever on top. For dessert, on Mikey's plate would be a large black-and-white cookie from Arnie and Richie's Deli or the Rascal House. For breakfast the next day, it would be chubs, nova, bagels and cream cheese. As it had been for Henry Wolf, Jewish food wasn't just good, it was our link to who we were and who we would always be, even though we lived in a Christian land of pork.

I wondered how Doc Wolf would have reacted to the Postville Hasidim had he been in his prime when they first arrived in Postville. None of the Hasidim had been patients of Doc, and he had no interactions with them until he asked Barbara Stockstill to contact them as he lay dying. If he had been younger, not battling the cancer that ended his life, would he have sought the Hasidim out, seeking to share the religion he sensed but never practiced? Judy Deweber told me that one of the first calls every new Methodist minister in Elgin had to make was to visit with Henry Wolf. Doc was an intellectual. He appreciated the opportunity to talk theology, whatever denomination it was. Certainly, Doc would have liked the Postville Jews' access to all that good Jewish food. But would he have been able to be friends with the Hasidim?

The biggest question is whether Doc Wolf would have been for or against the annexation of the slaughterhouse land. How would Doc have felt about the larger struggle going on between the locals and the Jews? Where did Doc fit in, and which side would he have taken? None of Doc's children said that Doc ever mentioned the Hasidim, but before he entered Good Samaritan, he certainly had to be aware of the cultural war going on in Postville. Did Doc look at the Hasidim as a foreign body in his midst? Were they Moishes-come-lately? Would their vociferous form of Judaism conflict with his internalized sense of religion, order, and morality?

Postville people were loyal to Doc Wolf. They respected his word. If Doc Wolf had good things to say about the Hasidim, then he could have been a rallying point for the Jews, perhaps even drowning the locals' attempt to annex the slaughterhouse land. But even though Doc was a leader in his community, his alliance with the Hasidim during the last days of his life swayed few locals to change their feelings about the

Jews. Both sides interpreted Doc's behavior as they wanted to. When I asked pro-annexation proponent Leigh Rekow about it, he looked at me with a knowing nod. But so did Ida Mae and Cliff Olson, who thought the Hasidic Jews were Postville's last salvation. Everyone had his or her own reason for why Doc did what he did, and as far as I could tell, no one switched allegiance because of Doc's final actions.

The battle lines in Postville had been so fiercely drawn by the time Doc died that several locals told me the only reason the Hasidim had acceded to Doc Wolf's deathbed request for a bowl of chicken soup was because the Jews wanted to garner support from the locals in the fight against annexation. They said it was a calculated attempt to buy votes through sympathy—that if Doc showed that much respect to the Hasidim and the locals loved Doc so much, then the locals surely would back down on the annexation issue. It seemed that the Postville Hasidim had engendered such bad feelings among Postville folks that the locals figured the whole weeklong Hasidic vigil at Doc's bedside had just been politics.

CHAPTER 20

The Derailment

August fifth was a still, hot day without a trace of breeze, just about the time of summer when an Iowa farmer's corn crop ought to come up to his shoulder. But on this day, the corn in Postville may very well have stopped growing. This was judgment day, the day of the annexation vote. It was time for the showdown, time for all the bluster and bravado to stop. The Hasidim had drawn a line in the pure Iowa soil, and today was when the locals would see whether they could muster enough votes to call the Jews' bluff.

Polls opened an hour after sunrise and would close at eight that evening. In addition to the signboard that someone had posted at the corner of Tilden and Lawler Streets, a curious flyer started circulating around town. It was copied on white paper with black-stenciled lettering and a crooked, hand-drawn frame around it. No one owned up to printing and distributing the flyer, but that wasn't surprising. People filling up at Home Oil saw it, as did anyone who ate breakfast at Ginger's or the Postville Bakery. The flyer carried a mixed message, a warning of sorts:

BE CAREFUL OF

THE TOES YOU

STEP ON TODAY...

BECAUSE THEY MAY

BE CONNECTED TO

THE ASS

THAT YOU MIGHT

HAVE TO KISS

TOMORROW!!

In its own way, the little poster really was ingenious. Who was stepping on whose toes, and who would want to kiss *anyone's* ass? That's what most of the locals thought they'd been doing ever since Aaron Rubashkin bought the slaughterhouse ten years earlier. If anything, the flyer was meant to enrage the locals, to get them off their tractors, out from Ginger's, and into the lobby of the high school to vote to kick the Hasidim out of Postville. Someone had put out the flyer, but who? It could have been dozens of people— Leigh Rekow, Stanley Schroeder, Rosalyn Krambeer, Marie Schlee, Beverly Schaeffer, Dawn Schmadeke, Whitey Meyer, Alicia Gustafson, even Harold Schaufenbuel. The very name of the high school where the voting was taking place to-day—Dr. John R. Mott—was proof enough to them that Postville didn't belong to the Jews. If anyone owned Postville, it was the locals who carried on Mott's legacy of Christian goodwill.

That flyer wasn't the only campaign literature. Someone had piled another stack of anonymous flyers near the check-out at Moore's IGA. These, printed on bright goldenrod paper, were more to the point:

VOTE YES
IT'S FAIR. IT'S PROGRESS
IT'S UNITY
YOU CAN BE PROUD TO BE A PART OF
POSTVILLE

On the backside was an explanation of how annexation would work, with this underlined: "THERE IS NO PROJECTED TAX INCREASE FOR POSTVILLE RESIDENTS DUE TO ANNEXATION."

As far as I could tell, there was only one anti-annexation flyer circulated around town. It had been mailed August first, with no return address, to anyone with a box at the post office:

DON'T FORGET
VOTE **NO** ON AUGUST 5 FOR
ANNEXATION!
SAVE OUR TOWN.
ANNEXATION MAY MAKE SENSE, BUT
ONLY WITH PROPER PLANNING AND
KNOWING THE END RESULT! ANNEXATION
WITHOUT PLANNING IS FINANCIAL RUIN.
BEWARE! BE EDUCATED! **VOTE NO**
IT'S **OUR** TOWN!

I had arrived in Postville the day before the vote and had checked into my usual quarters at the Pines, the room with the green shag carpeting, the Lysol stink, and the winking cow outside the window. It had been ten months since I last was in Postville, and even though I had broken bread with Aaron Rubashkin and his family in Brooklyn last fall, I didn't think Sholom would talk to me. I thought he would still be smarting over my tracking down Stillman and Lew, the interviews

I had had with the illegal aliens who worked at Agriprocessors, and most of all, my refusal to become a *baal teshuvah*. But I was wrong.

When I called the slaughterhouse, the harried secretary patched me through to Sholom right away. When I asked him whether I could swing over to visit, he said, "What's there to talk about?"

"About the election today. Who's going to win?"

"The side that should win, that's who's gonna win."

"Is that your side?"

"What do I know? It's no good to talk about the future. It's out of our hands."

"But you think you're going to win?

"Again with the election!"

"I'll be over in ten minutes."

"Who's stopping you? It's a free country. Come if you want. See what I care."

Such a welcome. It had been more than a year since I was at the abattoir, and once again the stench along the killfloor from the split-open carcasses was overwhelming. Again, I was hit by the nauseating, almost cloying, smell of fluttering chickens going through the kill line, four rabbis methodically slitting the necks with razor blades. Up the creaky staircase to the second floor, I practically bumped into Lazar Kamzoil, who was barreling down the steep steps. He had dark circles under his eyes, his skin the same sallow hue I had remembered. Rosh Hashanah was early this year, in three weeks, and the plant had been operating eighteen consecutive hours.

"Shlomo, that you?" Lazar asked, his nose almost pressed against mine. "What are *you* doing here?"

"The election. I came for the election."

"You drive all this way from your home just for this election? So important?"

"I want to see which side wins."

"And which side are *you* on?" Lazar asked, suddenly pulling back his head, peering at me over his glasses, as he had done before.

It was a question I had asked myself many times since I had first come to Postville, and now two years later, I knew which side I stood on: I wanted the locals to win, hands down. I was curious what would happen if the Hasidim lost. Would they pack up and leave, as Sholom had threatened? Would Postville become a ghost town of boarded-up shops lining Lawler Street, one more heartland town abandoned by elders who had died and children who had left? Or would the Hasidim stay, continuing to ignore the locals, looking through them? If the Hasidim lost, I couldn't imagine that they'd ever buckle under to the demands of the locals and allow their land to be annexed.

Perhaps the Hasidim would prevail in the vote today. No matter what anyone could say or think about them, the Hasidim had, after all, supplied 350 jobs to the local economy of a town that had less than fifteen hundred people in it. Business was booming in Postville. No one could deny that. Merchants like Glenda Bodensteiner and Roberta Dreier had never been busier, as were the bankers and real-estate agents, men like Jim Lage and Toey Kelly. Postville probably hadn't seen this kind of nonstop growth for more a century. Even historian Stanley Schroeder would have to concede that. Maybe the locals could get beyond how the Hasidim treated them and look inside their wallets: Financially, almost everyone was better off with the Jews in town.

For me, though, there was a simple reason why I wanted the pro-annexation forces to win: They deserved to win. It was finally time for the pleasant, accepting Iowans to stand up to the Hasidim. If they couldn't get angry (with the exception of Harold Schaufenbuel), I hoped they would get some *cojones,* neither an Iowa word nor concept. The locals had to know that they had been abused and ridiculed. Now it was payback time—even if it meant the Hasidim might take with them the goose that laid Postville's golden eggs.

Lazar suspected the answer to his own question, and he grimaced. There was an uncomfortable pause; the eighteen inches between us on this narrow stairway suddenly seemed as wide as the Iowa River. I was a lost soul, not only leading Mikey astray from his faith, but now siding with the *goyim.* I was the secular Jew in a T-shirt and jeans, who drove on the Sabbath, swam in the same pool with the *goyim,* who even ate bacon. We stared at each other for a couple of seconds, not speaking, in a stalemate of sorts.

"How are Bielke and the children?" I asked, breaking the impasse.

"And how *should* they be?"

This was the Lazar I knew. I smiled.

"They're fine. *Baruch Hashem. Zayt gezunt!* And Moishe, how's he?"

I took a photograph from my wallet, and just as I was about to show it, Lazar asked, "with or without *kippah?*

"Without."

Lazar shook his head in mock anger. He scrutinized the snapshot, staring at it at arm's length, then bringing it closer, almost to the tip of his nose, then back out to arm's length again. "To tell you the truth, Shlomo, he doesn't look like you at all. No similarities whatsoever. Very handsome, this boy."

There was another pause, this time not awkward, almost deferential. At that moment, I think, Lazar and I had reached some sort of tacit understanding of how his family lived its life and how mine lived ours. Lazar and I may have come from the same parents thousands of years ago, but now all we shared were some common prayers, a smattering of Yiddish words, an affection for the same food, and a profound love for our families. Face to face in this narrow stairway, listening to the grunts of steers queued to be slaughtered in the killroom, Lazar and I were as close as we'd ever come to acknowledging the differences that separated us, perhaps even accepting them. It was a comforting, almost sublime, moment.

"Shlomo, listen to this. You gotta hear this one. Last week, I'm taking a plane back to New York with just the baby and Bielke, and I'm holding the baby and this stewardess comes over to me and says, 'How adorable! Is he your first?'

"'Are you kidding?' I says to her. 'It's my eighth!'

"You should have seen the stewardess's face. She was shocked. Really shocked.

"'Mister,' she finally says to me, 'I think it's about time you moved your television set into your bedroom!'"

So, Lazar and Bielke had added another child, a little boy, to their family since I last saw them. But before I could congratulate him, Lazar bounded down the rest of the stairs, keys in hand. The slaughterhouse screen door slapped shut. "In a rush, gotta go," Lazar shouted, already in the parking lot.

I made my way up to the second floor and found Sholom padding through the maze of offices. As soon as I took a seat, Sholom started in, slapping the back of his right hand into the palm of his left. "Since the destruction of the Temple, we've always allowed ourselves to be pushed around. Never in a million years would we have moved here if we knew that the plant would be annexed. Never! What they are doing is immoral. Lazar says that Rekow at the church is telling everyone that we're busing in people to vote against annexation. They think we'd do *that*? Can you imagine?"

"Are you?" I asked.

Sholom shook his head and gave me a look, narrowing his eyes. "Are you kidding? We don't need to. These people will come around. You just wait."

"Maybe you should take annexation as a compliment," I tried. "The Postville locals want to share in your success. If you were a failure, they wouldn't want to have anything to do with you."

"But I don't want any partners. I don't work that way."

"What happens if you lose today?"

"Whadda they tell you?"

"Who's they?"

"Whadda they say?"

"Don't ask me. Ask them."

Sholom ignored my answer. "We have to take the cards dealt to us," he said in a slow, lugubrious tone, shrugging his shoulders. "We have no choice."

"But will you leave if you lose?"

"We shall see," he said, his eyes suddenly going distant.

I wanted to find out how the voting was going, so I walked over to the high school, and along the way, on West Greene, I passed Tindell Shoes, the shop Glenda Bodensteiner ran that had reminded me of my own father's shoe store. As I walked in, an old-fashioned bell rang, the same ding-a-ling jingle as on a girl's bicycle.

Glenda had been one of the staunchest supporters of the Hasidim, but when I asked her whether she was going to vote against annexation, she shook her head. "Things have changed," she said, almost apologizing. Leah Rubashkin still bought her children's shoes from Tindell's, but more and more, the Postville Hasidim were buying at the chain stores or on trips back home to Brooklyn. Glenda had allowed some of the Hasidim to start charge accounts at the store, and, she said, "that has turned into a total mess. They don't pay on time."

But Glenda could get by that. All had jobs at the slaughterhouse, and eventually, she hoped, they would settle their accounts. What was most upsetting to Glenda was a nasty altercation she had had with one of the slaughterhouse rabbis who had placed an order for butcher-knife sheaths several months ago. Glenda handcrafted the leather sheaths, as she had done more than a hundred times before for the *shochtem* at the packing plant. But when this rabbi returned to pick up his order, he said he had already paid for it. That was impossible, Glenda said. She went through each ticket she had made out for every sale, and there was nothing for the sheaths. But the rabbi wouldn't budge. He said he had paid fifty dollars for the sheaths, and when Glenda shook her head, he said the other woman at the store, Glenda's sister, must have pocketed the money. Then, the rabbi grabbed the sheaths from the Formica counter. Glenda again asked the rabbi for the money he owed her, and this time, he told her to keep quiet. "Never raise your voice to me! Women are not to do that—ever! Do you know how rich I am?," and then turned his back on her, walking out the store with the sheaths.

"I'd never heard someone brag like that, and I will never forget it for as long as I live," Glenda said. "It really changed my way of thinking about the Jews. I used to have faith and

trust in them, but I'm not so sure any longer." If any of the locals knew the Hasidim, Glenda did. She knew and liked their
families. She had seen their children grow up. But Glenda
had been affected by the incident, and I could see it. Just as I
was about to leave, tears began to well up in her eyes. "I'm
not going to hold it against all of them, but I see more and
more how important money is to them, and how they will do
anything to get it. Money to them is a major ordeal. They always say that their family is everything, but money is very,
very important to them. They take advantage every chance
they can." I could plainly see that Glenda was pained to voice
such a harsh assessment. It wasn't how she was raised, and it
wasn't how she lived her life. But now she knew—many of
the Hasidim were just as Harold Schaufenbuel had described
them.

Over at Dr. John R. Mott High School, Joyce Kuhse, Marjorie Schultz, Betty Kostman, Karen Schutte and Lavon Kregel
were the poll workers. From the official poll register, Joyce
and Marjorie checked off the names of everyone who lined
up to vote, and then Betty and Karen handed a ballot to each
voter. Next, voters went to the other side of the lobby, inside
one of the seven metal voting booths, each with a red, white,
and blue curtain, to mark their ballots with a no. 2 lead pencil. Lavon made sure the ballots were deposited in the safebox
and the pencils were returned.

To cast a ballot, residents had to have been registered
eleven days prior to the referendum. There were 1,220 eligible voters registered, 1,057 in Postville. If the annexation
passed, 703 unincorporated acres would be folded into the
Postville city limits, thereby adding $8 million in taxable
property to the city's $23 million property-tax base. Agri-
processors wasn't the only business that would be annexed if